BYZANTINE
AND
MEDIEVAL
CYPRUS

A Guide to the Monuments

by

GWYNNETH DER PARTHOG

Illustrated by Judith Davis

INTERWORLD PUBLICATIONS

1

*This book is dedicated to the
astonishing people of Cyprus,
who kept faith down the centuries*

Byzantine Double-Headed Eagle
(Ayios Ioannis – Nicosia)

JLD

Front Cover: Panel painting dd 1356 now in the Byzantine Museum, Nicosia;
Sketch of the Frankish Castle in Kato Paphos by Judith Davis

Back Cover: Photograph of Arkhangelos Mikhail Church,
Vizakia by Ena Burton

3

Published in England
by Interworld Publications, part of
Tophill Advertising & Promotions Ltd.
12 The Fairway, New Barnet,
Herts. EN5 1HN – England
Fax No 0181-447 0599

First Publication – 1995

International Standard Book Number
ISBN – 0 948853 20 4

Designed & Planned by Tophill Designs - London
Typeset by Sunset Typessetters - London
Printed by SOGEK,
Tel. 482361-2, Fax 487614, Nicosia - Cyprus
Cyprus Agents:
Hellenic Distribution Agency (Cyprus) Ltd

"Undoubtedly the most important event in the Roman period, one which fundamentally altered the whole subsequent history of Cyprus, was the introduction of Christianity."

Sir David Hunt, Footprints in Cyprus.

"Cyprus lies to the north and west of an area of submarine earthquake activity in the Eastern Mediterranean Basin. During Roman times the earthquakes which occurred circa 15 BC and 76 AD facilitated the construction of new monumental buildings."

from Ancient Kourion Area ed. Swiny (source Professor Soren).

"Proportionate to its population, Cyprus contributes more monks to the monastic enclave of Mount Athos in northern Greece than any other Orthodox country."

Marc Dubin, Cyprus the Rough Guide

CONTENTS

Ayia Napa Monastery
(see page 239)

8

FOREWORD

The Byzantine and Medieval Guide has been written to help all interested and independent-minded visitors to explore Cyprus a bit further. It tries to bridge the gap between detailed specialist publications and general guides. However, the author wishes to make it clear that she has no qualifications as a Byzantinist or any other kind of historian, but is writing as a layman for other laymen. Ancient history is well covered already – one has only to go along to the Cyprus Museum to discover that; but the Byzantine period is not, and it has been too long the preserve of the specialists alone. So take my book, if you will, and make your way to some of the places recommended on its pages. A few you will find to be deserted and in ruins, but many are in daily use and an integral part of the lives of the local community. That is what is so rewarding in this field: whereas the villas and temples of Greece and Rome are legacies of civilisations long past, the Byzantine and Medieval monuments are still part of the living culture of the island, of its people. Go soon, though, because as a way of life Byzantine Cyprus cannot survive much longer.

The plan of the book is as simple as I could make it. After a short general history, the island has been covered district by district, starting with the chief towns. The Troodos area, although not a district in itself, has been treated separately; and the most important monuments in the Turkish-controlled north are noted, together with a brief comment on each. In this way, all the places most worth visiting have been included. The list is by no means comprehensive. There are, for example, several thousand small churches – often estate chapels – scattered throughout the countryside, some even with a certain amount of wall-painting inside.

Small print. It is used where a place merits further detailed description which is not necessarily of general interest.

Names in Greek. I have tried to keep the spelling of names and dedication of churches in their Greek form, and favoured the Greek ending –os rather than the Latin –us (e.g. Lazaros), although I am aware that I have not been consistent in this. Commonly-shared saints such as St. George, familiar to us in their anglicised form, have not been changed.

Getting about. Apart from the towns, which are generally better tackled on foot, I have given directions for reaching destinations by car. The alternatives are: by village bus – make sure of your return journey; by taxi – not as expensive as you might think; by seat in a shared taxi – a network running at fixed times between the main towns and good for places like Kourion and Kolossi.

N.B. Do not attempt off-track monuments after the winter rains have arrived without a four-wheel drive.

In order to have enough time to see the painted churches of Troodos properly, I recommend lodging for a night or two, first at Kakopetria for the Solea and Marathasa valley areas, and again at Agros for the Pitsilia area.

Crossing to the occupied area. As a visitor you may obtain a day pass to visit the occupied part of Nicosia. To do so, make your way to the check-point at the old Ledra Palace Hotel. It is about a third of a mile north of the Paphos Gate roundabout, along Markos Drakos Avenue. Take your passport. A charge is made. Always remember that the local people are not allowed by the Turkish administration to do this, so please tread delicately here.

Inside the painted churches. Always ask if you may use a camera. In the nine churches on UNESCO's World Heritage list, photography is prohibited altogether unless the Department of Antiquities has given written permission. To obtain this, write to The Director at the following address, giving a valid reason: Department of Antiquities, The Cyprus Museum, Nicosia.

In all churches in Cyprus: do not enter wearing shorts or, for women, with bare arms; respect the sanctuary area, where women are never allowed and men only on condition they do not cross in front of the altar; make a small contribution to the church funds.

Acknowledgements

I wish to express thanks to the following for help received:

The Department of Antiquities for permission to photograph
Archbishop Makarios III Cultural Foundation for allowing me to reproduce the icon on the cover
Renos Lavithis for his patience, advice and encouragement, and for his hard work on the production side
Peter Megaw for answering my questions regarding early Byzantine sites
Dr Rowland Mainstone for drawing plans to scale for my use
Gerald Hennings for information on the castles at Limassol, Kolossi and Kato Paphos
David Pearlman of Exalt for taking me to monasteries and churches in the Dhiarizos and Xeropotamos valleys
A.X. Roussonnides of Kykko Study Centre for Research
Eleni Prokopiou of the Archaeological Museum, Limassol
Also and throughout:
My husband John for the time and energy he has expended in driving me all over the place and translating the village Greek: he turned everybody into a friend
Sunvil Holidays for allowing me a room to work in and use of their facilities.

Apology Any mistakes that occur in the following pages are mine and I must take responsibility for them. I can only pray that they are few, the discrepancies, the omissions and the errors of judgement, and confined to detail only. If that turns out to be the case, then they can be corrected, and I shall be content.

CYPRUS
BYZANTINE & MEDIAEVAL

◆

The Mediaeval Age in Cyprus can be said to date from about the middle of the tenth century to the coming of the Turks in 1570. However, to get the most benefit from the monuments, museums and art of the period, we need to understand how things evolved; and for that we must go back much further in time: because this is part of the history of a people, a living past that grew from small beginnings into a complete civilisation.

THE BEGINNINGS
History
The story starts around 46 AD with a visit to the Island of St Paul and St. Barnabas. It was a prosperous and peaceful land then, a full province of Rome, and the antique cities abounded in altars to Greek and Roman gods, with the temples of Apollo and of Aphrodite crowning the heights. Not surprisingly, after the preceding three hundred years under the Ptolemies, Greek, not Latin, was the common language; and Cypriot life was carrying on its old ways and customs side by side with the Roman civilisation. An organisation existed called **To Koinon ton Kyprion** – *the Union of Cypriots* – which acted as the voice of the people and protected their rights. Through the ages, this Union had played a considerable role in preventing the native culture from being crushed under foreign domination. Nevertheless, it was a cosmopolitan society, with a variety of religious creeds, and included a considerable Jewish community.

Among the last were a number of Christian converts whose ranks had been swollen in the past decade by refugees from Palestine, scattered after the stoning of Stephen (36 AD). Barnabas was a Jew born at Salamis, and John Mark was his cousin. So, when the Church at Antioch decided to send some of their brethren to spread the Gospel in Cyprus, who better to choose than Barnabas? Paul must already have shown potential, but he was the younger and less experienced man. So the three arrived.

Strong traditions tell of their landing at Lapethos and making a circuitous journey across the Troodos mountains to Paphos with a guide whom they baptised en route. His name was Herakleidios.

Apart from the famous conversion of the Pro-consul Sergius Paulus, in Paphos, Paul and Barnabas seem to have done a lot of hard work in the months they were in the Island, and at least paved the way before they left for a structured, organised Church.

When Barnabas and John Mark returned four or five years later, they continued what had been begun; but the Cypriots consider that, without question, St Barnabas is the true founder of their Church. The names of at least three bishops have come down to us from those days: Bishop of Salamis, Barnabas himself; Bishop of Kition, Lazarus the friend of Christ; Bishop of Tamassos, Herakleidios. But there is no written evidence for this.

A work purporting to be by the Apostle has turned out to be a fifth century invention – though it may have preserved within it an oral tradition now lost. Unlike Paul, Barnabas had no need to write letters to his Church because it seems likely that he seldom or never left it, remaining on the Island until he died – some time between 54 and 68 AD – killed by a mob in his native city.

Little is known about the fortunes of the new foundation over the following couple of hundred years. One sect among many, it was generally tolerated, occasionally persecuted, but emerged intact into history in the fourth century when Constantine the Great convened the first Church Council in Nicaea in 325: three bishops from Cyprus attended. Lack of documentation dogs Cyprus history, not only throughout this early period, but also through the whole of the Byzantine and later Middle Ages, continuing right up to the coming of the Turks in 1570: then there is almost too much! Only accounts by passing travellers and spasmodic Church records afford glimpses of local conditions. However, the Island's collective folk memory is exceedingly retentive, and time after time tradition is borne out by archaeological evidence.

THE FOURTH CENTURY

The Age of Constantine

It seems fairly certain that Helena, mother of Constantine the Great, landed near Larnaca in either 325 or 327 AD; that she found the region to be greatly run down, depopulated and snake-infested after a prolonged and severe drought. She had been to Jerusalem on a mission to discover the Cross on which Christ was crucified, and apparently was successful. To hearten the struggling Christian community, St Helena founded churches and monasteries on the Island, the best known of which is Stavrovouni Monastery; and she left pieces of the True Cross in several.

Monks were sent from Palestine, a shipload of snake-killing cats from Constantinople! Cats are still much in evidence at Stavrovouni, and they were once even more so at St Nicholas of the Cats near Limassol, where mediaeval travellers were taken to watch them stream in, tattered and torn, for their dinner.

The fourth century was a key to change in several ways.

First, Cyprus had the interest and practical help of St Helena; after that – perhaps not unconnected with her visit – more monks began to arrive from Palestine. (Among their number was one Epiphanios who was later to become a most outstanding archbishop, his name revered to this day.)

Then, in 330, Constantinople was inaugurated: that great, intricate Christian city, whose citizens considered themselves Roman but spoke Greek, and whose civilisation we know as Byzantine. It was to become the most important city in the world and the most magnificent; and it was to stand for eleven hundred years. Its impact upon Cyprus was total and ineradicable.

Thirdly, in the middle years of the century, several severe earthquakes occurred, devastating Paphos, Salamis and Kourion in turn. Paphos never recovered, Salamis had to be rebuilt and Kourion was wrecked but survived. The able and, we gather, irascible, Epiphanios was elected Archbishop now: he was the man for the hour. He found a Church choked with petty division and he rooted the factions out.

So when in the year 380, Christianity was made the official religion of the Roman

Empire, St. Barnabas's Church, reorganised and united, was ready to meet the challenge and cope with the programme that lay ahead.

For every district, a church had to be provided, for every See, a cathedral, for every cathedral, a baptistry; all to be suitably equipped and decorated. The need to recruit, instruct and ordain clergy would have been urgent, too.

The majority of the stricken people, with the noise and terror and loss of the earthquakes still a living memory – and the famine experienced by their grandparents not far behind – must have been willing converts. The old gods had betrayed them, their faith had been misdirected and they were being offered new hope through Christ. But the task was still enormous.

Apollo had been worshipped in the land for about as long as Christianity has been established in England; Aphrodite, in one guise or another, for twice as long. (In 395, the Byzantine Emperor was obliged to issue an edict banning the rites of Aphrodite at Old Paphos; he was not very successful.) The following year, the Roman Empire was finally divided into the Empire in the East and the Empire in the West: Cyprus ceased to be governed from Rome and came instead under the jurisdiction of Antioch.

THE FIFTH CENTURY – *Early Byzantine*

Expansion

As the Island moved into the fifth century, it came into a much-needed period of peace and prosperity which lasted right through the sixth century as well. Except for one thing! In the year 410, the Patriarch of Antioch wrote a letter to Pope Innocent I in Rome protesting about the behaviour of the Church of Cyprus, which was appointing its own archbishops, ignoring Antioch to whose See it now belonged.

Thus started a battle that continued for the best part of the century. The outraged Cypriots insisted that they had an Apostolic foundation in no way inferior to Antioch's, and went on consecrating their archbishops as they always had done. If the Patriarch had prevailed, the history of the Island might well have been different.

As it was, in 488, the remains of Barnabas were discovered near Salamis, where John Mark had buried him secretly over four hundred years before. The relics, and a copy of St Matthew's Gospel in Hebrew, found with the Saint, were rushed to the Emperor Zeno. He was greatly impressed and accepted as established beyond question the independence of the Church. Moreover, certain unique privileges were conferred upon its archbishops which are still exercised today.

They are: to wear the Imperial purple on Feast days; to sign documents in red ink, as did the Byzantine Emperors; to carry an Imperial sceptre in place of a pastoral staff; and to bear the title 'Most Blessed'.

So, vested in this great authority, the Church of Cyprus grew to be a powerful force in the land. Like the priest-kings of old, whose successors they were, the archbishops became the leaders of the nation throughout the long, later years of domination, culminating in the person of Makarios III, in 1960 first President of Cyprus, and the most powerful archbishop of all.

Meanwhile, the building programme went on apace; but initially, it seems, there was not much money to spare. Old foundations were built upon, dressed stone,

Roman columns and capitals were salvaged from the earthquake rubble of forty years before and used again. The bishops must have been hard-pressed to find funds to purchase the fine marble and mosaic needed to decorate their cathedrals. No wonder we find two chapels for offerings placed strategically at either end of Kourion Cathedral. Set in the floor of one is a quotation from Psalm 76: *Vow and pay to the Lord thy God*. The generosity of a son of the city, Eustolios, in providing a comfortable hostelry and baths is recorded in another inscription. Judging by the thousands of pieces of tessera that have been found, numbers of churches in the Island were richly decorated, so appeals for funds must have been answered.

In style, these buildings were Roman basilicas, with a clerestorey, an apsidal east end and an atrium or portico to the west. Inside, apart from the mosaics, the walls were covered with sheets of mother o' pearl and friezes of white marble carved in low relief. On the floors would have been mosaic carpets and opus sectile work, with the less costly local soft marble being used in the passages. The universal problem was how to cover these large expanses of wall; there being so far in this early period, only a limited imagery – sufficient for the catacombs, but quite inadequate now. Ships and anchors, vines and grapes, lambs, streams and palm trees were used, for example, with a limited number of Biblical scenes and a beardless, very youthful Christ, resembling the Apollo He was supplanting. Craftsmen filled in with what they already knew, using Roman Nilotic and hunting scenes, geometric patterns and acanthus leaves.

THE SIXTH CENTURY – *The Flowering*

Throughout the Empire

By this time, complete sequences illustrating the Life and Passion of Our Lord, Old Testament themes and Lives of Saints and Martyrs were well established, their treatment recognisably Byzantine. The style had developed from the mingling of East and West in Constantinople; Hellenistic grace and realism blended with the Oriental propensity for asceticism and flat, abstract design. The balance varied according to time and place, but it was a union of opposites that, when successful, became a new and dynamic form of art. Years were to pass before it could be used to full effect. Until then, the mosaics on the church walls proclaimed the Emperor, whom God had chosen to rule His people and in whose person were invested both religious and political power in God's name.

The Byzantines were obsessed with order, rank and symmetry. The Imperial Court was based on a hierarchy reflecting that of the hosts of Heaven as set out in the Scriptures. The Christians seem to have been the first to use wall mosaics on a large scale. Although the Romans adorned niches and similar small areas with mosaic-work, they kept largely to the floors, and their walls were painted. Once released from the floor, where the surface had to be smooth, the potential for the use of tesserae opened up. The art of setting the pieces at varying angles and depths to catch or avoid the light and so create a three-d effect and a vibrance, was explored.

The colour-range was quite small, but the skill was enormous. Portable icons were about also, some made with tiny tesserae, some with paint. They are said to derive from Egyptian funerary portraits and had always been popular.

Justinian 527-565
Ruling as we do over our Empire, which God has entrusted to us by His Divine authority . . . Introduction to the Digest.

On to the stage now steps the most famous emperor after Constantine; work-a-holic, brilliant, unpopular, zealously Christian and, forcefully by his side, his wife from the brothels of Constantinople, the Empress Theodora. They can both be seen in contemporary mosaic in the Church of San Vitale in Ravenna, positioned directly beneath Christ in Majesty; and Justinian's role as Christ's viceroy is quite apparent.

He extended the frontiers of the Empire, produced one of the world's best legal codes, developed a new concept in building using vaults and domes, (the astonishing St Sophia Cathedral is his). From the Imperial workshops, his jewellers, metallurgists, sculptors, stonemasons, workers in ivories and enamels, mosaicists and painters produced work of the highest standard. Not without cause is this century often called the first golden age of Byzantium.

In Cyprus
The Island reaped full benefit. The Persians, perpetual thorn in Justinian's side, harassed the mainland but left Cyprus in peace. Several thousand Persian p.o.w's were transferred there, though, just about the time when the secret of silk production had been wrested from China. (Two monks smuggled silkworms' eggs out of the country in the hollowed-out handles of their staffs in about 552AD).[1]

The industry was soon thriving in Cyprus: Persian textiles and designs had always been sought after, so now, with an experienced workforce to hand and a ready market, a reputation for figured silks and embroidered cloth was established. Also, the Island became known for its enamels and illuminated manuscripts. Oriental influence becomes apparent once more.

Only two examples of wall mosaics survive from the sixth century: one is Hellenistic and the other shows distinct Oriental attributes. Apart from these, and one or two partly-preserved church floors, nothing remains of the splendour that must have graced all the cities then. The reason is the Arab Raids.

THE DARK AGES – *mid-seventh to mid-tenth centuries*
I THE ARAB RAIDS
In 1902 in the ruins of Lapethos, a once thriving Roman port on the north coast of Cyprus, villagers unearthed a câche of early Byzantine gold and silver objects, among which were nine silver dishes known as the David plates. Between them, they illustrate scenes from the life of David. The control stamps on the backs show them to date from the first half of the seventh century, when Heraclius was emperor. They may be commemorative. (At Ninevah, in 627, Heraclius defeated the commander of the Persian army in single combat and beheaded him as David did Goliath.) As Lapethos was obliterated by the Arabs in 653/4, it is highly likely that this treasure was concealed at that date and never retrieved. Every coastal town was devastated at one time or another. It signalled the end of the antique cities.

---

1. Footprints in Cyprus p. 141.

In 632, the Arabs had exploded in a Holy War inspired by Mohamed. They conquered Persia, left weakened and in disarray after the onslaughts of Heraclius, and with incredible speed became lords of the coastal lands from Syria and Palestine through to Egypt. Constantinople, also weakened by the interminable Persian War, was unable to protect her provinces; indeed, by 672, the Arab legions had reached the walls of the city and were only just held off.

With success had come undreamt-of riches and also a sizeable navy, which the Arabs had previously lacked. Now lords of the seas, they set sail for Cyprus, and they arrived off Salamis in 649 with 1,700 ships. This was the first of three hundred years of pulverising raids. The Island had been thriving and was brimming with good things: the raiders razed Salamis, pillaged the countryside and made off with seventy shiploads of loot.

It was during this expedition that the Lady Umm Haram died, adored foster-mother of the Prophet. Within five years, Cyprus had an Arab army of occupation imposed upon it based at Paphos. For a period, the country was tossed like a bone between the Byzantines and the Arabs, and often found itself paying heavy tribute to both for protection. In 688 an extraordinary measure was taken by the Byzantines: the entire Cypriot population was packed into boats and resettled in a safe part of Asia Minor. Ten years later, they all came back again! So ended the most awful fifty years.

In the eighth century, some kind of organisation was managed and all the Byzantine provinces were put on military alert. Farmer-soldiers, called **Akrites** and trained on the old Roman lines for frontier defence, were settled on the vulnerable borders. Co-operating with these bands were two naval contingents. Communication was by a chain of beacons which flashed news of attacks across Asia Minor to the Capital. This organisation acted as the eyes and ears of the Empire for two hundred and fifty years. In Cyprus, the Akrites proved so effective that the Island was never completely occupied by the Arabs as Crete and Sicily were. It had its own internal system of beacons which could speedily give warning of a raid across the countryside. Two are known to have been located on the peaks of St Hilarion and Kantara above Kyrenia, and their fires would have been visible on the mainland, forty miles away.

The exploits of these soldiers were celebrated in heroic ballads which have been handed down in popular song and story to this day. The great hero was Cyprus's own Dighenis; and in the 1950's his emotive name was chosen as the non-de-guerre of Grivas, when he arrived secretly from Greece to lead the EOKA fight for freedom from British rule. Between the Akrites and the Church, the ordinary people in eighth and ninth century Cyprus kept heart and faith.

One of the worst raids occurred in 806, despite all precautions. It was in reprisal for the Emperor's refusal to pay tribute-money. *I have read thy letter,* thundered the Caliph Haroun-al-Raschid, *O thou son of a misbelieving mother. Thou shalt hear, thou shalt not behold, my reply.* It exceeded anything that had gone before and thousands were killed or taken into slavery, the archbishop among them. The Imperial Court in Constantinople must have felt very remote at such times.

All in all, the Island changed hands eleven times at least and, according to the historian Stephen de Lusignan, was subject to twenty four full-scale Arab attacks. Throughout the period, the true leaders of the Cypriots were the priests and the monks, who never deserted the people and shared their vicissitudes. It was then that the character and structure of Cypriot society and mores were bonded.

II THE ICONOCLASTS 726-843
Throughout the Empire

We had our Puritans, so did the Byzantines. An iconoclast is literally *'a smasher of images'*. Only a single religious point was involved, but it was so fundamental that it affected everyone, and innumerable priceless works of art were destroyed. At the outset, a decree by the Emperor Leo III, fully supported by his Eastern bishops, banned all pictorial representations of Christ, the Virgin and the Saints on the grounds that they were being misused and worshipped like idols. There was some truth in this. The knowledge that both Judaism and Islam excluded all figures from their art was a strong influence, too. The opposition, including all the monasteries – one of the chief sources of icons – claimed that pictures were needed because most of the population could not read, yet needed instruction; also, icons helped one to pray.

During the years of iconoclasm, abstract motives or a simple Cross replaced the traditional scenes and portraits. Meanwhile, monks were exiled – often to Cyprus – treasured icons were hidden and painters persecuted. In the end icons were allowed again, it being made quite clear that a painted image is not an object of worship but is venerated only for what it represents; venerated, in fact, precisely as the Holy Cross is. Nevertheless, everything beautiful from the earlier years had disappeared from churches everywhere, torn out and smashed.

Oddly, it was Theophilos, the last of the iconoclastic emperors, who commissioned the most richly fantastic creations to adorn the Great Palace, inspiring W.B. Yeats' poems on Byzantium: a golden throne supported by metal lions that roared, a hammered tree with mechanical singing birds on its branches.

> . . . Such a form as Grecian goldsmiths make
> Of hammered gold and gold enamelling
> To keep a drowsy Emperor awake;
> Or set upon a golden bough to sing
> To lords and ladies of Byzantium
> Of what is past, or passing, or to come.
>
> *from Sailing to Byzantium, W B Yeats*

MID-BYZANTINE – *(9th-13th century)*
Throughout the Empire
I THE MACEDONIANS 867-1056

Although the Arab menace was not finally overcome until the middle of the tenth century, the end of the icon dispute had already opened the way for new ideas in the ninth. In 867, a new dynasty had been founded in Constantinople under the first Macedonian Emperor, Basil I. An illiterate peasant himself, he encouraged progressive thought and culture in the capital – and the city must have been full of painters and intellectuals lately returned from exile. A wave of interest in the ancient world developed and resulted in a neo-classical revival.

In art, this had the happy effect of preventing religious painting becoming too severely oriental as a result of the excessive influence exerted by eastern prelates earlier.

Moreover, a change of emphasis occurred whereby Imperial imagery slowly gave way to a Patriarchal one on the walls of the churches, and the Founding Fathers exhorted the worshippers in paint instead of the current Emperor in mosaic. Basil brought in a new type of architecture. Originating in Armenia (whence came his forebears), it was basically a cross-in-square design and supported a central dome. It became the pattern for countless small churches still found today throughout the Orthodox world. It presented a challenge to the artists in that its internal surfaces called for a new plan of decoration; and a scheme was evolved that has remained standard ever since. In it, Christ is in the highest place, the dome; the Virgin, as Mother of God, occupies the next most exalted position, the conch of the apse; the walls and vaults set out scenes from their time on earth; beneath these stand the saints and martyrs. Squinches, arches, pillars, the sanctuary and side-chapels, too, have their appointed roles in proclaiming the Christian message to the worshippers. The medium used was either paint or mosaic, but more often paint, being more versatile and less expensive. The art was two-dimensional, shadowless, linear and stylised, yet, at the same time, it incorporated a classical grace and rhythm. The scenes were large: two to a vault. The figures moved through a timeless landscape, their gaze fixed somewhere in eternity.

In the Palace workshops, guilds of craftsmen were once more producing silks and ivories, illuminating manuscripts and setting cloisonné enamels and precious stones in gold or silver-gilt. Mosaicists and master painters went out to the provinces to establish schools. A visit today to the Treasury of St Marks in Venice can give some idea of the excellence and richness of the products: reliquiary and Gospel covers, patens and chalices, psalters and caskets can be seen there, looted during the Sack of Constantinople in 1204. Most of the work is religious because the whole city of Constantinople was informed through and through with a religious outlook. Nearer home, exquisite examples of ivories can be seen in the Victoria and Albert Museum.

II THE COMNENIANS 1057 – 1203
The Rise of the Turks
A remarkable Emperor, Alexios Comnenos, turned Cyprus into a military base when dealing with this next menace. He took over power in 1081 after the Seljuk Turks had rampaged up and down the Middle East for ten years, threatening the very existence of the Empire. At that date, almost the whole of Anatolia and most of the Syrian coast was controlled by them; also Jerusalem. Furthermore, in the West the Normans, who already occupied Italy and Sicily, openly had Constantinople as their objective.

Alexios inherited a kingdom that had quite suddenly run out of territorial possessions, money and fighting strength. But he was good at delegating authority, a fine diplomat and an experienced campaigner; and in the twenty-four years of his reign he restored the realm to something approaching its former capacity. Although half Asia Minor was by then the Turkish Sultanate of Rum, and Sicily and the Adriatic irretrievably lost, the redrawn borders were firmly fixed and no longer easy to breach. Jerusalem was in the hands of the Crusaders.

Art Through the Twelfth Century
Because so much has been destroyed in Constantinople, any provincial work that has survived from this and the preceding century has a rarity value and is all the more appreciated. Bear in mind that less than one per cent of the whole output of Byzantium has survived to the present day.

A number of examples exist in Cyprus and more continue to be discovered, concealed under whitewash or later plaster. Fresco was now the universal medium and far less mosaic was used. As the century progressed, a feeling of movement can be observed in the frescoes, as if a breeze had begun to blow, fluttering the robes of angel and saint. The substitution of paint for mosaic undoubtedly contributed to the greater freedom in presentation; but it is more fundamental than that, it is the neo-classical style taken further; here are the first stirrings of the Renaissance. Architectural backgrounds developed elaborately during this time, giving us an idea of the actual buildings of the day.

Persisting from the Early Christian period, though, is the absence of natural perspective – a feature that can be disconcerting until the eye accepts it. This was deliberate and was done for the same reason that shadows were omitted: to affirm the other-worldliness of the scene, the action being out of time. Often backgrounds, buildings, furniture are in reverse perspective. Figures, too, may have little relation to distance, their size relating more to their importance (familiar to us from Saxon carving).

Portable icons were just as affected by developments as wall-paintings, and influenced a far wider public, because travellers took them to the far corners of the known world. The best-known example is the Virgin of Vladimir, painted in Constantinople in 1125, which shows the Mother tenderly, wistfully, laying her cheek against her Son's.

Towards the end of the century, for the first time, artists began to sign their work and to be acknowledged by their patrons. Only the masters, though, and most of the painters remained anonymous as before: their work was for the glory of God, not for themselves; they were simply craftsmen and were paid to do their job; the people who got the credit were the lords who commissioned their services.

In Cyprus

It was not until 964 that Cyprus was finally recovered from the Arab grip – and it was a changed land. Gone were the cities and buildings of the old Roman province, gone or passing were Paphos, Lapethos, Constantia (Salamis), Kition and Kourion; the new towns were called Ktima, Famagusta, Limassol, Larnaca and Kyrenia. A new capital had been growing inland – Nicosia.

A spate of building began and every church was given a dome – or three – or five! The old basilica-style churches, now being restored, demanded a series of domes to span their vast spaces. Refugees from Turkish-occupied Syria possessed the skill to construct such domed buildings. Painters from the mainland began to arrive to teach how the new wall-surfaces should be decorated, and schools of painting were formed. Most colours could be obtained from local mineral deposits, Cyprus being rich in such things; only gold and ultramarine needed to be imported.

Two peaceful centuries were to pass in which the Island blossomed again, and the only enemy seems to have been the Imperial tax-collector. One Muqaddas, a Palestinian, reported in 985: *It is full of populous cities and offers Muslims many advantages in their trade thither, by reason of the great quantities of merchandise, stuffs and goods which are produced there.*[1] He continues, *The island is in the power of whichever nation is overlord in these seas.* A very perceptive remark.

---

1. Excerpta Cypria, page 5

Meanwhile, Governors were once more appointed. They proved an unreliable lot, often corrupt. The Church of Cyprus, too, resented them because the appointments deprived it of political power. With the crowning of Alexios Comnenos, all the wheeler-dealing disappeared. His policy was to give civil and military authority only to diplomats and soldiers of the highest quality, and after a while only putting in as governors members of his own family whom he could really trust. The Island was eventually fully garrisoned and used as a base to guard Imperial interests on the coasts of the mainland. The old watchtowers on the Kyrenia heights were turned into fortresses.

The reputation that Cyprus had in mediaeval times for breeding fine horses was established now: such a concourse of high-born officials and military leaders demanded good mounts. The most renowned of them is the Cyprian Bay acquired by Richard Coeur-de-Lion years later, thereafter and ever his battlehorse. It was during this period that Kykko Monastery was founded, ca.1100, under the patronage of Alexios. Pre-eminent senior religious house in Cyprus to this day, it possesses one of the three holy icons accepted by the Orthodox Church as being painted by St Luke; it was previously kept in the Imperial Palace.

By the twelfth century, the Island had become feudal. The aristocracy had been buying up large tracts of land and were now powerful local lords. This was happening throughout the Empire. The first of hundreds of tiny churches and chapels began to be erected on these estates now, and not one records a humble origin. Notable among them in Cyprus is at Asinou and the inscription informs us that the Governor, who was a duke and a son-in-law of the Emperor, had the church built in 1106. More monasteries were appearing also, but they were invariably founded with funds and charters obtained from Constantinople.

THE FINAL SEPARATION FOR CYPRUS

The Crusades

England is a country beyond Romania on the north, out of which a cloud of English with their Sovereign . . . sailed towards Jerusalem. The wicked wretch . . . sold our country to the Latins for £200,00 of gold.

These words are from a letter written by a recluse, Neophytos, probably in 1196, from his cave near Paphos, and is a solitary cry expressing the feelings of the people. *"The wicked wretch"* was Richard Coeur de Lion and the reason for his presence was his involvement in the Third Crusade of 1191.

All had been going well for Cyprus until the middle of the twelfth century. In 1099, the First Crusade had freed Jerusalem from the Turks and the Island had benefitted from a steady flow of pilgrims passing through on their way there. Venetian merchants arrived: Western influences multiplied. Alexios' well-run military base seems to have deteriorated as the century progressed, though; understandably, as the last Comnenian rulers of Byzantium were in desperate straits elsewhere and impoverished. Lacking strong leadership, Cyprus fell victim once more to a series of depredations by pirates, extortionists, and adventurers over a period of about thirty years.

The cause of Richard's interference was the latest of these, a minor member of the Comnenian House called Isaac, who in 1184 had falsely set himself up as 'Emperor of Cyprus' and was proving a hated tyrant. The English fleet had been on course for Acre when a storm arose, scattering the ships. Berengaria of Navarre, Richard's future queen, and also his favourite sister Joan, were on board the ship that sought shelter off Limassol, the captain sending messengers ashore asking for some aid. Instead of help, they received insults and provocation from Isaac. Some days later, Richard arrived, landed his cavalry, pursued the tyrant across the countryside to the Kyrenia mountains, blockaded the forts and cornered him in the Karpassos, where Isaac surrendered. Richard then married Berengaria in the Chapel of St George in Limassol Castle and, leaving garrisons in every town, continued on his way to join the Third Crusade. All this took place in a matter of weeks!

The English King now had an island that he did not want, and he found it something of a trial. First, he sold it to the Knights Templar: in 1192 the Cypriots revolted and were massacred in their hundreds in Nicosia on Easter Day: the Templars gave Richard his island back. Another adventurer, but on the Crusader side, was a Frank from Aquitaine called Guy de Lusignan. He was offered the lordship of Cyprus in compensation for his loss of the Crown of Jerusalem (to which he had a right only through marriage). He accepted. A condition of his tenure was that it was for his lifetime, no longer.

Two years later Guy died, but Richard failed to claim the Island back and Aimery de Lusignan succeeded his brother. This was the man who, by guile, cast off allegiance to the English Crown and acquired the title of King of Cyprus for himself and his heirs. Now the land was well and truly lost to Byzantium, for the rule of the Franks went on to last for a further three hundred years.

UNDER THE FRANKS 1192-1489

Henceforth, all hope of freedom was gone for the Cypriots. The Franks implemented an elaborate feudal system with a hierarchy far more rigid than that of the Byzantine landowners of the previous centuries. The great estates were either held by Frankish barons in fiefs or were a domain owned by the King. A few Cypriot families managed to keep their land, but they had to pay an annual tithe to the new rulers.

Apart from this remnant of the indigenous aristocracy, the majority of the people were now serfs known as Paroikoi, and they were tied to their respective overlords. Slightly better circumstanced were the Freemen, and it was from them that eventually a native middle-class emerged. As well as a third of their produce, both categories had to give two days a week free labour to their masters.

There was no crossing of the social boundaries either, and Franco-Cypriot marriages were forbidden. The regime was suppressive but not cruel, and legislation existed to protect the Paroikoi from abuse by their lords. Nonetheless, the Lusignans were well aware that they held Cyprus by force, and that they had to guard against insurrection. Immediately, they began strengthening all fortifications. The existing chain of defences on the northern mountain range was reinforced, also Kyrenia Castle, guarding a good harbour below: thus were ensured both an escape and a supply route, easily to be reached from the Capital. There a new palace was being built, with a fortified tower adjoining it.

Meanwhile, what of the Independent Apostolic Church of Cyprus? How was it faring under the new conditions? The answer is: terribly! At the outset, Aimery, as one of his moves towards the Crown, had invited the Pope to set up the Latin

Church on the Island, it to have authority over the Greek. For years, relations in general between the Church of Rome and the Orthodox Church had been strained; by the end of the twelfth century, it could be said that they detested each other: witness the sack of Constantinople by the – Catholic – Venetians on the Fourth Crusade. That was still a few years in the future, but submission was a no less bitter pill for the Church of Cyprus to swallow. *The Latin clergy*, says one writer, *treated the natives with contempt; the natives gave them snarl for snarl and bite for bite.* [1] Nevertheless, twenty years later the last Cypriot bishop had been turned out of his cathedral, and Latin Mass had replaced the Greek Liturgy in every town.

Finally, in 1260, the Bulla Cypria appeared. It was a Papal edict directing the displaced bishops – reduced to four out of an original thirteen – to swear fealty to the Latin Archbishop, to hand over all Church revenue and not to replace their own Archbishop. If the Pope was hoping to make the Island Catholic by such measures, he underestimated the tenacity of the opposition. Curiously, it is at about this date that the small monastery churches in the Troodos foothills started to be done up and to acquire sturdy protective roofs.

Numbers of 13th and 14th century Gothic monuments have survived as reminders of these years; but by pure chance the best are almost entirely located in what is now Turkish-occupied territory. The most outstanding are: St. Sophia Cathedral in Nicosia, Bellapaise Abbey near Kyrenia and Famagusta Cathedral.

After the fall of Acre in 1291, an influx of knights, their families and entourages gave the courtly life of Nicosia a boost; and the Christian merchants of Syria adopted the deep-water port of Famagusta as their new trading centre. Cyprus had now become the only Christian country left in the east Mediterranean. Goods from the Orient poured in to Famagusta, making that city rich and famous and outdoing even Nicosia in luxurious living. This advantage soon spread over the whole Island, and for much of the fourteenth century Cyprus was at a peak of material prosperity.

In the eyes of the world, too, it was once more a desirable place. *And the tongues of every nation under heaven are heard and read and talked.* Several visitors from the West recorded their impressions during that time. Speaking here is Ludolf von Suchen, a German priest, and he gives a picture of the life-style of the nobility. They amused themselves, he writes, in spear-fighting, tourneys and, above all, in hunting, and they even used cheetahs to bring down the wild moufflon. *The princes, nobles, barons and knights,* he continues, *are the richest in the world . . . but they spend all on the chase. I knew a certain Count of Jaffa who had more than five hundred hounds, and every two dogs have their own servant to guard and bathe and anoint them, for so must dogs be tended there.* [2] (If, gentle reader, you ever see, as I have done, a starving mongrel hound in Cyprus, remember its ancestry and give it a crust of bread.)

An affluent society attracts predators. For Famagusta, this meant above all the Venetians and the Genoese, jealous rivals for the Cyprus market. After an incident in 1372, the Genoese invaded and took the main towns, robbing and plundering as they went. They were bought off after two years of upheaval, but they retained Famagusta and exacted a crippling annual tribute as well.

1. Hepworth Dixon, 'British Cyprus' 1879
2. Excerpta Cypria page 20

Famagusta profited them little, however, because the trade had been lost through their own rapacity: but they remained like an irritable dog-in-the-manger to plague the Franks right up to 1464.

Meanwhile another, safer, source of income was the production of cane sugar. Previously manufactured in Syria and Palestine, the canes had been brought to the Island by the Crusaders retreating from Acre and were thereafter cultivated in large plantations, chiefly at Kolossi, Episkopi and Old Paphos. Cyprus remained one of the chief exporters of sugar until competition from the West Indies killed the industry.

By the end of the fourteenth century, the hey-day of the Franks was over. A Mameluke invasion in 1426, a battle ineptly lost resulting in massive slaughter in the streets of the capital and a king, Janus, prisoner in Cairo, pointed the way to the end. In 1489 the Venetians quietly walked into power and Cyprus became part of their Republic. It is not within the province of this handbook to recount the history of this period in more detail. Yet, from Guy de Lusignan through to the last Queen of Cyprus, an extraordinary pageant of rulers passed by, and their exploits make lively, entertaining reading. It is sufficient here to mention three: Peter I, Queen Helena and Katerina Cornaro.

King Peter I (1358-1369) was a flamboyant monarch who took his wife's nightgown on campaigns with him and always wore a naked sword round his neck as visible token of his vow to recapture Jerusalem. He did capture and sack Alexandria, though, with help. He also arrived at Westminster while fund-raising for a fifth Crusade and was feasted by King Edward III, it is claimed, along with the Kings of Scotland, France and Denmark. He is mentioned by Chaucer in The Canterbury Tales and is still remembered in Cypriot ballads.

Helena Palaeologina (1441-1458) was the formidable niece of the last Byzantine Emperor, Constantine Palaeologos. She married the king of Cyprus and dominated the government for sixteen years. So great was her influence that the possibility of Cyprus being reunited with Byzantium was being considered when Constantinople fell to the Turks in 1453 and any further moves in that direction were obviated. After this alliance, the ban on mixed marriages could no longer be taken seriously. The status of the Orthodox improved enormously and it was through her that a Greek bishop was permitted to take up residence in Nicosia once more. (He was Archbishop in all but name and his church, now known as the Bedestan, was referred to by the Cypriots as the Greek Cathedral.) The Pope expressed his concern about now at the influence the Eastern Church was having on the Catholics on the Island: but in fact the banished Church had been quietly making inroads on the Latin supremacy for years.

Katerina Cornaro (1474-1489) was the last Queen of Cyprus and she was Venetian. Her husband, James II, was the last full king of Cyprus and he married Katerina in a diplomatic move to gain a powerful ally against the Genoese, whom he had succeeded in turning out of Famagusta. The move backfired. There was much treachery abroad in those times and Venice coveted Cyprus. Within two years, James was dead after suddenly falling sick, his baby son survived a year, and Katerina became a figurehead queen. She ruled for fifteen years, but the real power lay in Venice. Finally she was persuaded to retire and the Island was governed openly by the Republic. Titian had painted her.

UNDER THE VENETIANS 1489–1570

The truth was that Venice was more concerned with the strategic position of Cyprus than with its inhabitants, providing, as it did, an urgently needed base for her Fleet against the increasing Turkish threat and also welcome revenue from the Levantine trade routes.

Nevertheless, initially the new governors tried to establish a good relationship with the populace, promising to treat them well: they did not want a rising any more than their predecessors. A bonus was that the Paroikoi could buy their freedom, that no additional taxes would be imposed and that everyone with estates could keep them. But the old feudal lords were dispossessed in another way, because they were all replaced in public office by Venetians. Deprived of any real power, they tended to side with the already disaffected Greeks. Moreover, as the top-ranking administrators themselves were replaced every two years, the gap between them and the people grew wider for lack of understanding; diplomacy suffered, whereas self-interest and extortion flourished. Eventually, the regime became so unpopular with all sections of the community that many appear to have emigrated, the desperately poor paroikoi in particular; and the countryside became depopulated. The Venetians partially dismantled the Lusignan strongholds in the Kyrenia mountains, fearing that they could be used by the Cypriots in the event of an insurrection.

Pilgrims to the Holy Land, passing through, give us an insight into life and manners towards the end of the fifteenth century. One, Felix Faber, writing of his visit in the reign of Katerina,[1] recounts his horror at the decadence of the Catholic Church. The Roman Sees were actually being offered for sale, the higher clergy departed abroad for long periods and the most unsuitable persons were posturing and preening as monks and bishops. Furthermore, he discovered a Greek and a Latin church not far from each other that shared a priest between them who officiated in both rites, a custom of the worst kind. This state of affairs continued with increasing laxity throughout Venetian rule. The truth was becoming even more apparent that the Latin Church on the Island was inch by inch being edged out by the Orthodox. One can still find examples of defunct 16th century Latin chapels sharing one roof with a far more substantial Orthodox church. The village of Kiti, near Larnaca, possesses one.

The eyewitnesses of the period almost all remark on the ruinous and deserted look of the land, especially of Larnaca and Paphos. Baumgarten in 1508 depicts Cyprus in springtime in this manner: *Very fruitful of corn, abounding in silkworms, silks, oil, sugar and wine. Here are very beautiful hills, most pleasant and delightful valleys, always resounding with the melodious singing of birds . . . Yet, notwithstanding all this fruitfulness and pleasantness, neither its cities nor its villages are much frequented, but as if it was barren and a deserted place it is inhabited only by a few people that live in cottages. It has no cities but Nicosia and Famagusta . . .*[2]

As the sixteenth century progressed, so did the Turkish advance become more of a threat. By 1522, Egypt and Syria had been engulfed and Cyprus was beset on three sides by the aggressor. Defence became a priority. Gunpowder had been invented since the Lusignan fortifications were built and those would be little use

---

1. Excerpta Cypria page 47
2. Excerpta Cypria page 55

against the new artillery. To withstand cannon-fire, the Venetians constructed the massive walls of Famagusta, Nicosia and Kyrenia Castle, much of which still exist.

The Martengo bastion at Famagusta is considered one of the finest examples of military architecture to be found, incidentally. The circular wall surrounding old Nicosia went up between 1567 and 1570 but was not completed in time for the Turkish invasion. Preparations for the anticipated battle involved flattening all existing cover outside the new walls, and many historic buildings were destroyed to this end, including the beautiful Monastery of the Dominicans, resting place of many of the Lusignan Royal House.

When the Turks reached the city in 1570, it fell within seven weeks due to the incompetence of its commander. Around 20,000 Christians are thought to have been massacred in the days that followed. Rupert Gunnis in his book 'Historic Cyprus' writes evocatively about the fall of Nicosia:

Few of the Italian officers or the Cypriote nobles escaped the general holocaust . . . The Turks, when they captured Cyprus were peculiarly bitter against members of the Roman Catholic faith, and especially persecuted them. Therefore such members of the Latin aristocracy as escaped . . . found it expedient to change their names and their religion and were gradually absorbed into the Greek Cypriote peasantry. Where, now, is Nores? Where d'Ibelin? Where Giblet? Gone in name, perhaps, but not in blood; somewhere still run these noble strains; diluted and thin they may be, but they are there. The peasant in the village, the policeman in Nicosia, or the priest in the Carpass may, if they but knew it, have bluer blood in their veins than half the aristocracy in Europe.

Famagusta put up an heroic resistance for a further year under siege conditions whilst waiting for the promised relieving force from Venice which never came. Surrender there brought its own horrors.

ARRIVAL OF THE TURKS – 1570

At first, the bonded peasants looked upon the Turks as saviours. Gone were their oppressors, gone was the Latin Church and the entire feudal system had been wiped out virtually overnight. For them, the Turkish rule began well. The Orthodox Church regained its former standing and it was the Latin buildings that were converted into mosques: the onerous taxation was reduced and for a small sum the paroikoi found themselves owners of the land they had toiled on for so long.

Nevertheless, the Church looked further ahead because it now had a secular responsibility and the Archbishop represented the voice of the people to the Turkish Bey. The population was desperately poor, their country in ruins and the larger part of its leaders and educated class lost. The Church decided to revive To Koinon tou Kyprion.

Another three hundred years were to pass before this latest yoke was to be lifted, and in all that time very few of the Turkish governors were anything but petty and rapacious tyrants. Oppression, corruption and excessive taxation were once again the order of the day. In the seventeenth century, the office of Grand Dragoman was created. The holder was always a Greek appointed by the Archbishop; he had direct access to the Sultan in Istanbul and a hard task – and sometimes a short life – as spokesman for the Cypriots in secular affairs.

When the British took over in 1878, they found a run-down, neglected backwater – a far cry from the fruitful, prosperous and cosmopolitan country it once had been. Yet, at the head of his sorely abused people, the Archbishop of the Church of Cyprus still proudly signed his name in red ink, was addressed as 'Most Blessed' and carried an Imperial sceptre in the style of a Byzantine Emperor.

POST-BYZANTINE ART IN CYPRUS
(13th to 16th centuries)

Briefly, in the thirteenth century, church wall painting degenerated as schools closed and the masters departed. Yet some good panel paintings exist from this time, as if artists were still to be found if the demand were there.

After the fall of Acre, the future began to look rosier for the Cypriots because artists and craftsmen returned along with the dispossessed Crusaders and merchants from Syria. Renewed contact with the mainstream of Byzantine art, the new Western influence and a continuation of conservative, traditional methods produced a variety of styles. Throughout the fourteenth and fifteenth centuries, demand for portable icons was considerable, for they were commissioned by wealthy families of all creeds to present to their places of worship. Invariably, the donors would be represented kneeling below in careful portraiture, affording us a glimpse of the fashionable society of the period.

Another source of icons came from the monasteries, which have always kept the Orthodox tradition alive through years of oppression. The difference between religious painting as done by the monks and that produced by the schools of Constantinople is marked: in general, the first is conservative and tending towards eastern austerity, whereas the other is more progressive, fluid and classical. More icons were needed about now to fill the new iconostases – tall, three-tiered screens – which were replacing the older and simpler templons, made up of painted wooden panels and posts, before the Sanctuary.

When, in the fourteenth century, exchanges between Cyprus and Constantinople were possible again, the latest evolution in Palace art under the Palaeologue emperors reached the island and some superb work resulted: although the influence is less apparent in the wall painting. Its characteristics are elegance, sweetness of expression, delicate colouring and attention to detail; there is an absence of passion, an air of fin-de siècle, a reflective glow of diffused light as in some tranquil summer evening. It is, in sum, a very sophisticated final phase of the art of Byzantium.

On the other hand, local Cypriot work continued after the thirteenth century to co-exist with the Palaeologue on the Island, in monastery and village churches and in chapels run up by wealthy landowners. It was derived from earlier periods and came from painters' manuals, cards, transfers and old illustrated manuscripts. Often brightly coloured and stiffly executed, the profusion of small scenes depicting the Passion of our Lord, the life of the Virgin, the Miracles and so forth, with a string of saints below, are enchanting and quaint to the modern eye; but they achieved their purpose – which was to teach illiterate people the message of the Bible.

After the fall of Constantinople in 1453, the presence of Helena Palaeologina in

Cyprus attracted a flood of refugees over. During the following decades, some churches received new and beautiful paintings. But when a large church was built at St Neophytos Monastery, artists familiar with the schools of Crete and of Mystra seem to have been at work; because on those walls are some outstanding examples of Palaeologue art. The icon screen there holds a series of fine icons, nearly all of which were produced by a single artist in 1544.

In the early days of Venetian rule, an attempt was made to blend Latin and Byzantine styles to create an Italo-Byzantine school of painting in Cyprus. It had varying degrees of success, the accolade going to examples in the apse of a monastery church at Galata of 1502. The movement was short-lived.

Western influence, however, continued to manifest itself even in traditional painting. Some scenes showed it more than others. The Nativity, for instance, was affected hardly at all; whereas the Crucifixion, once stark and containing three dignified figures only, had often become an over-crowded, emotional occasion, losing much of its spiritual content in the process.

One or two artists are known by name in the first quarter of the sixteenth century: Philip tou Goul, Symeon Axenti and Titos for example. Their work is good and almost purely Byzantine in a late, local manner. Although they have recognisably personal styles, the workbooks they used were often the same and even here Latin features are evident.

After 1570, when the Turks came, fresco work slowly came to an end and few panels were painted. Later, icons began to reach the Island from abroad, particularly from Crete where there was a flourishing school, and from Venice itself, which supported a sizeable Greek and Cypriot community.

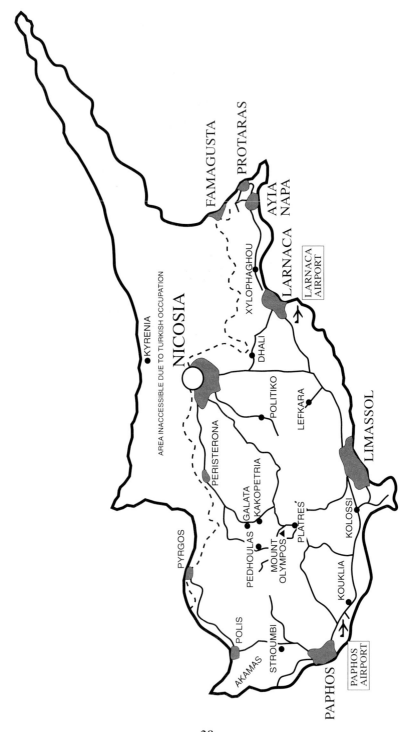

FAMAGUSTA

PROTARAS

AYIA NAPA

XYLOPHAGHOU

LARNACA

LARNACA AIRPORT

KYRENIA

AREA INACCESSIBLE DUE TO TURKISH OCCUPATION

NICOSIA

DHALI

POLITIKO

LEFKARA

LIMASSOL

PERISTERONA

GALATA

KAKOPETRIA

PLATRES

KOLOSSI

PYRGOS

PEDHOULAS

MOUNT OLYMPOS

KOUKLIA

POLIS

STROUMBI

AKAMAS

PAPHOS

PAPHOS AIRPORT

28

THE TOWNS & CHIEF MONUMENTS
OF EACH DISTRICT

PAPHOS

History of Paphos

Paphos today is unhealthy, unsafe and practically uninhabited

(Enlart in 1899)

The modern town of Paphos has two parts: Ktima on the cliff and Kato, or Lower, Paphos by the sea. Kato Paphos is the descendant of Nea Paphos, which was founded in about 325 BC and was so-called to distinguish it from Old Paphos, nine miles to the south-east at Kouklia.

Roman AD 46 to AD 330

When Paul and Barnabas came to Paphos in the time of the Emperor Claudius, the city had been the capital of Cyprus for two hundred years and was in its prime. It had a population estimated at around 30,000. The Apostles entered a thriving, peaceful city-port, rebuilt within its walls on the Roman grid plan sixty years previously after a bad earthquake. On high ground west of the harbour stood the palace of the Roman pro-consul; adjacent, the fine patrician residences of his colleagues; and half-a-mile across the bay gleamed the white marble columns of the Forum.

The life-style of the Roman officials was inclined to be showy, but the culture was in the main a continuation of the Hellenistic, and Greek the common language. From inscriptions, it is evident that shrines and temples abounded and that a number of different gods were worshipped: Mithras, Apollo, Dionysos, Hera, Aphrodite and Artemis, to name the most popular. The port was also used by pilgrims who came to visit the Temple of Aphrodite at Old Paphos. To the Establishment, Paul and Barnabas would have appeared to be trouble-makers, disturbers of the peace; and tradition has it that they were thrown into the city gaol. (The tale of the whipping has less foundation.) In due course, they were summoned before Sergius Paulus, the pro-consul, who wished to know what they were preaching. Bar-Jesus was present in his capacity of official soothsayer: he was also a Jew, and he tried to destroy the Apostles' case for the new sect. At last, Paul turned on him, called him the son of the devil and struck him blind in the name of the Lord. *Then the pro-consul believed, when he saw what had happened, for he was astonished at the teaching of the Lord:* Acts 13 vi-xiii. Whether this impressive conversion helped the Apostles make more converts is not known.

In the following century, it appears that Christians suffered periods of persecution here in common with the rest of the empire, as the catacomb of Ayia Solomoni and occupation of the Tombs of the Kings testify. It is claimed that the first bishop of Paphos was Epaphras,[1] one of the seventy disciples of Christ, consecrated in AD 67 by St. Herakleidios (the same that was created bishop of Tamassos by Barnabas).

Early Byzantine 330 to 649 AD

By the 4th century, the bishop of Paphos had apparently become the Metropolitan for Cyprus, taking precedence over the rest of the bishops, by then numbering some fourteen or fifteen. In 325, Bishop Kyrillos attended the first Church Council at Nicaea, with Yelasios of Salamis and Spyridon – of Corfu fame – of Tremithousa.

In 332 and again in 342 severe earthquakes caused widespread destruction along the entire south coast as far east as Salamis. That city was quickly rebuilt. More easily reached from Antioch when the Roman Empire came to be divided, Constantia was destined to be the new capital of Cyprus: but not yet. Paphos was also restored, the island was still governed from Rome, and the city limped on.

The appalling earthquake that extinguished Kourion in the summer of 365 also hit Paphos, and may have been the deciding factor in transferring the seat of government. It was probably in that year that the western half of the city was abandoned. By 368, the move had been effected. The new Metropolitan was now Epiphanios of Constantia, the first acknowledged full Archbishop of Cyprus.

Paphos was never to regain its proud Roman title of *Augustus Claudia Flavia, sacred metropolis of the cities throughout Cyprus;* and in 391 St Jerome records that *it had only its ruins to show what once it was.* Yet the cathedral that rose on the site of the ruined forum at the end of the 4th century was the largest and most impressive on the island. Moreover, Paphos continued to rank high in the Church hierarchy – and its bishop is to this day second only to the Archbishop in authority.

---

1. History of the Churches of Paphos: Tsiknopoullos

For the next two and a half centuries, the town was a quiet, provincial place, still with a skilled work-force (as excavations have revealed). The Governor's Palace, for example, was rebuilt and refurbished in a sumptuous style, indicating the, at least occasional, presence of high-ranking officials; and, at the beginning of the 5th century, a beautiful church went up at the port, Panayia Limeniotissa.

The Arab Invasions 649 to 964

Because of its remote position, Paphos was particularly vulnerable to Arab attacks, and seems to have had little help in repelling them. The second raid of AD 653 laid the city waste; and when, following this, an Islamic garrison of 12000 men was settled on the island, Paphos is thought to have been its base, for only here have Arabic inscriptions been found. The garrison remained for thirty years; and any Christian monuments that had survived the raid were destroyed during that time. (These included the cathedral and the church of the port, Limeniotissa.)

By now, the Cypriots had moved eastwards, creating a suburban district outside the walls. At this point, Paphos disappears into obscurity, possibly engulfed by the Arabs, who may have even settled here. An indication of the power of survival of the Church can be found at Yeroskipos, where the substantial five-domed church of Ayia Paraskevi was being built – or rebuilt – during this time.

Mid-Byzantine 965 to 1191

The fortunes of Paphos continue to be obscure right through the 10th and 11th centuries. It was a time when many small churches were built, frequently as private chapels on the large estates which were arising now peace had returned. The cathedral was rebuilt on a less ambitious scale, likewise the church of the Port. The new settlement at Ktima grew, and once more master-craftsmen came from Constantinople to establish schools.

When we hear of Paphos again, it is the start of the 12th century, and the city has become a leading port of call for ships on their way to Syria, Palestine and Egypt. Pilgrims to the Holy Land now often put in here: Erik the Good, King of Denmark, died while on pilgrimage and was buried in the cathedral in 1103; another distinguished pilgrim was Erik Magnusson, King of Norway, who came in 1110/1111.

A castle is known to have existed because it surrendered to Coeur de Lion's men in 1191: and before that a contingent of Scandinavian soldiers (known as Varangarians) were stationed somewhere in the vicinity.

One night in 1159, a violent earthquake occurred which ruined fourteen churches, including the restored cathedral and church of the Port. The event was recorded by a young man called Neophytos in his Retreat in the Paphos hills. The disaster struck just as Byzantine control over the island had begun to weaken, and it seems likely that the damaged buildings were patched up rather than rebuilt. The last thirty years saw Paphos again at the mercy of pirates and adventurers. Further damage to stability and the economy of the city would have been inflicted by the tyrant 'emperor' Isaac Comnenos and his extortions. Likewise, the fall of Jerusalem to Saladin in 1187 would have resulted in loss of trade and an idle port. History awaited the Third Crusade, which brought Richard Coeur de Lion to Cyprus and a new look to Paphos.

The Frankish period 1192 to 1489

After the initial disruption caused by King Richard's capture of the Island and its eventual leasing by Guy de Lusignan, the port appears to have picked up. But how the Cypriots resented their treatment is made clear by the then famous Neophytos writing in 1196: *Strange things and unheard of have befallen this land, and such that all its rich men have . . . sailed away to foreign lands. And those who could not fly – who is fit to set forth the tragedy of their sufferings? The searches, the public prisons, the exaction of money squeezed from them . . .*

The south-west area was to be a rich source of revenue for the Crown, with its huge yield of grapes, its silk industry, its cotton and, later, its plantations of sugar-cane. The estates merely exchanged their hastily departed Byzantine overlords for their Latin counterparts; the best, such as Kouklia, being selected for royal dhomaines.

In Nea Paphos, which they called Baffo or Baffe, the Franks were a considerable presence, and over the years the town became virtually French. Its past status of district capital was restored and its defences strengthened; a new castle was built to protect the harbour, and a sea-tower. (When the castle was ruined by earthquake in 1222, the sea-tower became a fort, joined to a second tower on the mole by a curtain wall.) The Latin Church established itself at the outset and had its own bishop in the town by 1196. Steps were taken to reduce and subordinate the Orthodox clergy; and in 1230 the Greek Bishop of Paphos was expelled. He went to Arsinoe (Polis); and the exile continued until at least 1500. Meanwhile, more Greek churches were being built throughout the district, purposely small and unnoticeable. Their Latin counterparts, on the contrary, were magnificent and among the finest Gothic structures in Cyprus – although few remains are visible today.

At some point, the harbour lost its capacity: the inner basin silted up, and the long breakwater that protected ships at anchor in the outer basin from westerly storms sank into the deep. 15th and 16th century travellers remarked on the exposed harbour and also on the unhealthy air of Paphos – caused by new stretches of marshland. Nevertheless, sugar and cotton continued to be exported from the port. By this time, sugar-cane had outstripped the grape as a valuable harvest. New aqueducts conveyed the essential water to the processing factories at Akhelia, Kouklia and, probably, at both Lemba and Emba; but the headquarters were at Kouklia, where a manorhouse had been built. Kouklia, site of Old Paphos, was known now, not for its temple but for its sugar.

In the 14th century, Genoese ships had become a menace, first appearing in 1316 to ravage the district and in 1373 actually occupying the fort, which they held for a year. In 1426, after winning the Battle of Khirokitia, the Mamelukes sacked the town. Afterwards, and for years to come, the revenue from the sugar industry was used to help pay towards the annual tribute demanded by the Caliph of Egypt; and that must have affected Paphos trade considerably. Then, around 1470, plague raged throughout the island for two and a half years, killing three-quarters of its population, according to report. Therefore, when a certain Nicholas le Huen travelled to Paphos in 1487, he may not have exaggerated when he wrote, "There were very noble churches there in times gone by as can be seen, even though the place now lies deserted."

The Venetian Period 1489 to 1570

Among its ruins, the ancient town persisted. It was still the capital of the south-west district, its defences were kept in repair and merchant ships continued to call at the port to load sugar and cotton as before. The list of bishops of the See of Paphos now has an Italian ring. Although the Church was corrupt, with sees for sale and absentee prelates, there were in Paphos at least some caring bishops, one of whom restored the neglected Latin cathedral out of his own pocket.

But, although in 1540 the population was thought to be about 2000, the town was in a slow decline. The Venetian engineer, Ascanius Savorgnano, assessing it in 1562, noted "a dearth of houses" and a harbour which could be enlarged to hold up to 200 galleys but not much use as it was. Finally, when the Turkish invasion was only months away, the Venetians dismantled the fort and sea-tower.

Turkish period 1570

Referred to as "Baf" or "Baffa". The only way that the change from Venetian to Turkish rule benefitted the Paphians was in the toleration of the Orthodox Church. The Bishop of Paphos returned promptly from Arsinoe and once more established his cathedral on the site of the 4th century basilica – where the smaller church of Khrysopolitissa was waiting.

The Turks restored and garrisoned the harbour fort but left the seaward tower derelict. Certain churches were selected to serve as mosques, as was the custom. Minarets appeared beside the Byzantine church of Ayia Sophia in Ktima and, it is thought, the Franciscan church below. The nearby Frankish Baths were rebuilt in Turkish style and also the handsome bath complex at Ktima.

Paphos became the centre of a military district, commanded first by a Pasha, then, from 1640, by a Bey. Perhaps the death of the sugar industry, a shrinking population and a neglected, silted-up harbour accounted for the subsequent rapid decline of both Kato Paphos and Ktima during the 17th and 18th centuries (or Old Baffo and New Baffo as they were then called). At some point, possible in the first quarter of the 18th century, the Turkish governor, the Bishop and the majority of the people had abandoned the coastal town for Ktima. The new cathedral and bishopric were at Mousallas and Paphos had shrunk to a poor village in a vast field of ruins and rubble, the harbour capable of receiving small boats only. The truth was that Paphos had simply outlived its usefulness. Early in the 19th century, the first antiquarian interest had began to manifest itself.

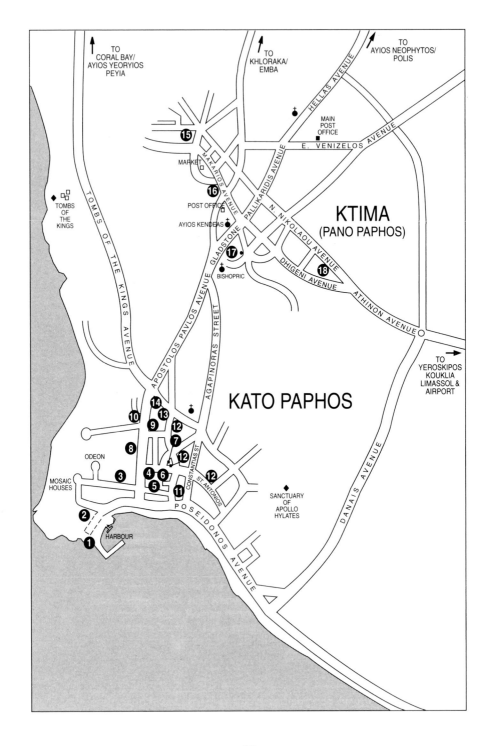

TO
CORAL BAY/
AYIOS YEORYIOS
PEYIA

TO
KHLORAKA/
EMBA

TO
AYIOS NEOPHYTOS/
POLIS

HELLAS AVENUE

MAIN
POST
OFFICE

E. VENIZELOS AVENUE

AVENUE

MARKET

MAKARIOS AVENUE

PALLIKARIDIS AVENUE

N. NIKOLAOU AVENUE

KTIMA
(PANO PAPHOS)

POST OFFICE

AYIOS KENDEAS

GLADSTONE

DHIGENI AVENUE

ATHINON AVENUE

BISHOPRIC

TOMBS
OF
THE
KINGS

TOMBS OF THE KINGS AVENUE

APOSTOLOS PAVLOS AVENUE

AGAPINORAS STREET

KATO PAPHOS

TO
YEROSKIPOS
KOUKLIA
LIMASSOL &
AIRPORT

ODEON

MOSAIC
HOUSES

CONSTANTIAS ST

ST ANTONIOS

SANCTUARY
OF
APOLLO
HYLATES

DANAIS AVENUE

POSEIDONOS AVENUE

HARBOUR

36

THE MONUMENTS

Note: * Indicates monuments of particular interest
        ** Indicates monuments of outstanding interest

THE FORT

There were two very strong castles on the sea, whose walls were always washed by the waves. Stephen de Lusignan, 1580.

Dating: Built 1222, repaired 1391, strengthened 1473, destroyed 1570, restored 1592.

Description: This is a small Frankish keep within a Venetian wall. The plaque over the entrance ascribes the construction of the fort to the Turkish governor of Cyprus in 1592, Ahmed Bey. On the ground floor is a central hall, partly covered with stone vaulting. Rooms on each side lead to prison cells beyond which are small courtyards; and underneath is a basement containing two dungeons. The rooms on the upper floor were originally connected in pairs by a wooden bridge and stair. Here, the central room was used as a mosque by the Turkish garrison. At that time there were eight cannons. The British used the fort as a salt store until 1935, when it was designated an ancient monument. Steps lead to the roof, from which a good all-round view may be enjoyed.

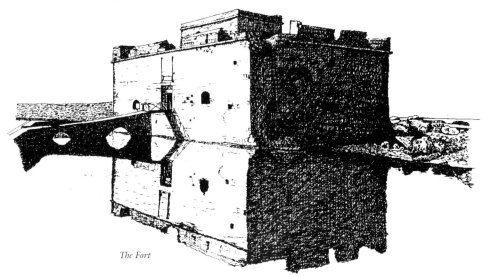

The Fort

History: After the loss of their first castle in the earthquake of 1222, the Franks built a replacement on the ancient mole at the west end of the harbour, where an earlier sea-tower may have existed. The new fort consisted of two towers connected by a curtain wall.

In 1373, the fort was captured by a raiding force of Genoese, and they held it for a year, successfully repulsing two separate assaults led by the Lusignan Prince of Antioch and James, Constable of Cyprus respectively. It was relinquished only when the Genoese had acquired Famagusta by treaty.

In 1391, James had the towers restored: now King James I, he was an indefatigable builder of defences against the Genoese. Seventy years later, the fort was involved in the contention between James II and Charlotte, his half-sister, for the Throne. 1473 saw the first Venetians in command as part of a universal show of strength in support of Queen Katerina. It was probably

38

then that the old keep was enclosed in an outer shell.

At the time of the Turkish invasion, almost a century later, the two towers were destroyed with explosives. Between 1580 and 1592 the Turks reconstructed the main tower, leaving the seaward tower in its ruined state. Nevertheless, the castle is still, as Hill states[1], a Venetian fortress incorporating a Lusignan tower.

PANAYIA LIMENIOTISSA:
Church of Our Lady of the Port.

The earliest church on the site was a basilica built at the beginning of the 5th century. It was destroyed by the Arabs in 653. It had three aisles divided by two rows of marble columns, a single apse, a narthex and atrium. The floors were paved with brilliantly-coloured mosaics in geometric patterns and also with rectalinear marble opus sectile. These show affinities with floors found in the nearby Governor's palace.

The Arabs robbed the wrecked church to construct simple dwellings round it, among them a hall paved with some of the marble. An inscription in Arabic was found.

A new basilica was built on the same site as the first, but reduced in size. Possibly 10th century work, it collapsed during the earthquake of 1159.

A small chapel came next. It stood within the nave of its predecessor, put up in the Lusignan period. It became ruinous under the Turks, but it was still standing comparatively recently.

SARANDA KOLONES: The Frankish Castle

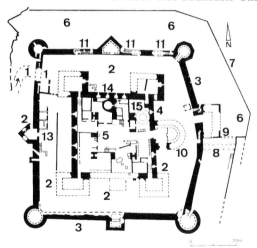

PLAN OF THE CASTLE

(1) Access (current entrance)
(2) Enceinte
(3) Curtain Wall
(4) Castle
(5) Courtyard
(6) Ditch
(7) Counterscarp
(8) Site of Bridge
(9) Gate Tower
(10) Entrance Tower
(11) Sally Ports
(12) Postern Gate
(13) Barracks
(14) Steam Bath
(15) Donkey Mill

Dating: Built 1200, destroyed by earthquake in 1222.

Description: **The square keep** of the castle is protected by a surrounding curtain wall and a ditch. Four massive rectangular towers project from the corners and a fifth, U-shaped, forms an entrance-tower on the east side. Within the castle, thick piers round a central courtyard once supported vaults and an upper storey. (Note the lower treads of a staircase.) It is thought that the chapel might

1. Sir George Hill, History of Cyprus.

have been on that level, above the entrance. In three of the piers are latrines – the waste was carried to the sea through a covered drain in the ditch. Features on the east side include: mangers for horses; two donkey mills – later installations; a stoking-room; and, on the north-west side, the vaulted furnace of a small circular steam bath. A platform behind this is edged with three fine marble pedestal basins, spolia from antiquity. In the central court is a stone trough containing a pile of sling balls.

The outer wall was strengthened with a number of granite columns taken from the old Roman agora.

Towers. It has eight of varying shapes: the four at the angles are circular; the one on the north is an arrow-head – giving cover for the sally-ports; the south is a rectangular bastion – perhaps to accommodate a ballistic machine; on the west, a pentagonal postern gate; and on the east a great rectangular gate-house – reduced now to its base, but note its position relative to the castle entrance. A wooden three-arched bridge formerly crossed the ditch at this point.

The barracks were in the western part of the enceinte (outer courtyard) by the postern gate. Here numerous bolts from crossbows were found. In the angle made by the north-west tower of the keep and its north wall, a trap-door admits to a small vaulted room under which is a deep chamber, possibly a dungeon. Beyond the west curtain wall are some Hellenistic remains: a well, a chamber tomb and a large, bottle-shaped cistern. (The ramp here is a legacy of the Franks themselves, made when they removed the castle stone for use elsewhere.)

Finds: quantities of mediaeval pottery of the 13th century – which gave an end-date to the occupation of the castle – and a hoard of seventy-six Byzantine bronze coins, thought to have been hidden when the Arabs sacked Paphos in 653.

History &
Tradition

The castle became known as Saranda Kolones or Forty Columns because so many grey granite columns lay on the unexcavated mound. For a long time it was thought to be the site of a Temple of Aphrodite. Local people recounted how a man once found his way in and, lost in a dark labyrinth, wandered on and on to emerge eventually in Ktima. Another story told of a barking dog, similarly trapped. Excavations began in 1957 and continued at intervals until the mid-eighties. At first the castle was considered to be Byzantine, but subsequently proved to be entirely Frankish. It has been partially restored.

Saranda Kolones

It is not known why the Franks decided not to rebuild this strong castle after the earthquake and constructed the lesser fortification by the mole instead. It was a Late Crusader type of building of an advanced concentric design, and it had commanded the harbour. Possibly it needed the expertise of the Templars to rebuild it.

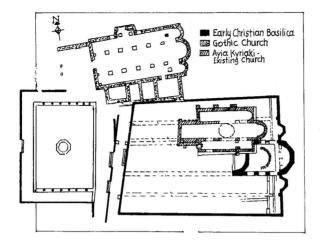

*Ground plans of the
Cathedral,
Gothic Church and
Ayia Kyriaki*

THE EARLY CHRISTIAN CATHEDRAL

Dating: Built late 4th c., rebuilt 6th c., destroyed 653 AD.

Description: **The first basilica** had seven aisles, making it the widest ever found in Cyprus. It had three apses, with a double central apse, again unique in the island, but not unknown in the Empire. It probably had galleries overlooking the nave, and a clerestorey. The aisles were divided by rows of twelve marble columns crowned with Corinthian capitals of acanthus leaves. The roof would have been wooden and either exposed or closed with a flat ceiling. Four immense granite columns – still in position – supported a double triumphal arch over the inner sanctuary between the apses. Soaring above the arcaded nave, the effect would have been dramatic, exercising a dynamic pull towards the apse. Some of the fine mosaics that adorned the floor may still be seen, predominately floral or geometrical in design. Parts of two panels of a series, halfway down the central aisle, contain naturalistic figurative motifs with inscriptions taken from the New Testament. The one in a guilloche has clusters of purple grapes hanging from a vine with a sheep gazing up at them, and the words: *I am the True Vine.* (John XVI).

The other is of a stag drinking at a stream: *As the hart panteth after the water brooks, so panteth my soul after Thee, O God:* Psalm 42. Both were popular allegories of the early Church.

The atrium is on a grand scale, having all the width and half the length of the basilica – although it is out of alignment with it. Formerly, it had colonnaded porticoes, and the broken columns lie about in profusion with here a Doric capital, there a Corinthian and elsewhere portions of the entablature. The line of the south colonnade can be established from the row of bases visible. In the centre of the atrium is a fountain with octagonal sides and an elegantly patterned floor.

The second basilica. In the 6th century, considerable modifications were made – possibly necessitated by the earthquakes that virtually destroyed Antioch in 526 and 528. The number of aisles was reduced to five, and the double apse replaced by a single one placed between the great pillars: also, the

41

area behind was raised in accordance with 6th century practice – probably to hold a clergy bench as was done at Kourion. At the same time, much flooring was renewed, the central aisle being covered with costly opus sectile, with marble slabs laid at the west end and new mosaic over large areas of the side aisles. For an example, see the visible part of the north aisle. There, an inscription attributes all the changes to a Bishop Sergios (otherwise unrecorded). A curious feature that is more apparent on plan is the trapezoidal shape of the modified building: it is slightly splayed, the south side being five metres longer than the north.

At the west end, three doorways with steps admit to the narthex, a narrow vestibule running the width of the Cathedral, also paved with mosaic. Beyond this, other doorways open on to a passage, which probably led originally to the Bishop's Palace on the south.

History: The Cathedral rests on Roman foundations and is thought to be on the site of the Forum – a conclusion reinforced by the presence of a very large number of marble columns. In the Roman and Byzantine periods, the low cliff on the south side was washed by the sea. Records are sparse but the building was in use for almost three hundred years before being destroyed by the Arabs in the second half of the seventh century. And Arabic inscriptions found here imply their continuing presence. In the 14th to 15th centuries, the Latins erected a large Gothic building over the south aisles, flanked by paved courtyards. A wine press appeared on the site of the atrium . . .

KHRYSOPOLITISSA CHURCH –
also known as Ayia Kyriaki.

Built circa 1500. This Byzantine church occupies the northern aisles of the

Khrysopolitissa Church

42

old cathedral. It replaced the, slightly longer, 11th century church – no doubt the new cathedral – to which Eric King of Denmark was brought for burial in 1103, and which was brought down in the earthquake of 1159. Khrysopolitissa is a cross-in-square, three-aisled church with an extended west arm, no narthex and a high, octagonal lantern.

Outside, hugging the south and east walls, the lower courses of the 11th century church can be seen.

Khrysopolitissa served as the cathedral of Paphos until the Episcopate moved to Ktima around 1734.

THE GOTHIC CHURCH: Church of the Franciscan Monastery, known as the Frari.

Dating: Built in 1312, repaired late 15th/early 16th c., collapsed in 1600.

Description: Here stood a large three-aisled church, possibly with rib-vaults. The bases of two rows of five columns can be discerned, with a sixth engaged at the west end. Their capitals, found during excavation, were decorated with grapes, flowers and rosettes, and seem to be without counterpart. In the north wall are the remains of a chapel behind pointed arches; it contains two niches.

At about the time of its bi-centenary, the church was repaired. A few sculptured pieces in late Renaissance style have been found, the most remarkable being four limestone angels, almost life-size, supporting a canopy. (Now in the Paphos Museum.) The walls were frescoed but the paintings were later concealed under plaster and whitewash, suggesting a Turkish presence. For its last thirty years, therefore, the church may have become a mosque. Beneath the building are four vaulted rooms, purpose unknown.

History: Little is known about the Franciscans here, beyond an occasional mention in the 14th century. As in 1486 it is referred to as the **former** Franciscan church, it appears that the Order had already left the monastery by that date. Around the turn of the century, the church was repaired and adorned with the sculptures, presumably by the Latin bishop.

Tradition &   Sts. Paul and Barnabas are said locally to have been preaching the Gospel
Legend: here in the Roman forum in 46 AD when they were arrested, and that Paul, at least, was tied between two pillars on the portico and flogged with a whip of forty tails less one. Then both Apostles were locked up in the prison.

Until current excavations, a marble pillar west of the Gothic church was railed off to preserve it from those who would chip off a piece for a potion or souvenir. The pillar is easily identifiable by its reduced and rounded shape. This is a late legend and rather doubtful: another pillar stands a little to the north near the Frankish Baths in a similar state. But that a prison did exist on this spot is given more credence because of the four unexplained underground chambers under the Gothic church. Jeffery[1] considers that the

1. Historic Monuments, page 403

site was probably deliberately selected by the Franciscans because of its associations.

Below the church which belonged to the Friars Minor is a prison where St. Paul was bound and kept for some time with St. Barnabas while preaching the Gospel: Le Huen, Carmelite monk, 1486.[1] Also, Fra Noel, writing in the late 15th c., refers to the prison as large and having seven cells.[2]

It was still being pointed out to travellers in 1599.

This is perhaps the most sensitive area under excavation in Nea Paphos: the heart of the city, redolent with ancient history, legend and the very beginnings of Christianity.

THE FRANKISH BATHS

One of the capitals drawn by Enlart

Situated about two hundred yards from the Gothic church to the north. One of the few remaining secular monuments of the Frankish period, these public baths were almost buried under earth and rubble until cleared and stabilised. As can be seen by the outworks, the building was originally more extensive; but it was rebuilt by the Turks in its present modified form and domes added. The entrance is through a courtyard on the west side. It is not far from the remains of the mosque – of interest today only for the carved stonework taken from a Gothic church and incorporated in the walls. Note adjacent fountain with carved capitals built-in.

Frankish Baths

1. Excerpta Cypria page 51
2. Excerpta Cypria page 53

THE LATIN CATHEDRAL

A church was visited where they sang in Latin, not far from the spot where the seven sleepers lay so long Le Sage, Flemish silk merchant, 1518.[1]

A solitary shaft, about two hundred yards south of Ayia Solomoni; west of the main road behind car-rental shops.

Ruins of Latin Cathedral
– drawn by Enlart

Dating: Built late 13th c., restored mid-16th; in use until 1570.

Description: Only an angle of the s.w. aisle remains, like a tower. Part of a vaulting rib is visible, supported by a moulded corbel. From this meagre information, it has been deduced that the cathedral had ribbed vaults, was exceptionally lofty and of first-class workmanship. The foundations have been uncovered but are somewhat overgrown.

History: The first Latin bishop of Paphos arrived in 1196, but this cathedral was not finished for almost another hundred years. There were twenty-six bishops in all, the most famous being Jacopo Pesaro (1496-1502) who is buried in the Frari Church in Venice. Pietro Contarini came in 1557 and found a very neglected Cathedral and restored it at considerable expense. The last incumbent was also a Contarini – Francesco – and he it was who bravely held a last service in St. Sophia, Nicosia, in July 1570, exhorting the people while the Turks bombarded the city.

Tradition: Locally known as the Foot of Galatariotissa (giver of milk), women scrape up earth from a corner of the shaft, mix it with water and give it as a potion to increase the milk of nursing mothers. Possibly a relic of the ancient fertility cult suppressed by the Christians: a similar custom prevails in Old Paphos.

AYIA SOLOMONI: Catacomb church

A small underground complex of Hellenistic chamber tombs adapted for use as a church.

Position: On the main road to the harbour approx. 300 yards from the junction with the Tombs of the Kings road (traffic lights); under the Handkerchief tree.

Description: A flight of steps leads down to a central court, four cave-like chambers and a well. The court is open now and resembles an atrium, but may formerly have been underground too. A further flight of steps, steep and worn, descend to the well, which still contains water. Two of the rooms interconnect and form the narthex, nave and sanctuary of the small church. On the walls of the apse and either side are remnants of paintings of the end of the 12th century. Further paintings can be made out in the nave, but blackened and obscure. Among the graffiti cut into the plaster are many names of 13th century Crusaders. On the doorways of the court, crosses have been carved.

---

1. Excerpta Cypria page 61

Decoration:	The remnants are poorly preserved but are of good quality. In the apse, six celebrating Fathers of the Church converge upon an altar in semi-frontal positions: at least three are wearing the polystavrion phelonian – an early example of its general use cp the apse of Arkhangelos Mikhail, Kato Lefkara, also end 12th century. Guarding the sacraments are a pair of angel-deacons carrying ceremonial rhipadia or fans. The Christchild is depicted twice, in both paten and chalice, as the Sacrifice; notice the face looking down from a veil above – a unique and controversial feature.*

*For further information on the subject see The Painted Churches page 349.

History & *Tradition:*	Obscure, but it is generally agreed that this is the Chapel of the Seven Sleepers, or the Seven Maccabees, to which almost every mediaeval visitor was brought. Thought to have been in use as a secret church by the 2nd century, the catacomb might have served for a Jewish synagogue before that – which would account for the parallel legends.

The seven sleepers were Christian youths said to have been walled up alive in a cave for their faith in 252 AD at Ephesus, only to emerge almost two hundred years later as if it were yesterday. The Maccabees were a mother and her seven sons, martyred for their Jewish faith in 168 BC and greatly venerated by early Christians, the mother being canonised as Saint Solomoni. *And others (Jews) that had run together into caves nearby, to keep the Sabbath day secretly, . . . were all burnt together . . .* II Maccabees vii. No doubt, there has been a tragedy in this place.

The well is a sacred spring, or Ayiasma the water from it used to cure eye ailments. The tree is also sacred, a relic of pre-Christian pantheism; it is festooned with handkerchiefs and strips of garments left by the afflicted (to which tourists have added their quota).

AYIOS LAMBRIANOS

Across the road from Ayia Solomoni is another Hellenistic tomb complex which was apparently used for Early Christian worship. It has a large atrium and, on the east, rock-cut chambers. The western part extends under the side-road and still awaits excavation.

PANAYIA THEOSKEPASTI CHURCH, *(covered by God)*

Panayia Theoskepasti

Position:	About 150 yards s.e. of the Basilica.
Description:	It stands on a high, squared-off rock, perhaps the base of the old Eastgate tower, a rather ugly church built in 1922 to replace a previous one. It contains an icon said to be one of seventy painted by St. Luke. (The Orthodox Church recognises only three, one of which is at Kykko.) A piece of marble by the steps is carved with antique crosses and may have come from the Early Byzantine church which escaped the Arabs in 653 AD.
Tradition:	The church got its name because as the Arabs approached the city it became shrouded in a thick mist and was thereby saved from any damage.
	N.B. Although on a high rock, Theoskepasti is indeed an elusive church to find sometimes!

THREE SMALL BYZANTINE CHURCHES
IN THE EAST SUBURB:

1. Ayios Yeoryios: ruined but contains tombstones of the Beduin family – who were among the first Franks in Paphos. South-east of Theoskepasti Church.

2. Ayios Antonios: about 175 yards from Theoskepasti, beyond the city east gate. Originally a two-aisled church but south aisle lost; it has a high dome and a later narthex. It is surrounded by wild yellow chrysanthemums in springtime. Until very recently it was leased to the Anglican Church, but R.C. and C. of E. services are now held in Khrysopolitissa Church.

3. Ayia Marina Chapel: a small 15th century whitewashed building with a belfry. Near the old north-east gate of the city.

AYIOS AGAPETIKOS and AYIOS MISITIKOS: *the Saint of Love and the Saint of Hatred.*

Between the n.e. gate and the corner of Fabrica Hill are these two chapels dug out of the sandstone. The former is easily seen from the road. Only the east end remains; and the altar is tended, a lamp sends out a tiny light and lovers come to pray. According to Gunnis, the names are a corruption of two local hermits: St. Agapetos and St Themistos.

THE ROCK OF DIGHENIS

Near Ayios Agapetikos below Fabrica Hill, a large rock rests on a smaller one. It is part of the folk-lore of Paphos which was engendered at the time of the Arab raids when the Akrites were here, whose exploits later became legendary. In this one, the heroic Dighenis was wooing the Queen of Paphos, who promised to wed him if he brought water to Kato Paphos. After great labour, he managed this, only to be told the Queen had changed her mind! From the heights of Ktima, the furious suitor flung a rock at her as she sat in her palace here. The Queen's spindle, which she hurled back, can still be seen two miles away below Ktima cliffs – an isolated column of granite.

KTIMA

Citizens from Paphos moved to Ktima for three prime reasons: to escape the Arab raids in the 7th to 9th centuries; because of severe earthquake damage; and finally because the formation of marshy land brought malaria and pestilence round the port area.

This new settlement was not mentioned until the Lusignan aristocracy arrived towards the end of the 12th century and made it a Royal Estate. ('Ktima' is Greek for 'Estate'.) By the 15th century, no-one willingly lived at Baffa, but sought the higher ground and healthier air. By 1540 the upper town had a population of ca. 2000; but Kato Paphos had already dwindled into a poor village. Under the Turks came a marked decline and in 1815 Ktima was reported to contain only about 200 dwellings, 150 of them Turkish, and to be divided into a Turkish 'Metropolis' on the north and Greek Ktima in the Moussalla district. (The old Turkish quarter and the lanes below the Greek Cathedral at Exo Vrisis are worth exploring.)

The Monuments: Only two, other than the Queen's needle already mentioned and the museums; but Ktima itself is a monument to a way of life that has not yet been sacrificed to tourism.

DJAMI KEBIR MOSQUE
formerly Ayia Sophia Church.

Position: About 150 yards north of the market on Hadji Ali Street. (The large dome stands out.)

Dating: Built 15th c., converted into mosque 1584.

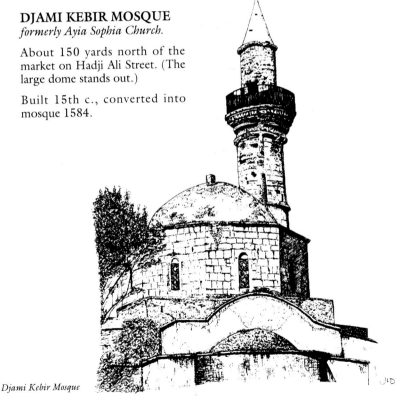

Djami Kebir Mosque

Description: A lofty Byzantine church with a large dome and high octagonal lantern. Its wall-paintings have been whitewashed. Note the women's gallery on the south, the mihrab on the south-east and outside the monumental west

49

doorway and the S.E. entry – now blocked off to take the mihrab within. A Latin church once stood nearby.

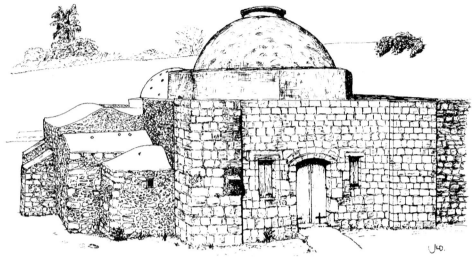

THE TURKISH BATHS

South of the market below the cliff. The baths are considerably older than the days of Turkish rule, dating back certainly to mediaeval times and possibly even to the 12th century. Ancient clay pipes once conveyed water underground from nearby natural springs. The Hamam appears to have been a Latin building used first by the Franks. Allowed to lapse into a ruinous state since 1974, it has recently been restored by the Department of Antiquities. Plans are in hand to open it as an art gallery and exhibition centre.

THE PAPHOS MUSEUM

Half a mile along Grivas Dighenis Avenue, the main road going east, on the left. Contains: Early Christian capitals, carvings and inscriptions, including some from Peyia basilica and Shryvallos baptistery; sculpture from the Latin periods, including the four Renaissance angels from the Gothic Church; a sizeable collection of Byzantine pottery and glass.

The pottery. Look out for:

Case I – 13th c: sgraffito dish with stylised bird showing tripod firing dots.
Case II ca 1200: finds from Saranda Kolones, including splendid capering goat and, top shelf, Byzantine gold-painted glass scent bottles elegantly painted with birds.
Case IV 14th c: sgraffito, especially large bowl in centre with cross design.
Case V 14th c: deep bowl with four vertical rows of projecting faces
Case VI 15th/16th c: fine glass-ware (majolica).

50

THE BYZANTINE MUSEUM Situated in the Bishopric, entrance in Ilission Street.

It consists of a collection of icons, vessels and vestments from all over the district, well displayed. There are good examples of icon-painting from the end of the 12th c. to the beginning of the 19th. Look especially for:

End 12th c., the Virgin Eleoussa, from the Monastery of St Savvas tis Karonas;

ca 1500, the Archangel Michael; and a number of fine 16th c. examples, often by named artists, including:

1520 St Nicholas from the Monastery of St Nicholas by Nikolaos;

1521 Virgin and Child by Titus, from Mon. of St. Savvas;

1562 John the Evangelist and donors by Tzenios, from Church of the Archangel, Ayios Nikolaos.

1570 Virgin and Child by Silvestros, from Church of St. Marina, Philousa.

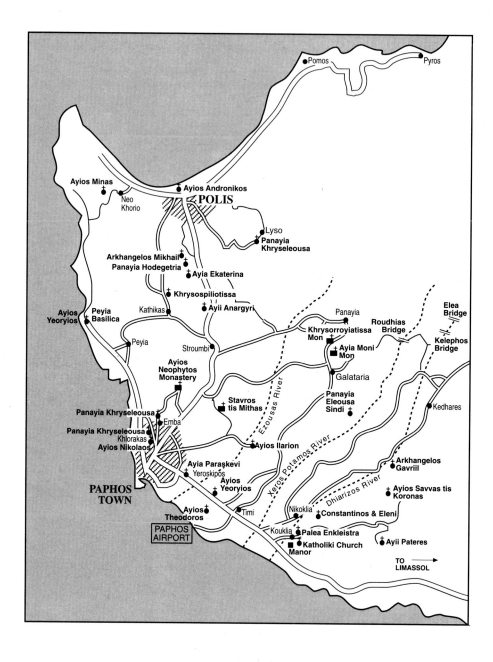

PAPHOS DISTRICT

THE MONUMENTS

Note: * Indicates monuments of particular interest
         **Indicates monuments of outstanding interest

AYIA PARASKEVI, *Yeroskipos:* Five-domed basilica.

Position: Two miles east of Ktima, in centre of village.

Dating: Built before 843, decorated 10th, 12th and late 15th c., west extension 19th c.

Description: A three-aisled vaulted basilica with pierced arches cp Ayios Lazaros Church; but in addition to the three domes in line along the nave, two smaller domes span the side-aisles and so form a cross. This is a Cypriot development and a second example has survived at Peristerona in the Nicosia district. The outer walls are four foot thick, the internal three foot and the whole structure immensely strong, despite the removal of the west wall. On the south wall of the north aisle is

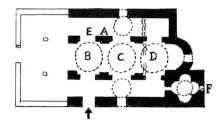

Ground plan of Ayia Paraskevi

(A) Consecration Cross   (E) Processional Icon
(B) Christ (lost)   (F) Blocked Entrance
(C) Virgin & Child
(D) Cross

painted an ancient cross on the bare stone which must date from the consecration. The chapel on the south-east encloses a small, quatrefoil-shaped space under a dome; almost certainly an early baptistery and, if so, this part of the church at least could date from well before the Arab raids.[1] Until recently, a mediaeval tomb lay across its east portal, which had been blocked – suggesting the chamber's later use as a chantry chapel. Now a vestry, when Jeffery saw it in 1918, it was *a dust-hole and cut off from the rest of the church.*

History: No-one knows the age of this most interesting church. It stands on the ancient pilgrims' road which led to the Temple of Aphrodite. Here was the goddess's Holy Garden (Ieros Kipos) tended by countless maidens. To the south-west of the Church is a large grotto containing a sacred spring, now sealed because of pollution. The presence of Corinthian capitals and columns suggest a Roman temple in the vicinity, spolia perhaps that was used in the first church. So deep-rooted was the worship of Aphrodite that the idea of a mother-goddess seems to have been perpetuated in the central dome with the Virgin in the place of highest honour. Moreover, Aphrodite's feast day was on a Friday, and the church is dedicated to Ayia Paraskevi, a female saint whose name means *Friday.*

Decoration: **8th/9th c:** In the east dome above the altar.
A damaged aniconic design in red, green and yellow of a Cross against a background of radiating beams, each of the three surviving arms ending in a stylised flower. It is bordered by a Roman guilloche and a broad outer band with a looped ribbon pattern.

Possibly 10th c: (south central arch, on the reveals)
Two prelates with two half-length figures above.

---

1. *After the sixth century . . . the detached baptistery disappears.* Oxford Dict. of Byzantium.

Ayia Paraskevi – Yeroskipos

End 12th c: (below central dome, north lunette)

Part of a Dormition, the Virgin appearing through the later Crucifixion.

Late 15th c: all else, central and west nave – apse programme missing.

Central dome: Virgin Orans with Christchild in front and surrounded by Her prophets; in the squinches, the four Evangelists write their Gospels.

Western dome: remnants of the Pantocrator and the Heavenly Host; in the squinches are the Sacrifice of Isaac (normally found in the bema as it pre-figures the Sacrifice of Christ), St Paul dictating to a scribe (rare subject but appropriate for Paphos).

The Gospel story: unfolds in thirteen scenes, starting on the south-east and moving west. They are not all in sequence and the Annunciation and Presentation of Christ in the Temple are lost. Among the most successful are the Raising of Lazarus and the Entry into Jerusalem; the Betrayal is exceptionally well done under smoky torch and lantern. Most interesting is the Crucifixion, made into a complex scene through influence of Western art, full of action, crowds and stress, yet still holding to a Byzantine style. Notice the Temple 'rent in twain', the man about to break the Good Thief's legs – to hasten death, we are told – the Good Centurion and the fainting Virgin. The helmets of the departing soldiery helped date these paintings, being types worn ca 1480.

The Virgin of Yeroskipos: on an icon-stand in the north aisle is a large portable processional icon dating to the 15th century with 16th c. overpainting. On the reverse is the Crucifixion. Considerable areas of both surfaces are missing, but what remains is very fine. It was found by chance in a field last century. *(Most of the information on the paintings is taken from A & J Stylianou's Painted Churches of Cyprus.)*

FOLK ART MUSEUM, *Yeroskipos*

Affords an insight into the traditional way of life of the Cypriot villager, hardly changed for centuries, but now virtually disappeared in the space of a decade.

Position: Off the Paphos/Limassol road: first turning right beyond the main square going east.

Description: The building is a traditional, stone-built Cypriot house of the second half of the 18th century, complete with hards and outbuildings. The upper floor was added soon after 1800.

Ground floor: Each room contains the utensils and apparatus appropriate to it. Some are rough, others well-crafted, and all are practical – witness the pair of boots with neither left nor right foot, so that by changing them round regularly they give longer service. The best room has been arranged for a wedding reception and decorated with the bride's best handwork. Some fine dowry chests are kept here.

Upper floor: A long, absorbing room showing dress of different districts, textiles and embroidery.

Outbuildings: Homemade rope-making (including cannabis) and a portable silk-spinning kit may be seen in the inner courtyard. The west side has stabling, ovens and stores, a complete shoemaker's workshop and a tinsmith. The last room celebrates Cyprus potteries, vanished or vanishing.

History: This is the house of Andreas Zimboulakis who, in 1798, so impressed Sir Sydney Smith i/c East Mediterranean Fleet during the Napoleonic Wars that he was appointed by him Representative of the British Government in Western Cyprus. The young man identified so closely with his benefactor that he adopted the name of Smith, and the place came to be known as "Hadji-Smith Zimboulakis' house". It first opened as a museum in 1978.

AKHELIA (About five miles from Paphos)

In mediaeval times, Akhelia was one of the centres and place of export for the local sugar-cane industry, a lucrative Lusignan estate. The name is a corruption of L'Eschelle, which means 'port' or landing stage cp La Scala at Larnaca.

THE CHURCH OF AYIOS YEORYIOS

Position: On the main road from Limassol just before the turning into the village proper.

Dating: Early 16th century; rebuilt 1745.

Description: Single-aisled rectangular building in the Franco-Byzantine style, the earlier structure having had a portico at the west end with arcading and a cobbled floor. In the extensive rebuilding – probably made necessary through earthquake damage – five external buttresses were added on the north and south. A small doorway on the north-west now gave admittance to female worshippers, who had their own gallery cp St George's, Arpera, of the same date. The west doorway has Frankish-style decoration and the date of rebuilding above. Among the gargoyles are four in animal form and one of a man's head (note his hands). At the east end are three ornate Latin crosses.

Note: *Shortly after the rebuilding, a small, exquisite icon screen was installed in St George's where it remained for one and a half centuries. Then, in 1889, the Bishopric sold it in a London auction room for a small sum and it went to the V&A. Recently it disappeared only to turn up in the Berlin State Museum 'exact provenance unknown.' It should come home.*

THE CHURCH OF AYIOS THEODOSIOS

Position: Five hundred yards down the earth road opposite St George's and screened by trees.

Dating: Built 12th century, painted ca 13th c. and 16th c. Considerably restored.

Description: It is a cruciform, barrel-vaulted building with a central dome cp Kouklia & Khlorakas. A Roman cippus supports an altar table which is an inverted carved marble slab, also Roman: lotus leaves and fruit alternate in a band round the sides.

Decoration: A few paintings remain on the walls.

Of the first period: west arm, south side: St Peter and St Paul in a large donor fresco. Each had a deceased figure, two-thirds the size, standing on the left dressed like twins in identical garments, one in white and the other in green, and both with a napkin drawn through a loop: their eyes are open but their hands are crossed on their breasts. Also, three saints on horseback: the remnants of a St George on the north wall, north arm; possibly St Demetrios on the west wall and another. Between them are indications of a deacon with chalice and censor.

Part of fresco showing napkin

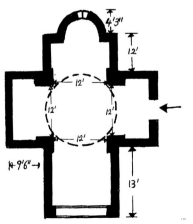

*Ayios Theodosios (Akhelia)
Paced Ground Plan*

57

Ayios Theodosios – Akhelia

Of the second period are the standing saints and the Virgin: west arm, north side are Sts. Anastasia, curer of poisons, and Andronicos with wife Athanasia. North arm east side are three prelates next to the Virgin: St Nicholas, St Gregory and St Theodosios (depicted here typically with a neat gray divided beard). These have a touch of a master's hand.

History: Obscure, but it could well have been a monastery church. Theodosios the Cenobiarch was a 5th century monk from Cappadocia who was appointed head of all communities of monks in Palestine and who died near Bethlehem aged 105.

OLD PAPHOS, (Palæ-Paphos)

In Roman times, Aphrodite's Temple continued famous throughout the Mediterranean and attracted thousands of pilgrims annually. From Augustus through the Severan Emperors, the ancient city received royal patronage, and their statues graced the sacred precincts alongside those of the gods. Titus made a personal visit in AD69 and consulted the oracle – with a favourable prognostication! But the remains of the Roman sanctuary buildings to be seen now date from late 1st or early 2nd c.AD and are probably a rebuilding after the destructive earthquake of 76/77 AD. Numbers of well-to-do Roman families lived here, chiefly in the western quarter, as the richly appointed tombs and the mosaic floors of the houses attest.

In 400 AD, Palae-paphos was still well populated, and buildings of the Late Roman period extended right down to the coastal plain. The Koinon ton Kyprion had its headquarters here. It organised the religious festivals, authorised statuary and inscriptions and controlled the bronze coinage. It was the instrument through which the authority of Rome was impressed upon the people through the cult of the Emperor. This cult did not die with the adoption of Christianity and the enforced closure of all pagan shrines in 395. The Byzantine Emperors, heirs of Rome, relied on Divine Right for their authority and fostered it. The Emperor's domination of religious ceremonial lasted right through the Early Byzantine period, to be replaced by a Patriarchal one only in the Macedonian Age.

In Byzantine times, Old Paphos slowly decayed, deprived of the Sanctuary which was its mainspring. Undoubtedly, Aphrodite continued to be worshipped despite the decree, but the patronage, the pilgrims and the revenue had all gone. A Roman presence can still be traced up to the time of the Arab raids in the 7th c. but thenceforward nothing more is heard of Palae-paphos until the coming of the Lusignans: a gap of more than five hundred years. The Byzantines appear to have kept well away from what, to them, would have been a notorious and sinful city.

KOUKLIA

In the Lusignan period, the area became a royal domain, extensively farmed for sugar-cane; and a sugar-processing plant was built on the site of the Sanctuary, with a second, major factory at Stavros on the plain below. Conspicuous on the headland of the old western quarter stood the Chateau de Couvoucle, or Pavilion (Fr), a magnificent 13th century fortified manor house of which only part of the east wing has survived as built.

For nearly three centuries, La Couvoucle was the headquarters of all the King's Paphos estates and the name became synonymous with the city site, corrupted eventually into 'Kouklia'. Next, it became a Turkish farmhouse or Chiftlik and then a deserted ruin which was rescued and restored by the Department of Antiquities; but only the Gothic Hall and some masonry and an arch on the south-west are Lusignan.

THE LUSIGNAN MANOR HOUSE or COUVOUCLE

Its Gothic hall is one of the finest surviving secular buildings of the Franks. Steps lead down to its 13th century floor, which is well below the level of the present courtyard. Internal measurements are about 100 x 25 feet and the hall is divided into four bays. Diagonal ribs support the vaulting, and the arches spring from small capitals or abacuses which rest on corbels. The style pertains to the South of France in the 13th century and has helped to date the Hall. The fine-cut stone used in building carries numerous masons' marks of the same origin. The outer wall is reinforced by four sturdy buttresses; note the three very small arrow-slit lights.

Lusignan Manor House – Kouklia

A ramp leads to an upper floor, replacing the original external flight of steps. Here is another single room which has been carefully restored from the evidence left by its wreckage: small square windows, centre post and struts supporting heavy wooden beams under a wooden roof. The room further up the ramp is a restored Turkish addition.

Both the upper rooms now house a well-set-out and informative site museum.

The Sugar Industry at Kouklia

I came near a castle called Baffa, in the lordship of the King of Cyprus, in which castle is made a great quantity of sugar: Martoni, 1394.[1]

---

1. Excerpta Cypria, p. 28

60

The Lusignan kings derived a major part of their revenue from their sugar plantations in the Paphos district. These lay at Lemba, Emba, Akhelia and Old Paphos; but the chief of them was at Old Paphos, where too was the administrative centre.

In the 14th and 15th centuries, sugar was being produced in areas all over the Mediterranean and competition to sell in the western markets was keen. The Paphos factory at Stavros was geared to a high output. It is one of the few refineries in the Middle East virtually intact in all essentials: its excavation confirms and clarifies contemporary accounts of the methods and stages of processing the sugar-cane.

THE REFINERY

Position: The factory is located below the Couvoucle, seaward of the main road, down an earth track. Turn right at the fork and continue for about two hundred yards.

Dating: First built end 13th century; reconstructed possibly early 15th; destroyed late 16th.

Description: The lay-out is in three separate working units: mill, refinery and furnaces. A stretch of the aqueduct is visible in the field beside the earth road. It brought water from the Oritis Forest, several miles north-east, and supplied the Couvoucle first.

The Crushing Hall: The chopped raw cane was first pulverised on the huge mill-stone, a vertical grindstone of rough conglomerate being turned by donkeys. The resulting pulp collected in the sunken basin. (The grinder can be seen among others on the far bank.)

The Mill-house: Here the juice was extracted from the pulp by a horizontal, water-driven turbine wheel, which turned millstones of a smaller size: a sophisticated technique that was employed from the outset – an earlier wheel emplacement having been uncovered beneath.

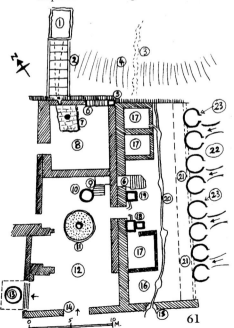

PLAN OF KOUKLIA REFINERY

(1) Aqueduct, above bank
(2) Stepped channel containing tapering pipe (for pressure)
(3) Bath
(4) Slope
(5) Retaining wall
(6) Staircase
(7) Wheel emplacement
(8) Subterrace Mill House (2nd stage)
(9) Steps
(10) Sunken basin for juice
(11) Mill base
(12) Crushing Hall (1st stage)
(13) Early Sugar Press
(14) Wide entrance for bringing the raw cane
(15) Outflow under arch (blocked)
(16) Refinery (3rd stage)
(17) Water Basin
(18) Collection
(19) Juice Collection
(20) Conduit
(21) Boiling Vats
(22) Store house, access down ramps
(23) 8 Furnaces in pairs (at lower levels)

61

The Refinery: Contained in one large hall were the pot-washing basins and the juice containers on the north side and the boiling vats on the south. To convert into sugar, the juice was boiled here in copper cauldrons of various sizes, and there were eight hearths. (The best quality required three boilings).

The Furnaces: They were eight, arranged in pairs, and each had a narrow pointed opening to enable the stoking and clearing work to be done from outside the hall.

N.B. An additional mill was built to the north-west of the complex at a later date. It was purely water-powered and intended only for pulping more cane to increase output.

The excavation was carried out by a Swiss-German archaeological mission under Professor Maier. The three metres of debris found on top of the collapsed factory indicate that the final destruction was accompanied by a severe fire.

CHURCH OF PANAYIA KATHOLIKI, *Kouklia*

Position: On outskirts of village, north-east of the Temple precincts and about 100 yards up the road from the modern entrance.

Dating: 12th c. with 16th c. additions. Paintings 14th c. and later.

Description: A cruciform building, barrel-vaulted with a central dome and arched recesses on the south and north cp Ayios Theodosios at Akhelia – a familiar 12th c. construction. The west arm was extended later, probably early in the 16th century judging by the two transverse ribs. In the same period, an arcaded

Panayia Katholiki – Kouklia

portico with pointed arches was added to the outside on the south and west: notice the grooving for shutters. The west entrance carries a fan-shaped decoration under a massive lintel-stone; and the two round holes may have been for banners: over the south door is carved a cross of Lorraine. A pig's-head gargoyle ornaments a gutter. These 16th century features suggest a Latin presence, and it is most likely that this was the church for the Couvoucle at that time. There are remains of a small extension on the south-east, possibly for a tomb, or a priest's entrance to the diakonikon.

The stones used throughout have obviously been taken from the Temple ruins and several bear inscriptions.

Decoration:	Not much. The original painting is lost and only a little post-Byzantine work remains. Of this, the best is a 14th century portrait of Therapon, 8th c. Saint and Bishop, on the walled-up entrance to the diakonikon; and the most curious is the rivers Tigris and Euphrates, flowing in twin streams of paint from lions' masks on the west wall (being part of a vanished Last Judgement). For the rest: Christ Pantocrator survives in the dome with a liturgical inscription; St Peter occupies the north pillar of the west arm, and a Birth of the Virgin above; further west part of a mounted St George is visible, the water-pot boy behind, and, on the west face of the pillar, the donor.

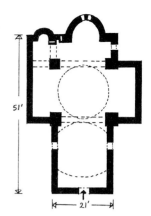

Ground plan of Panayia Katholiki

Tradition: The site is so imbued with the 2,000 year old presence of Aphrodite that there is a certain confusion here between the goddess and the Virgin. Offerings are still made to Aphrodite both at a stone by the west wall of the church and at one in the North Stoa of the old Roman Temple, mainly by nursing mothers; but now she is called Panayia Galatariotissa, Our Lady the Giver of Milk. The church itself was formerly dedicated to Panayia Khrysopolitissa, Our Lady of the Golden City – and unofficially, it is said, Panayia Aphroditissa!

AYII PATERES, *Pano Arkhimandrita.*

Position: Seven miles north-east of Kouklia on a good road. Look for sign on right as approaching village. The short road ends in steps.

Dating: Uncertain, but 14th century wall-paintings.

Description: A tiny cell, 10' x 4', with a stone bench at its east end. Adapted from a Roman tomb. Behind a grill in the north wall is an ossiary containing some twenty skulls and bones, apparently those of monks from the nearby monastery of St. Theodosios (a very old foundation): the skulls seem remarkably small. Images of saints once covered the walls, and two can still be identified: Onoufrios, guarding the entrance, and a 9th century saint, Peter of Athos.

History: According to the Paphos Bishopric,[1] this is a shrine to the memory of the 318 Church Fathers who participated in the first Oecumenical Synod. The reference may be to the First Council of Constantinople, convoked in 381 by the Emperor Theodosios.

Tradition: The village tradition is that 318 Christians from Syria, led by their bishop, landed at Pissouri and travelled inland to this place, only to be massacred by heathens.

---

1. History of the Churches of Paphos, Tsiknopoullos

THE MONASTERY CHURCH OF CONSTANTINE AND ELENI

Position: Just over a mile north east of Kouklia on the Pano Arkhimandrita road, turn left onto an earth road signposted 'Souskiou' and continue ¾ mile to small bridge. Almost immediately turn right and follow a dusty white track, turning right at forks. The road ends at the church, which stands slightly north of the Phatalas river-bed, with its impressive southern cliffs.

Dating: Uncertain but possibly of 12th century origin; restored 1976 with new vaulting and roof.

26'

19'

Ground Plan

Description: Same style and proportions as Asinou church but lacking the narthex ie. domeless, single-aisled with a barrel-vault and arched recesses on south and north – a common Byzantine construction. Narrow, deep recesses in the parabema, also arched, each contains a pair of cupboards. No trace of the monastery remains, but the gong still hangs from the tree by the west door to call the monks to prayer.

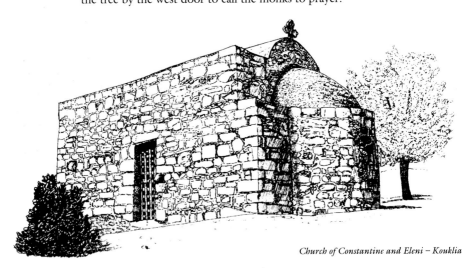

Church of Constantine and Eleni – Kouklia

Decoration: Considering that the church was roofless for years and that the paintings were also damaged by local Turkish herdsmen, it is surprising that anything has survived. Two periods of painting can be discerned, but not enough of the earlier to date it. What we do have is early 16th century. In the south recess, east wall are Constantine and Helen; facing each other on the north east and south east piers are two saints, one being identified as Romanos the Hymn-writer; in the apse, Christ is depicted twice (Byzantine-style) in the Communion of the Apostles; the six officiating Fathers of the Church below include Athanasios, Epiphanios, Chrysostom and Basil; on the north wall of the semi-dome is a striking Sacrifice of Isaac and opposite is the

64

Entertainment of the Angels. Under an acanthus design, the north parabema arch is divided between what must be St Stephen and Christ of the Utter Humiliation.

PALAEA ENKLEISTRA, *Kouklia*

Position: From Constantine and Eleni Church, a quarter of a mile to the south in a steep cliff-face. Follow the faint line of the track as it descends right beyond the church and becomes a path which crosses the river-bed; the cave is a few yards further right.

Dating: 15th century.

Description: Largest of a group of three small caves, hollowed out of the limestone: all have been inhabited. The first two are badly eroded but retain some fragments of fresco. The third is intact and has kept a lot of its decoration in a clean, fresh condition, its inaccessibility preserving it from fires and sheep (although not from the attentions of Turkish shepherds, who have damaged the faces). From being 15ft wide and 7ft high on its east side, the chamber tapers to about half this size on the west. Its only structural feature is a tomb-recess in the east wall.

Decoration: The saint by the entrance is surely Onoufrios. Inside, either side of the recess, stand Cosmas and Damian, the medical saints who gave their services free, with the martyred prelate Hermolaos overhead. To the right of the entrance on the north wall are the Three Youths in the Furnace, George and the Dragon and Mary of Egypt with St Zosimos. The saint to the south is Anastasia, holding her salves against poison. On the low ceiling west of her, the Evangelists Mark and Luke write their Gospels, John the Theologian with Prochoros and Matthew being opposite on the north-east. The subject of the ceiling is The Trinity in place of the more usual Christ Pantocrator. God the Father is portrayed next to His Son and the Holy Spirit is above them as a dove: they all have haloes with crosses, the words O ΩN – '*The Eternal*' – on the arms; and they are all inscribed *Iesos Christos*. They are framed in two quadrilinear shapes, superimposed to form an eight-pointed star, and the whole is set in a roundel. Around this moves the Heavenly Host of Archangels, Angels, seraphim, cherubim and wheels.

Style: A skilled artist carried out this work: delicate and detailed where necessary, sure and bold elsewhere; the faces carefully built up in a suffused Byzantine light, the brushstrokes of hair and beards meticulous, the colours gentle. A & J Stylianou consider there are affinities here with Mystra.

Content: The roundel on the ceiling contains more than meets the eye:
a) for the doctrinal point of 'Filioque' (used only in the Western Creed) see The Painted Churches of Cyprus p. 397.
b) The Orthodox Church never depicts God the Father as such, because He has not become incarnate – yet He is so portrayed in this instance.
c) Also involved here is the symbolism of number and pattern (see footnote to St. Sozomenos Church, Galata).

History: An unknown hermit is thought to have lived and been buried here in the 14th century.

Tradition: Confusion with St. Neophytos led to a local claim that this was that saint's first cell – hence its name 'Old Retreat.'

AYIOS SAVVAS TIS KARONOS, *near Prastio, Paphos.*

Position: In the Dhiarizos valley. Take the road through Nikoklia and continue to Ayios Yeoryios village. About three miles beyond, look for a conspicuous new chapel on a rock across the river; the earth road to the monastery goes past it. To join it, take the stony track that runs down to the river right of the main road just before a bend and a culvert (a sheepfold up the hillside left): it leads to a bridge over the river. Keeping right, drive on a good earth road for ten minutes, winding uphill to the monastery.

Dating: Founded circa 1120, restored 1501, rebuilt 1742, renovated 1989.

Description: A tall, rectangular building commanding a magnificent view across the valley and north-east to Mount Olympus, it has a single aisle and a sloping, tiled roof. It is buttressed in the Franco-Byzantine manner and reinforced with two internal ribs. The east end has a single apse, five-sided externally, and in the apex a round window of pierced stone displaying a floriate cross: a similar window at the west end has no cross.

Ayios Savvas tis Karonas

The three doorways have Gothic hoods and moulded frames, and each has a different feature: the north, five semicircular steps; the south, a cross of Lorraine above; and the main door on the west an older lintel bearing this weathered inscription: *It must be a king first built this monastery, which time has so damaged. May God on the awful Day of Judgement remember the Exarch of this monastery, who in 1501 repaired and beautified this church.* (Trans. Rupert Gunnis in Historic Cyprus). In the tympanum above, a more recent inscription refers to the second restoration of 1742. High on the west wall are three stone brackets, probably dating from 1501. The object they supported may have been a gutter or even a portico; but note the carved face gazing down, Venetian style.

Built into the masonry in several places, but most visible on the south-west corner, are finely-cut stones, chevron-patterned, some engraved with large Greek letters, part of an inscription which Gunnis considers once ran round the west portal. The foundations of the 12th century church extend eastwards by more than twenty feet, its walls were three feet thick and divided the interior into a wide nave and two narrow side aisles.

The shells of the monastic buildings stand on three sides, their ground floors buried under banks of rubble. Still in position in one room are the huge storage pitharia, special to Cyprus. On the south-west, by the main gateway, lies the Synod Hall, spanned by a graceful 18th century arcade, its dimensions ruined by clumsy partitioning circa 1910. Outside, until October 1992, was a large marble basin into which water ran, the outflow being from the mouth of another carved face. It is there no longer, having been stolen together with the Corinthian capital that supported it.

The interior is unpainted and the icon-screen without gilding. Embedded in the walls at intervals are broken water-jugs, an acoustic device. In Gunnis's day, the screen still held a number of fine icons of the 13th, 15th and 16th centuries now in the Byzantine Museum in Paphos. The sole remaining icon is a modern one of St Savvas, and that has been damaged by a hunter.

History: Founded at a time of peace and prosperity in Cyprus in a century of monasteries. In the 13th century it is thought to have been occupied by Latin monks, an entry in a document of 1234 recording the annual donation of money to Nicosia cathedral by one Baldwin de Morpho from the revenues of St Savvas which he held by Royal grant.

Two hundred and fifty years later, the monastery appears to be back in Greek hands and still paying revenue to the Crown, this time in bushels of wheat and barley. A letter written by the Abbot Gerasimos to King James II in 1486 begs him to waive the tax explaining that during the night of December 7th *the monastery was struck by lightning and devoured by fire, so that all the monastery, save the church, was destroyed, all the upstairs and downstairs rooms, our clothes, wheat and barley, all were burnt, and so great a damage was caused to us that we are utterly ruined.* King James did – on condition that Masses were ever said for his soul[1] (Acknowledgements to David Pearlman for highlighting this place.)

ARKHANGELOS GAVRIIL CHURCH, *Prastio, Paphos.*

Position: From the main Limassol road, two miles east of Timi, turn left at the Nikoklia signpost. Keep right at the fork and continue for about ten miles along the left bank of the river Dhiarizos. When a huge rocky outcrop can be seen (about two miles beyond Ayios Yeoryios village) take a much-used track leading down to the river-bed; cross that and proceed on the opposite bank until level with the outcrop: the church stands on rising ground ahead.

Dating: Late 15th century.

Description: It is built on rock and incorporates river boulders and rough stones in its fabric, yet the four corners of this tall rectangular building, its windows and doors, are constructed of well-cut ashlar blocks. It has a sloping roof with a central ridge, reinforced inside with three lofty arches. Set high in the western wall is a stone round window, pierced with twelve small holes scattered unevenly round a cross and probably symbolising the twelve Apostles round their Lord. On the north wall by the icon screen is all that remains of a vast wall-painting of Gabriel, his halo thickened and moulded in

---

1. Mas Latrie: Histoire de l'Ile de Chypre, III 213.

relief. The screen itself is an elaborately-carved templon. The royal doors are surmounted by a pair of eagles, almost free-standing and lively, their heads straining round. Nearby is a panel of almost heraldic lions encircled by vines and grapes and supporting a stylised palmette: a small gem.

History: Not known. The church stands alone on the site of a vanished Turkish village, and even the village name is not Greek but Italian, being a corruption of 'Prati' meaning 'Fields'.

NB. Look out for the little chapel of St Elias on the other bank under the outcrop.

PANAYIA ELEOUSA MONASTERY, *Sindi*

Position: On the west bank of the Xeros Potamos. Take the Timi/Khrysorroyiatissa road to Pendalia village, turn right past the school and, as the road bends just past a building, proceed onto an earth-road on the left. Ignore a fork to the left but continue south-west on high ground towards the river. Superb views of Sindi as the track descends 2½ to 3 miles from Pendalia on a track which is sometimes rough. Drive or walk, but avoid the winter months.

Panayia Eleousa – Sindi

Dating: Built ca. 1500, restored 18th century, later monastic buildings.

Description: The monastery stands near the river, sheltered by the surrounding hills. Remains of cells and offices occupy three sides of a fairly spacious courtyard, the church itself being on the south. The church is quite arresting: lofty, well-constructed, a ground-span of 51' x 19' and a high octagonal lantern with four lights under a tile-covered dome – an astonishing monument to come upon in such a remote place. It has a tall three-sided apse containing a sizeable window under a hooded dripstone. Two of the three doorways have similar hoods: the immense main entrance from the courtyard, and the one at the west end. The smaller south door, now blocked, has a plain rectangular frame with a curiously-built double lintel – a mid-18th century style also found at the Tekke in Larnaca and at Arpera church. The walls are buttressed on the north and south. The interior is bare and bird-haunted, the icons long gone from the gilded screen; in the apex of the west wall is a

68

round window, now blocked. The monastic buildings have crumbled to low walls mostly, but stand jaggedly two storeys high on the east: they are late in date – perhaps even 19th century – poorly constructed and of different stone. (Look for the two carved stones conserved in an arch.) In the centre of the yard is a deep, stone-lined well.

History: Sindi was erected on land belonging to a Latin overlord named Gautier de Moine and could well have been occupied first by Latin monks. During the Turkish regime, it was put under the protection of Kykko Monastery who sent their own monks down. When Barsky visited it in 1735, he wrote that only three monks lived here, the small amount of land unable to sustain more. He records that the monastery was thriving and possessed two water-mills, one on either side of the river, a few fruit trees and land for growing corn.

Legend: This is a story of a craftsman-builder and his apprentice. The younger man was commissioned to build Sindi and, when he had finished the work, he invited his old master to come and look at it. The two climbed onto the roof to inspect the dome, of which the young man was particularly proud. From there, the master could see his own creation, the church of Ayia Paraskevi across the water (now a ruin), and he realised how poor a building that was compared with Sindi. In a fit of jealous rage, he pushed his former apprentice off the roof and he was killed immediately.

AYIA MONI, *The Holy Monastery*

Position: 3000' up on Mount Royia and superbly situated a mile south of Khrysorroyiatissa.

Dating: Founded ca 300AD. Basilica first built 6th century; rebuilt in 1638; renovated in 1798, 1885 & 1990-93.

Description: **The monastic buildings** extend round three sides of an exceptionally spacious courtyard. According to the inscription by the entrance, the monumental gate-house was erected in 1798 by Melianthos, Abbot of Kykko & Moni; but it was most likely first built by Abbot Nikephoros in 1638. (Observe the two blocked small windows framed in vine-leaves). At the far end of the yard, north of the church, is a compact stone building that has an air vent above the north recess: it is not a chapel, more likely a kitchen.

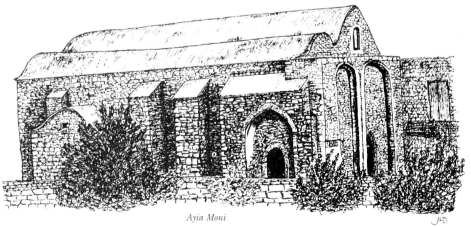

Ayia Moni

69

The church itself is a basilica that has lost its south aisle and colonnade, and its structure reflects its long existence. It stands on the site of a classical Greek temple of the 4th century BC, and material from that building has been incorporated into the fabric.

Under heavy covers on the west wall are two inscribed stones in Cypro-syllabic script, discovered in the foundations in 1885; the one on the left dates from about 1000 BC and the one on the right records the dedication of the temple to the goddess Hera by Nikokles king of Paphos. The four walls of the church differ in style. The south was given its blind arcading in the 19th century; the west front, vaults and roof date from the rebuilding of 1638, work commemorated in an inscription on the door-jambs of the main entrance; the north has a mediaeval look and features a porch, an arched recess and four buttresses, all neatly tiled.

It is at the east end, however, that the antiquity of the basilica becomes apparent; the high, flat apse wall with its massive cornerstones and the long, part-blocked window lighting the side-aisle belong to the reign of Justinian, 6th century AD. Against the apse wall are the remains of a low, two-chambered room from which worn steps and a narrow, underground passage once gave access to the Sanctuary.

Inside, the church is undecorated, the only embellishment being a frieze of acanthus in the apse and over the west door. The aisles are separated by four arches born on plain stone pillars, the end ones being engaged. Set round the head of the eastern window are five stones in a linear design. Memorable is the almost classic beauty of the apse.

History: Ayia Moni takes us back to the very beginnings of monasticism. According to tradition, it was founded around 300 AD by St Nicholas and St Eutykhios as a place of prayer and contemplation, making it the earliest such establishment in Cyprus. Both attended the First Church Council at Nicaea in 325.

A sacred relic which had been given to St Nicholas (miraculously), a piece of the cloak of the Virgin, was kept at the monastery until 1754.

In 965, Ayia Moni was visited by Athanasios, teacher and monk, who, a year or two previously, had introduced communal monasticism to Mount Athos. He remained for four years, and thereafter Ayia Moni received a lot of financial support from Mount Athos and came to be known as Moni ton Iereon, the Monastery of the Holy Fathers. The way of life seems to have been relatively unaffected by the coming of the Latins, the Paris Codex of 1588 recording the names of fourteen consecutive abbots between 1227 and 1407.

But, struggling to survive under the Turkish regime, the monastery was placed under the protection of Kykko and kept in good heart where others became run down or even abandoned. The abbot of Kykko resided at Ayia Moni after Kykko's devastating fire in 1751. Only the precious icon, Our Lady of Kykko, was saved and kept at Ayia Moni for one year: when it returned to Kykko, the piece of the Virgin's cloak accompanied it.

Recently, Ayia Moni was unoccupied for some years; but now the monks have returned under a new Abbot – a second Athanasios from Mount Athos – and all is well.

Visiting hours: 9 to 11 and 4 to 6 daily.

THE MONASTERY OF KHRYSORROYIATISSA,
(Our Lady of the Golden Pomegranite)

Position: Twenty-six miles north-east of Paphos on a spur of Mt. Royia, with extensive views over green and rich countryside. Drive ten miles up the Polis road and turn right at the signpost. The road is good as far as Pano Panayia; after that it is another mile to the monastery. Parking, wc's and, in summer, refreshments there.

Dating: Founded 1152, rebuilt 1770, restored 1967.

Description: The monastery is on two levels, the buildings alongside the road looking onto the roofs of the church, cloisters and winery. Everything is in the style of the 18th century, earlier building-work having been destroyed. The church is quite big. It stands in a neat, wedge-shaped courtyard which is lined with flowers and shrubs. Behind the colonnaded cloisters are the monks' cells and, above, the continuous balcony of the guest rooms, stone pillars on wood under a tiled roof, all pleasing to the eye. At the west

end is a fountain of the purest water. Behind the church, steps descend from the courtyard to the winery.

The church entrances are elaborately carved and painted under protective porches: the murals celebrate the Virgin, illustrating the Annunciation, Nativity and Dormition, and also the discovery of the icon by the hermit Ignatios.

71

Inside, the church has a barrel vault and five transverse ribs, the central rib being stopped with masks. Decoration inclines towards the ornate. The front of the women's gallery is heavily carved in small wooden panels, picked out in blue, red and gold, the underside being in a waffle pattern. An inscription states that Abbot Joachim had it made in 1802. The chandeliers – all different and no doubt all gifts – are unfortunate.

But observe the fine carving on the icon screen, throne, and pulpit, and, incorporated into the screen, particular, very special icons. Left of the royal doors is the Virgin and Child of Khrysorroyiatissa, the founding icon of the monastery, claimed to have been painted by St. Luke: every part save the faces is covered in silver-gilt, but the faces are distinctive. This icon is greatly venerated and among others who come to pray before it are wrongdoers and their families, asking for mercy. A copy, with the story of its finding, stands by the wall. To the right of the royal doors is a fine, late 16th century Christ Pantocrator: in 1848 the priest Polycarpos covered the hand in silver-gilt, having had his leprosy cured. The icons of St. Luke, John the Divine and John the Baptist date from 1773 and are remarkably good for that time. Among other prized possessions here is a copper-plate engraving of the Holy Icon made by John Kornaris in 1801.

Winery and icon workshop

The present Abbot, Dionysios, has revived the Monastery's wine-making tradition during the last eight years, with considerable success; the vineyards are above on the slopes of Mt. Royia. The wine is obtainable from the shop in the south cloister and the cellars may be visited. The abbot is an expert restorer of icons and conservation has been practiced at Khrysorroyiatissa since 1987.

History:

The Monastery was founded in 1152 by a recluse named Ignatios after he discovered the Holy Icon of the Virgin on a beach at Paphos and built a shrine for it on this spot. In time, a monastery grew round it that became one of the most well regarded in Cyprus, containing at its height twenty monks, fifteen deacons and thirty novices[1].

After 1571, the greater part of its property and possessions was taken by the Turks, and after years of pillaging and maltreatment nothing much remained except the Holy Icon; no records survived, so the Monastery's history is unknown before the 18th century. The itinerant Russian monk Barsky visited here in 1735 and found a very small domed church and only two or three cells. He observed that the monks were very poor but that they had one asset – the beauty and the quiet. At this time, as with Ayia Moni, Kykko took responsibility for the place and there was no resident abbot until 1770. Then one of the greatest bishops of the age, Panaretos of Paphos, breathed new life into the monastery and installed the monk Kalinikos as Abbot. Between them the church was rebuilt, the buildings were restored and a school set up to instruct local village boys in Greek history and religion.

The Turkish massacres of 1821 brought more tribulation but never a return to the desperate poverty of old. In 1967, a bad fire which destroyed much of the premises necessitated extensive rebuilding. With Archbishop Makarios providing the financial help, the Department of Antiquities restored Khrysorroyiatissa almost exactly in the style which had suited it so well.

---

1. Romantic Cyprus, Keshishian.

Tradition: The holy icon, painted by St Luke, was kept at Isauria in Southern Asia Minor until the days of iconoclasm, when a woman threw it into the sea to save it from the iconsmashers. It was washed ashore at Paphos, near the Moulia rocks, where a fisherman found it and hid it in a cave. Almost four hundred years later, the hermit Ignatios saw a great fire burning in that direction and discovered the icon, radiating light. Whilst carrying it back to his retreat on Mount Kremasti, he stopped to rest, and an angel in a vision urged him to take it instead to nearby Mt. Royia and enshrine it there, which he did.

STAVROS TIS MITHAS MONASTERY
(Holy Cross of the wild mint)

Position: Two miles south east of Tsadha village, off the Polis road, on a knoll.

Dating: Founded 1520, rebuilt 1745, restored 1971.

Description: A small, single-aisled church in the Franco-Byzantine style, similar to St George in Arpera of same date and also incorporating a women's gallery – here dismantled but see separate entrance on north west. The north wall appears to be of earlier construction. The west door has a marble lintel with nice moulding under; the south doorway is early 16th century, in Gunnis's opinion, and possibly from the first church. Small openings in the apex of the east and west walls are filled with pierced stone insets, best viewed from the interior: the west displays a floral cross in a roundel, the east a plain Greek cross.

The Holy Cross of Mithas, containing a splinter of the True Cross, stands in the north west recess: it shows signs of burning. The iconostasis is contemporary and carries an inscription recording the rebuilding by Bishop Joachim in 1745. Recently a Crucifixion crowned the screen but the panels have gone to the Byzantine Museum in Paphos. In the epistyle, top centre, is an icon of St Peter and St Paul, as pillars of the Church, holding an image of a church. Outside again, the modest cloisters with their attractive arches are 18th century with recent restorations.

History: The monastery formerly owned large tracts of the surrounding land, recently sold to developers for a golf course. It had some importance, being at one time a residence of the Bishop of Paphos and also possessing a splinter of the True Cross. But when the Russian monk Barsky came in 1735 it was ruinous. A miracle occurred in the 1830's when a fierce fire broke out. The Abbot of Mithas brought out the Cross and flung it into the flames, which were immediately extinguished; and, although its silver case had melted, the Cross itself was only slightly scorched.

In charge here is Brother Barnabas, very welcoming to visitors.

EPISKOPI: Retreat of St Hilarion: once a place of pilgrimage, and still revered. (Scenic, peaceful but scant remains)

Position: On the Ezousas river, about ten miles east of Paphos past Konya and Marathounda.

History: St. Hilarion (AD 290-371) was one of the Desert Fathers of Egypt and a disciple of St. Anthony, founder of Monasticism. His fame grew over the years until, besieged by crowds, he was forced to leave and eventually reached Paphos some time after 360 AD. By then an old man, he found solitude again in this remote cave. St. Jerome became his friend and later wrote a life of St. Hilarion.

Description: An area much affected by earthquake damage. The cave is on the right below the road at start of village; also a ruined church on earlier foundations. Note capital with acanthus leaves. The modern church above, dedicated to the saint, commands a fine view. The displaced bishop of Paphos came here in the 13th century before moving to Arsinoe (Polis) for the duration of the Frankish occupation hence the name of the village, which means 'Seat of the Bishop'.

AYIOS NEOPHYTOS MONASTERY: *Church, Monastery and Enkleistra or cloistered place* (cafe open weekends and holidays)

Position: Six miles north of Paphos through Trimithousa. 1,360' above sea level at top of narrow wooded gorge.

Ayios Neophytos Enkleistra

74

Dating: Enkleistra begun 1159; Monastery church built 1435.
Enkleistra painted 1183 and 1196; Monastery church painted ca. 1503.

Life of St. Neophytos 1134 to 1219 *(Taken from his own writings)*

He was born at Kato Dhrys near Lefkara of poor parents, and grew up unschooled. He taught himself to read and write during his years as a novice at St. Chrysostom Monastery. In 1159, wanting to join a reclusive community in Asia Minor, he came to Nea Paphos to take ship; but he was robbed of his passage money and imprisoned as a vagrant. On his release and penniless, the young man walked towards the mountains and discovered there an isolated cave in a cliff beside a spring: a haunt of birds and a place of wild beauty still. He decided to make this his retreat and he remained in it for the rest of his life.

History of the Enkleistra

Neophytos enlarged the three caves of his retreat himself, fashioning altar, bench, table and recesses from the rock.

1160   A tiny chapel dedicated to the Holy Cross and a cell were finished after a year's labour, sufficient for the solitary man.

1165   He managed after much striving to obtain a splinter of the True Cross.

1170   Urged by the Bishop of Paphos, he was ordained and took a disciple. Others came for instruction and so a monastery was founded. Neophytos drew up its Rule, the first Ritual Ordinance.

1183   The nave of the Enkleistra was completed: in the same year, a master painter decorated the cell and sanctuary.

1196   Nave decorated. Neophytos was now a legend and forced higher up the cliff to preserve his solitary life.

1197   January 24th. Now in his sixties and still excavating the new Enkleistra, he was nearly killed by a dislodged boulder.

Neophytos remained in his new retreat for a further twenty or so years, descending only on Sundays to preach and instruct. At all other times, he heard the Liturgy and received the Sacrament through a hole in the ceiling of the nave. He died at the age of eighty-five: he had woven his own shroud, made for himself a coffin of pine and cedar and chestnut and left these instructions:

After the burial, rebuild the wall . . . that no one may know where I have been buried. There my worthless body should stay in quietness until the common Resurrection . . .

From his tiny cell had issued a constant stream of writings, including hymns, letters, two Ritual Ordinances, reproofs and commentaries. As few could read and write then, it is the more astonishing to hear this lone voice from a remote corner of Cyprus raised in indignant protest at the invasion of Richard the Lionheart, whom he calls a wicked wretch. (See Introduction under The Crusades.)

1503   An inscription in the south-west corner of the nave refers to restoration of the Enkleistra *by the contribution and expense and much desire* of the monk Neophytos – almost certainly the monastery's new patron, or Ktitor, mentioned in the records.

In the Turkish period, the location of the Saint's tomb became forgotten until, one night in 1750, a treasure-seeking monk broke down first the wall and then the coffin-lid and received a great shock. Amid rejoicing, the shrivelled remains were transferred to the main church, where they are now: his skull in a reliquary beside the iconostasis and his body in a wooden box – despite Neophytos' expressed wish that he should be left alone.

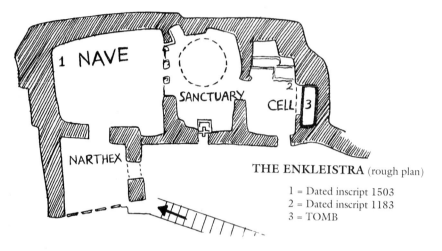

THE ENKLEISTRA (rough plan)

1 = Dated inscript 1503
2 = Dated inscript 1183
3 = TOMB

Description: **THE ENKLEISTRA**

The Cell and Chapel (comprising the original Retreat). Completed September 1160.

A low doorway admits to the cell, which measures approximately 11 ft by 8 ft. The place is exactly as it was: the stone table at which he wrote, the stone bench on which he slept and the stone tomb which received him when he died. Notice the niches for his writing materials. The large recess behind the bench used to have wooden doors. In the chapel is a stone altar and, over it, a wooden cross from the days of the Saint. Embedded in the north wall near the altar is a marble slab with an inscription in metre beginning:

Formerly I was allotted to be a habitation of birds
But I became Thy home, O Word.

and refers to it now being a consecrated place.

The Decoration of 1183

These paintings are lavishly accompanied by inscriptions, mostly quotations from the Bible or earlier saints. The work was closely supervised by Neophytos and reflect his life long obsession with death and resurrection. According to tradition, he had already done some decoration himself, in 1170. But the style of the wall-painting is that of a trained and gifted artist: he who wrote in a slight depression between the table and the tomb, *The Enkleistra was painted by the hand of me, Theodore Apseudes (The trustworthy) in the year 6691 from Adam* (= 1183 AD).

It was unusual, then, for the painter to give his name.

The style is Neo-classical after the school of Constantinople, and has something of the master painter of Lagoudera of 1192 about it, although at an earlier stage. The flowing lines, vigour and plasticity of the figures is there, though the feeling of movement has not yet reached its full development.

Paintings of the Cell:

On the north wall above the bench is a large fresco of Christ Enthroned, flanked by the Virgin and St. John as supplicants; below, Neophytos is on his knees: *Be merciful to him who beseechingly lies at Thy divine foot. . .* Here is a true portrait of the saint in middle age. The Prophets in three medallions overhead are Isaiah, Daniel and David, the paintings by the door are of military saints and the saint on the south is the rarely depicted Andrew – fool for the sake of Christ. The Crucifixion on the south wall has been damaged, leaving St John and the Good Centurion as the only mourners. Note the foot of Christ from a previous rendering showing through. In the tomb recess are the Crucifixion and the Anastasis separated by the Virgin and Child between two bishops (probably Chrysostom and Basil the Great). This Crucifixion, small as it is, conveys all the grief and dignity and beauty of this composition in Byzantine art before the Latins changed it. The Anastasis, eastern form of the Resurrection, is considered by A&J Stylianou to be one of the finest on the subject in the 12th century.

Paintings in the Sanctuary chapel

Taking up the entire upper west wall is an extraordinary scene: the Recluse is being borne aloft between the two Archangels, who have him firmly by his shoulders. His hands are folded across his breast as in death and he is wearing his Abbot's robes. The inscription beneath expresses his fervent wish that this vision should come true. Opposite, the apse-space is very cramped, and the Mother of God is on the same level as the officiating Church Fathers. (Of those, Neophytos' choice is Sts. Chrysostom, Basil, Epiphanios and Nicholas). Overhead, on an extremely difficult surface, the artist has managed the Ascension with Christ in a mandorla above the Virgin and an archangel, the amazed Apostles in varied postures, and even a landscape. Either side of the north door is the Annunciation. (Note the Gabriel especially, as a superb example of the new freedom of movement). The Pantocrater on the low ceiling is a restoration of 1503. On the wall below is a row of seven hermits with gentle human expressions. They should be compared with their intimidating brethren in the nave to see the difference in style and attitude between the neo-classical and the monastic painter.

THE NAVE. Completed 1183. It is entered through a narthex, end of the gallery, and was also hewn out of rock by the Recluse. He divided the nave by a templon from the first chapel, which then became the bema or sanctuary of the enlarged church. He made a recess in the east wall and therein placed a large wooden cross which contained his splinter of the True Cross.

Thirteen years later, a second painter covered the walls with scenes from the later part of the Christological cycle, manifestly in accordance with the wishes of Neophytos.

The Decoration – 1196 and 1503

Scheme:

It begins on the south with Abraham Entertaining the Angels and the Last Supper; the Washing of the Feet is on the west; thence the cycle moves clockwise through Christ's Passion and Crucifixion, ending east of the entrance with the Anastasis and later Appearance; the Ascension is on the ceiling. In the recess and guarding the Holy Cross are the archangels with Sts. Chrysostom and Basil and Gregory the Theologian: Constantine and Helena, who discovered the True Cross, are alongside. The lower register on the west contains a row of famous hermits.

The Paintings: The first three in the series were totally repainted in 1503. Abraham Entertaining the Angels links the O.T. with the Passion, being symbolic of the Last Supper. Note the odd seating arrangements in the latter, and the strange table-supports. The well preserved Washing of the Feet shows the puzzled disciples unstrapping their sandals against a backdrop of a Venetian palace. The rest of the work is that of the unnamed artist of 1196. It is linear and uncompromisingly, severely spiritual, as if challenging the neo-classicism of the earlier painting. It achieves its best expression in the Anastasis. This painter, too, skilfully adapts the uneven wall-surface to the subject: the Betrayal caught in an angle, the winding procession along the Via Crucis with Simon of Cyrene carrying the Cross just arriving at the east wall of the recess; then the Crucifixion directly above Neophytos' own cross.

Note that the treatment of the Crucifixion and the Descent from the Cross is less harsh than elsewhere, possibly because the artist is more closely following tradition. Below the Anastasis is the head of a monk ardently gazing upwards: he is thought to be the Ktitor of the Monastery who paid for the 1503 restoration – but it could represent Neophytos again. The Ascension on the ceiling is well-positioned as it enables Christ to disappear through the orifice, already there. Much of this painting is lost and faded, but notice at the lower left corner a nest of young birds and their parents, never forgotten by the Saint. By the bema on the west wall is Stephen the Younger, who was martyred for his defence of icons in 764 and is here pointing to an icon. By style, he appears to belong to the row of saints in the Sanctuary. To Apseudes, also, the Christ Enthroned seems to belong (right of the icon screen). Compare this head with that of the Pantocrator at Lagoudera.

N.B. Neophytos himself appears in a number of paintings in the nave: as one of the Apostles in The Last Supper, The Washing of the Feet, The Agony in the Garden and The Ascension; as Simon of Cyrene in the Via Crucis; as Joseph of Arimathea in The Descent from the Cross; and as Adam in The Anastasis.

The paintings in the narthex belong to the 1503 period and include the Annunciation, Peter, Paul and prelates.

Also: On the north side of the cell is a fourth cave, a church which the Saint dug out and dedicated to John the Baptist. Shepherds' fires over a long period have blackened the interior and damaged the paintings.

Neophytos' spring is located beside the small bridge below: to reach it, go down steps. The palindrome there comes from the fountain at St. Sophia, Constantinople and reads: NIPSON ANOMIMATA MI MONA NOPSIN – **Wash your sins not only your face.**

Subsequent History of the Monastery

It appears to have been respected by the Latins, who were probably impressed by the immense love the local people had for their saint, and it prospered. The existing church and principal buildings went up in the 15th century, 1435 being the date conjectured. The standard of the work and the size of the church suggest patronage at a top level. (The Lusignan king at the time was John II who was allied by marriage to the Greek Palaeologue dynasty).

The high order of its decoration, too, circa 1503, must be due to the determined efforts of the Ktitor Neophytos to bring over the best Byzantine painters. Some time in the 15th century, the Latins built their chapel against the west wall of the Greek church, and the monks were obliged to open new entrances for themselves in the north and south walls – hence the semi-circular steps. After the departure of the Latins in 1570, their chapel became the narthex of the monastery church. In 1585, the community was ravaged by Turkish soldiers. Barsky, the Russian monk, stayed for three days in 1735 and made his customary sketch. In the days of the 1821 massacre, Abbot Melissovouccas and his few monks fought for their lives from behind the refectory door – still scarred by Turkish bullets. They got away, but the abbot was later found, taken to Nicosia and killed.

The Monastery Precincts

They are reached by a splayed flight of steps on the west. Above the door is a modern mosaic of Neophytos. Inside, a broad pavement extends south of the church to the refectory at the far end. Halfway along is a large double headed Byzantine eagle done in mosaic. At a lower level on the south are the old monastery buildings, enclosing a charming small garden of shrubs and trees. The west end and main entrance to the church is reached by a short steep flight of steps. In this courtyard hang the metal and wooden oblong gongs and their hammers that are used instead of bells. The monks' quarters opposite are fairly recent.

THE MAIN CHURCH, dedicated to the Mother of God of the Enkleistra. It is a large, well-built basilica, with a high dome and barrel vaults. The nave and side-aisles are separated by two rows of four columns under round arches, and the capitals are ornately carved with acanthus leaves. The walls were once fully decorated and a fair amount of the paintings have survived. There is a fine iconostasis. The floor is of polished marble – note the doves. Entry is though what was the Latin chapel, built against the basilica's west wall; the dividing wall was taken down last century and the difference in height and style between the two buildings is clearly seen.

The Paintings: done by artists trained in the pure Byzantine style in its last flowering, as developed at Mystra in the 14th and 15th centuries and in Crete in the 16th. Mainly to be found in the apse and parabemas, south-east vault and north vault. A&J Stylianou consider that all the paintings in the church were carried out at the same period and are early 16th century. They vary greatly in scale, but in technique and treatment are all products of the refined late Palaeologue style as it developed after the fall of Constantinople in 1453.

> **Bema:** The Apse follows the traditional programme: the Virgin in the conch with the Christchild on her left arm; below her, the Communion of the Apostles, Christ depicted twice and with Paul replacing Judas on the right; and at altar-level six Fathers celebrate the Liturgy, all wearing the polystavrion. In the prothesis (north chamber) is St Stephen in the niche; and, flying down from a starry heaven, a weeping angel above Christ of the Utter Humiliation (damaged). In the opposite niche in the diakonicon (south chamber) a sorrowing angel-deacon displays the dead Christ on a red cloth, *I the Lamb lie before you, mystically slain* . . . On the adjacent pillar is the deacon Lavrentios, a young saint holding key and candle; and portrayed above is Sylvester, Bishop of Rome under Constantine.

> **Bema & Nave:** In the spandrels and soffits of the arches are ten saints: two in the north aisle, eight in the south aisle, east end, and two on the south-west. They include Cosmas and Damian the medical saints over the south east pillar, the wild figure of Alexios Man of God in the soffit under, and St. Hilarion on the south west.

> **South vault:** At the east end are three paintings: Joachim and Anna, parents of the Virgin, offer gifts at the Temple; they depart having had their gifts

rejected; Joachim prays. This last is a strong portrait of the despondent man just before the angel speaks. Almost certainly a lost cycle on the Life of the Virgin began here.

North vault: Almost a complete series illustrating the ancient Lenten hymn, the Akathistos (= to be sung standing); one verse for each letter of the Greek alphabet, one scene for each verse – making twenty-four altogether. It starts in the bema and runs in a continuous strip along the south of the vault, returning on the north side. (This is when 'fresco neck' makes itself felt!) Note that three phases of the Annunciation are shown in the opening scenes: surprise, repudiation, acceptance.

The quality and the strip effect are best appreciated by western visitors in the more familiar scenes – the five from the Nativity to the Flight into Egypt, where the sense of continuity in the events gains from the lack of divisions. Notice the soft, glowing colours set off by the dark sky, the meticulous way faces have been built up, and, despite the lofty elevation, the attention to detail. On the opposite vault come the remaining scenes (the two missing ones were on the old west wall of the basilica now demolished). They have no set iconography and are difficult to follow unless armed with a translation of the Akathistos. The last scene but one, *All we who psalm thy Son*, shows a Byzantine choir, wearing special white caps, with their choir-master on the left in a curious orange hat, beating time. The Hymn is illustrated elsewhere in Cyprus, done towards the end of the 15th c. (See the Latin Chapel, St. John Lampadistis Monastery.)

The Iconostasis

Thought to be contemporary with the church, it was restored and gilded mid 19th c. by Abbot Gregorios. He also contributed the throne and pulpit, the canopy over the icon of Neophytos on the screen and the wooden case and canopy containing his body. To the left of the screen on a ledge stands the engraved silver-gilt reliquary (mid 18th c.) holding the skull of the saint.

The Icons on the screen are later than the wall-paintings by about forty years, the Christ (top centre) being signed by the painter Joseph Houris and dated 1544. All but the bottom row appear to be his work. The central portion contains, on the top row, a Great Deesis, and beneath in twelve smaller panels the main feasts of the Church. The Christ, Virgin and Baptist were taken to London in 1980 as part of the Treasures of Cyprus Exhibition. They are very fine: slightly mannered but still Palaeologue in style, the chief influence here comes from the Cretan School of the 16th century. On the side screens are the rest of the Apostles (Simon missing far left), female saints and lesser feasts. The icons on the bottom row are by various painters: John Kornaris, famous Cretan artist, made the Neophytos portrait in 1806. The oldest icon must be the Mother of God of the Enkleistra, 1450, on a separate stand. Finally, on the Royal Doors beside his most prized Fathers of the Church, Basil, Chrysostom and Gregory the Theologian, stands Neophytos: the monastery has indeed honoured him.

AYIA EKATERINA of PHIDEFKIA, *Kritou Terra*

Position: Two and a half miles east of Kritou Terra down a good track. (Three quarters of a mile past the church, the track joins the Paphos/Polis road.)

Dating: Probably built and painted late 15th century; arcades and painting 16th century; severely damaged in 1953 earthquake and repaired; restored in 1992.

Description: Unique in the Laona area. Here is a domed building with three aisles divided by low arches which rest on built stone piers, each aisle ending in an apse. Of the north and west porticos, only the west is standing; it serves as narthex, or vestibule to the church and its arcades support three small domes. The base of the springing of an arch on the north-west corner suggests that a similar arcade once existed on the north. The church is known locally as 'the seven-domed' and it may be that the north portico also carried domes. The mystical number three, symbol of the Holy Trinity, is expressed in the design of the building; in the arches, domes, aisles and entrances.

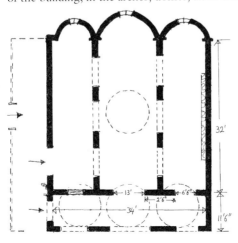

Ground plan of Ayia Ekaterina (based on paced internal measurements).

81

The decoration was almost wholly destroyed by the 1953 earthquake. St. Marina, 'Holy Martyr', is still visible on the south wall by the west entrance; and an elaborate monochrome design at ground-level opposite. At the east end is the Virgin on the apse wall, and faintly, in the south vault, Abraham Entertaining the Angels. In the west portico, the entire south wall is taken up by a large damaged figure of the Archangel Michael.

History: This monastery church was founded by monks sent from the famous Monastery of Saint Catherine on Mt Sinai and they still own it, although it has not been occupied in living memory. As late as the year 1900, the monastery owned large tracts of land in the Laona, and a monk would come annually from Sinai to hire it out to local farmers. Eventually, the land was sold off and the monks no longer visit. (From information obtained from the Muhtar of Kritou Terra.)

Ayia Ekaterina – Kritou Terra

Tradition: According to Kyprianos,[1] Katerina was the Christian daughter of a former Governor of Cyprus living in exile in Alexandria in the days of the tyrant Maximian. She was a highly educated girl. Upon the death of her father, she returned to Constantia (then the capital of Cyprus) and lived in her uncle's house where she openly professed her faith. Maximian had her forceably brought back to Alexandria, and she suffered a martyr's death. He had hated her father. In the Middle Ages, Katerina was a cult figure, her shrines became places of pilgrimage, and various legends collected round her saintly life and death.

Legend: When she was beheaded, instead of blood, milk gushed forth.
Her body was transported by angels from Alexandria to Mt. Sinai.

Cypriot legends about Ayia Ekaterina Monastery: milk was used to mix the mortar when building the church, no water being available. The hero Dighenis, who chased Rigena the Queen everywhere from Paphos to the

---

1. History of Cyprus 1788

82

Akamas, brought running water to the monastery at Rigena's request, his reward being marriage. She had thought the task impossible and, to escape wedlock, fled to the Baths of Aphrodite and down to the shore. Dighenis saw her sailing over the sea with her scarf as a boat and threw a rock after her (it is still in the sea there); but she kept right on until she got to Egypt where she built another monastery at Sinai.

KHRYSOSPILIOTISSA, *Pano Arodhes.* Catacomb cp Ayia Solomoni.

Position: About 1¼ miles east of the village. From Kathikas, drive to the junction with Pano Arodhes and turn right onto the signposted track.

Description: A Hellenistic tomb with an antechamber, both vaulted. Worn steps lead down to a small inner room – originally they may have continued to the customary well. The rock-face above has been worked and retains some of its fresco (suggestive of the Virgin between Archangels), work thought to be 14th century. The main hall is bare except for a rough apse with an altar built against the east wall in the Turkish period. The small chapel over this catacomb was erected in 1947 and has a reputation for miraculous healing.

History: None directly; its only record is a song. The area is called Thermoskrini and is known for its spring-water. Judging by the many catacombs and artefacts found in the vicinity, it may be the site of a Roman settlement. A small, isolated community was still here in the 16th century. Later, under Turkish rule, Khrysospiliotissa became one of the hidden churches of the Linovamvakoi or Flax-cottons, Orthodox Greeks who 'blew with the wind', outwardly turned Moslem to escape the crippling taxes on Christians while secretly attended the Liturgy.

Legend: The ballad tells of a Christian girl hidden in the catacomb from pagan threats, then martyred. Over the centuries, it has become embroidered. Now her name is Christina and she was hidden by her father from a rich Turkish landowner who desired her. She revealed herself because her father was being tortured, was tortured herself and finally she took some poison and died.

Tradition: Popular place of pilgrimage, especially for the sick. As at Ayia Solomoni, the catacomb is said to cure eye trouble: there well-water is the remedy; here, the well being lost, candle-black is resorted to. Down the steps, the lighted candle is held to a crevice and the resulting soot applied to the eyes like kohl.

AYII ANARGYRI, *near Miliou* (ref. to Cosmas & Damian, who healed the poor free.)

Position: Almost a mile from the main Paphos/Polis road. Look for a concealed turning on the left north of Yiolou and follow the signs to the Ayii Anargyri Hotel.

Description: A tiny monastery church of late date (1649), barrel-vaulted with two transverse ribs. The only point of interest is the plaque above the west entrance: two carved panels showing the Crucifixion and Deposition respectively. The monastic buildings were renovated in 1950. The site is attractively wooded and watered; it is also a spa and cures rheumatism.

ARKHANGELOS MIKHAIL CHURCH, *Kholi* (Formerly ded. to the Virgin, Panayia Khryseleoussa)

Position: On eastern edge of village in superb position looking across the sweep of the valley towards the Paphos mountain range. From main Paphos/Polis road, take concealed small road on left just before bridge at Skoulli. Kholi is less than a mile up the hill. Key with the village priest.

Dating: Church and decoration early 16th c. Tower built about fifty years previously.

Description: This is a small barrel-vaulted building with a single transverse rib, typical of its period. A portico has just been added along the north side – too late, though, to save numbers of painting inside from loss or damage from the damp. The church is built against the east wall of an earlier watch-tower, a doorway being cut through to convert its ground-floor into a narthex. Note the difference in floor levels.

The paintings

Arkhangelos Mikhail – Kholi

Once fully decorated in a local, post-Byzantine, conservative style, enough remains for the scheme of decoration to be followed: the north vaults illustrate the Life of the Virgin – naturally in a church dedicated to her – and on the south are scenes from the Life and Passion of Christ. Lost are most of the saints on the walls beneath. The painter's skill is perhaps at its best in the apse, in the faces of the converging Fathers of the Church and in the head of Barnabas on the north wall nearby. (Two of the Fathers are Cypriot prelates – Spyridon and Epiphanios.) The Crucifixion, west end, south vault, is well preserved: the figures are rather harshly drawn and have hard outlines, but the scene conforms to the essentially Byzantine concept of the minimum number of mourners, outward calm and deep inward grief.

On the north wall, west end, is a portrait of that emaciated beauty, Mary of Egypt, receiving communion from St. Zosimos: on the left is all that remains of The Last Judgement, an elaborate picture that was lost when the west wall was demolished. Many of the frescoes are being preserved by the Dept. of Antiquities.

The Watch-tower

It was possibly built at the time of King James II (1460-73) when Turkish expansion was a threat in the eastern Mediterranean, one of a network of observation posts and signal stations reaching from the south to the north coasts. The Tower of the Queen above the Baths of Aphrodite may have been another. Here at Kholi, the tower would have been three storeys high originally, with a flat roof and a cellar. An external stair would have led to a single entrance at first floor level. Traces of this can be seen in the north wall; and a door with steps is visible at the foot of the south wall, leading down to a cellar or cistern now blocked. The present north door was put in when the church was built.

PANAYIA HODEGETRIA

Below the Church of the Archangel is an attractive chapel dedicated to the Virgin. It is also built in the Franco-Byzantine manner but dates from the 15th century. It has a transverse central rib and arched recesses in the north and south walls and houses a fine but damaged icon of the Hodegetria, probably contemporary with the chapel. Some paintings survive, notably a rustic Baptism of Christ.

AYIOS ANDRONIKOS CHURCH, *Polis* (Paintings now being cleaned by the Dept. of Antiquities.)

Position: On the north-west of the town just beyond the pedestrian precinct by a car park.

Ayios Andronikos – Polis

85

Dating: 16th century.

Description: A single-aisle, barrel-vaulted church with pointed transverse ribs; a vestibule on the north. It was formerly fully decorated in a multiplicity of small scenes, which were whitewashed by the Turks when it was converted into a mosque.

The paintings cover the vaults in three tiers, illustrating the Life and Passion of Christ and the Appearances. On the walls below are rows of half-length saints with some emphasis on monastics and ascetics, suggesting that it may have been a monastery church. The style is flat and very conservative, the drawing is good and the colours lively, with much use of red on a blue ground.

PANAYIA KHRYSELEOUSA, *Lyso*

Position: Eight miles south-east of Polis on high ground. Half-a-mile south of Polis, from the main Paphos road, take a minor road left, signposted LYSO. After passing through Steni and Peristerona, keep left at the fork.

Dating: 15th century.

Description: A fairly large, striking church with a whitewashed exterior, it has both Byzantine and Gothic features, but not blended into the Franco-Byzantine style. It was probably the place of worship for the Latin overlords of the district. The well-preserved coats-of-arms carved on its north and south doorways include the bearings of the powerful Gourri family and of the Nevilles. At the east end, an attractive Gothic window of two lights supporting a roundel with stone tracery has been blocked from the inside.

On the south is arcading with capitals in the Gothic manner. Inside, the blocked east window now carries a painting of the Panayia Eleousa (Our Lady of Mercy); it is flanked by seraphim and has a top border of stylised birds – possibly ravens. The early 18th century icon of St Nicholas, set in the back of the bishop's throne, is worthy of note.

AYIOS MINAS CHURCH, *Akamas*

Position: About two miles west of Neokhorio on a rough earth road. Papakyriakos, the village priest, has the key. After leaving Neokhorio, ignore the first right-hand turning, shortly come to a fork and then keep right.

Dating: 16th century on 12th century foundations. Restored 1990.

Description: Ayios Minas is a single-aisled monastery church with a barrel-vault reinforced with three transverse ribs. All that remains of the monastic buildings are the footings of some cells on the north-east. Incorporated into the north wall is part of the architrave of an earlier doorway, possibly 12th century. Recent work at the west end has uncovered the original extent of the church, which has now been restored to its full fifty feet to include a narthex.

A limited number of frescoes have been recovered, mostly 16th century work. The best-preserved is a painting of Constantine the Great and St. Helen on the south wall. On the north vault opposite is the Transfiguration, part of a lost Festival cycle; and belonging to the first period of decoration, on the wall below, is St Theodore. On the central rib, freed from the grime of centuries, a small haloed head shines out.

History &
Tradition:
Ayios Minas was a dependency of the monastery of St George of Nikoksilitis near Drousha and six monks lived here. It was still functioning in 1834. The dedication is to an early Egyptian martyr. Minas was a Roman soldier at the time of Maximian (late 3rd c). He had fled to Egypt to escape persecution because of his Christian faith, and was tortured and finally beheaded for insisting that there was only one God. The implication is that the first settlement was by monks from Egypt.

PANAYIA KHRYSELEOUSA, *Khlorakas* (Our Golden Lady of Mercy)

Position: In the village, adjacent to its very large successor.

Dating: 12th or 13th century.

Description: This is a cruciform, domed building with barrel vaults, cp. Ayios Theodosios at Akhelia and Panayia at Kouklia. Its mediaeval paintings are either lost or hidden under later plaster: a George and Dragon can be seen on the north wall of the north arm; and in the west arm, south wall, where the plaster has been cut away, are two busts of saints, one being Ayia Kyriaki. A monumental west entrance of finely dressed stone has a Frankish coat-of-arms on the lintel in the form of a T. Above, is a window lighting an upper room. At some time, a Latin building was attached to the north wall of the west arm. Two blocked pointed arches visible on the inside indicate an open connection with the church – possibly a Frankish family chapel. It survived as the village school until 1920 when it was demolished.

AYIOS NIKOLAOS MONASTERY CHURCH, *Khlorakas*

Position: South-east of the village. From Ktima, take the first turning signposted Khlorakas. The very small, whitewashed church is by the sports ground.

Dating: 12th century.

Description: A compact, single-aisled building with a dome resting directly on four engaged piers cp the Church of the Holy Apostles, Perakhorio. At some later period, the west was extended to create a narthex, and this additional space was incorporated into the nave by widening the old doorway. The Frankish family arms, familiar from the village church, appear again here, above the

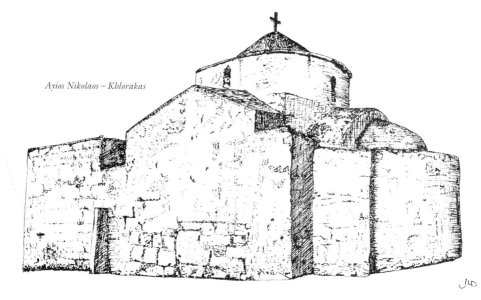

Ayios Nikolaos – Khlorakas

north door. Traces of painting may be seen in the apse, part, it seems, of the Fathers of the Church; also on the south wall of the nave.

The monastery functioned at least until the early part of the 19th century.

PANAYIA KHRYSELEOUSA, *Emba* (Eleousa = merciful)

Position: Off the old Coral Bay road, three miles from Ktima. In half-a-mile, after a sharp bend, take the first turning on the right (signpost). The church is at the beginning of the village on the left.

Dating: Built 12th century with later narthex. Decorated end 15th century.

Description: Now an attractive, weathered complex of walls, angles and curves, Emba church began as a simple cruciform building, domed and barrel-vaulted like so many of that period were. Later, it was altered to a cross-in-square design, and the spaces between the arms of the cross were enclosed – all except the south-east. The narthex was added in 1744 and it was also built in a cruciform with its own large octagonal dome, here topped by a small Roman marble column. At some period before the alterations, the church was monastic.

Decoration: Entry through the north-east doors brings one straight into the original simple church, where a magnificent Pantokrator looks down from the dome, surrounded by the Heavenly Host. The scene was painted towards the end of the 15th century by a master in a conservative, Palaeologue style. Christ is in a ring of shimmering light; motionless around Him, and also gazing down, are all the Powers as described in the Book of Ezekiel (I v.4-25), portrayed meticulously without losing spiritual force. The Virgin Orans is centrally placed between archangels below her Son, and the rest of the circle consists of Angels, Cherubim, Seraphim and Wheels. The outer ring contains the conventional O.T. Prophets framed in a slender arcade.

Six-winged Seraph

88

And the four beasts had each of them six wings about him; and they were full of eyes within: and they rest not day and night, saying, "Holy, holy, holy, Lord God Almighty, which was, and is, and is to come". Revelations IV v.8.

The decoration in the west vault has been, first, badly smoked and, secondly, atrociously overpainted, but is now being freed from this state: the paintings

Panayia Khryseleousa – Emba

on the south side are fully visible, those on the north – which include a Last Judgement – only partly so to date. They are revealed as contemporary with the work in the dome but done in a local, two-dimensional, post-Byzantine manner, bright and well-executed. The north vault carried three tiers of paintings, the two lower being a series of twelve small scenes depicting the Resurrection and subsequent Appearances of Christ, and the uppermost a row of saints.

N.B. Earlier decoration is known to exist underneath the 15th century plaster.

The iconostasis is 16th century and on it are displayed three particularly fine icons. Those of Christ and John the Baptist are by a local artist, Titos, the first being signed and dated 1536. For technique, look closely at the Baptist, not only for the ravaged, wild face, carefully built up, but also for the delicacy of the tiny scenes each side. The Virgin Hodegetria is of the same period, by another hand. St. Symeon the Stylite, end 16th century, is not in the same class. In a glass case is a two-panel painting of the twelve Apostles, Veneto-Byzantine, of high quality and probably from the middle of the 16th century. Other Venetian legacies are a painted coat-of-arms left of the north-east door, and a leatherbound Gospel of 1538.

History: In the 12th century, Emba was probably the hub of an estate already, with an aristocratic Byzantine overlord. Under the Lusignans, it became a royal dhomaine, and by the 14th century one of the important sugar-producing centres in the Paphos area. But it was under the Venetians that a Byzantine master-painter was commissioned to decorate the dome of the church, indicating that there was wealth, still, in Emba.

The steps to the roof: According to the village priest, there were cloisters where the narthex now stands, and the stairway gave access to the monks' quarters above. Until 1744 a traditional market was held under the arcades.

PEYIA BASILICA

Position: At Cape Drepanum, twelve miles north of Paphos on the coast between Coral Bay and Lara. Drive towards Coral Bay. At the last junction, do not turn left towards the shops but continue straight along the new road. Shortly after being joined by a tarmacked road on the right, the surface deteriorates. After two or three miles, the turning for Lara is signposted right and almost immediately the tavernas of Ayios Yeoryios appear ahead. Park by the modern church of St. George.

The area: Cape Drepanum is the geographical location; Drepanum was the Roman town on the cape; Ayios Yeoryios is the modern name of the settlement; Peyia basilica takes its name from the nearest village.

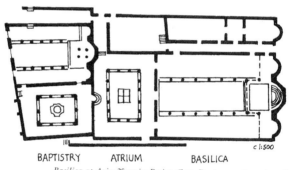

BAPTISTRY   ATRIUM   BASILICA   c 1:500

Basilica at Ayios Yeoryios Peyias, Cape Drepanum (w. ack. to Dr. Mainstone)

Drepanum, meaning a sickle, was a late Roman and early Byzantine town, mainly unexcavated. Almost certainly destroyed by earthquakes and now buried under scrub, its ruins cover about a quarter square mile; but its small harbour is still in use. The off-shore island of Yeronisos has on its west side remains of Roman buildings suggestive of a garrison for the town's protection. Among the twenty-odd rock-cut family tombs below the edge of the cliff, several display Christian crosses of an ancient design. A mile south, opposite another island, is the site of the deep-water harbour.

Excavations: Three churches and a small bath complex of the 6th c. AD were excavated in the early fifties. The enclosed site behind the fishermen's cottages contains Peyia basilica mid-6th c., a second basilica, late 6th c., and the baths. A third small basilica, of a still later date, exists several hundred yards to the south. On the sites of both the later churches, gleaming white marble capitals are lying, quite plain except for simple carved crosses. They are imports from Prokonnesos in the Sea of Marmara, centre of a thriving industry then.

First Basilica: time of Justinian (527-565)

A small complex comprising a three-aisled colonnaded basilica with annexes, treasury and offices, baptistery and chapel, the main floors being laid with mosaics.

Description: The modern entrance is on the north-west, which brings one first to the atrium. Lacking a narthex, access to the church was through one of three doors in the atrium.

The two aisles were separated from the nave by colonnades, the columns and their acanthus capitals being made of the Prokonnesian marble. The ambo was positioned halfway down the nave, and a stone screen protected the sanctuary, or bema.

Of the three apses, the central one is semi-hexagonal on the outside; within, the seats of the synthronon are still in place. Originally, galleries ran the length of the church over the side-aisles, and beyond them came the annexes under separate low roofs. At the north-east end of the complex is a small chapel for offerings, as at Kourion; and, moving west, a series of rooms, beginnings of stairways and then a rubble of columns, tiles and stone from the collapsed first floor. In the atrium, once more, turn west and ascend the decorative semi-circular steps to the Baptistery. Here, the font, instead of being in a recess as at Kourion, is a sunken circular pool in the centre of an open peristyle court – in line with contemporary Constantinople practice. It was probably galleried. Doors at each end of the north wall led into the baptistery chapel. This is a small transept basilica, unique in Cyprus, and the earliest of the buildings here. At some stage, the chapel was turned into a church.

The Mosaics

In the centre of the atrium is a large mosaic divided into four panels containing respectively a boar, a bear, a bull and a lion, all running as if being hunted. The floor of the nave, now mostly lost, was laid with a variety of geometrical designs; but a broad band to the east was divided into about forty small panels, each containing a biblical beast: of these only four remain, showing confronting lions and stags. (This section is in very poor condition.) The floor of the bema has an inhabited trellis design, appropriately filled with a variety of sea creatures and birds of the headland. Some of the best work can be seen in the baptistery's geometric carpets laid round the font: they are divided by bands of lotus in a frieze similar to the work at Paphos basilica of the same period. In the chapel, beneath the north wall of the transept, small, slender pieces of marble were found, cut into shapes (crustae) and in several colours. Fitted together, full-length figures of saints, flowers and a jewelled cross emerged. They would have been set into the wall. Similar work has been found elsewhere, but none in Cyprus. Falled glass tesserae under the apses indicate that they were also covered with mosaic-work.

History: None direct; but no previous building was on this site, and if this replaces an earlier church, new ground was sought for it, probably because of severe earthquake damage (for which there is an amount of circumstantial evidence).

91

AYIOS YEORYIOS CHURCH

Beside the track leading to the harbour stands a small Byzantine church: by the entrance is an ancient sacred olive tree, barely alive, but festooned with strips of cloth. In the sanctuary is an altar formed from two early Byzantine capitals, one upturned beneath the other. The church is much visited by local people, who come to pray here, especially if they have lost anything; and several legends and practices are attached to it. Rupert Gunnis relates the following:

> A story still told in the village is that during the sixteenth century pirates landed at Peyia and stole the son of one of the leading villagers. The distracted father came to the church and offered St. George a great gift if only his son could return. That evening the boy suddenly appeared in the village dressed in barbaric apparel, still clasping in his hand the basin of soup which he had been handing to the pirate chief and which, even more wonderful to relate, was still steaming hot.

The church is also resorted to by love-sick youths, who light a candle to discover whether their love is returned. If the candle continues to burn upside down, it is.

Baptistery at Peyia Basilica

92

LIMASSOL

History of Limassol

HISTORY

Early Byzantine: Limassol began to emerge as a town only towards the end of the antique period, when the classical cities of Kourion and Amathus were in decline after the violent earthquakes of the 4th century AD. As Amathus harbour silted up, vessels started to use the deep-water anchorage here instead, where the river Garyllis entered the sea. By the middle of the 5th century, the town was substantial enough to have its own bishop. Its most famous prelate was Leontios of Neapolis, first half of the 7th century, a younger contemporary of John the Almoner, whose life he wrote.

Mid-Byzantine: In the peace and prosperity that followed the final defeat of the Arabs in the 10th century, Limassol became a major port. The need for defence did not arise again until the last decades of the 11th century, when the Seljuk Turks were threatening: it was probably then that the first castle was built at the mouth of the river. This was likely to have been a small shore fort having a separate chapel in front, the whole standing within a walled enclosure. (The foundations of the chapel may be seen today on the lower floor of the present castle.)

In 1191, the leading citizens of Limassol welcomed Richard the Lionheart with open arms after his defeat of the tyrant Isaac Comnenos. The fort is his most likely H.Q., and the double ceremony in which Berengaria became first a bride and then Queen of England would surely have taken place there, in the protection of its walls, as tradition claims.

Latin: The Knights Templar, during their year's perilous rule over an island in revolt, built new fortifications, including a stronger castle at Limassol (1191/92). Yet, by the mid-13th century, this second fort had been replaced from its foundations by the massive square keep whose walls still stand today inside their Venetian shell. It constitutes one of the oldest examples of European Gothic architecture in Cyprus.

After the fall of Acre in 1291, the town and its castle were made over formally to the Templars jointly with the Knights of St. John. Upon the Templars' disbandment in 1313, their possessions in Cyprus were given to the Knights of St. John, who continued in residence in Limassol. The town flourished. A mid-14th century visitor commented on the number of splendid houses it possessed.[1] It was a short prospering, for over the next hundred years a series of disasters fell upon Limassol. In 1349, the Black Death decimated the population; in 1373 the Genoese ravaged and fired the place; there were several bad earthquakes; and in 1425 and 26 came the terrible Mameluke invasions. By the end of the 15th century, Limassol was in ruins, only the cathedral and the castle still standing. Fifty years on there was just the castle.

Present: The present old town is mostly 19th century and not without charm. It replaces the mud-brick dwellings of the Turkish period. Apart from its one ancient monument, the town has kept another link with the past: its wine industry. For wine has been made, bottled and exported from here ever since the Knights of St. John cultivated their acres of vines – probably longer. Still prized is their own Commandaria, perhaps the oldest named wine in the world.

---

1. von Suchen, Ex. Cyp.

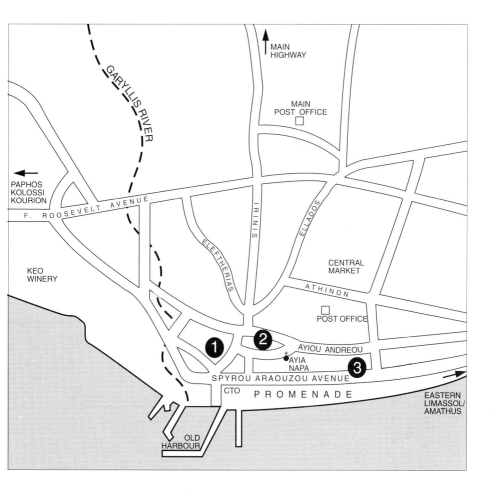

THE MONUMENTS

Note: * Indicates monuments of particular interest
              ** Indicates monuments of outstanding interest

THE MONUMENTS

LIMASSOL CASTLE (Originally, the castle stood on the seashore beside the river Garyllis; but the river altered course in the 16th century and is now 100 yards further west.)

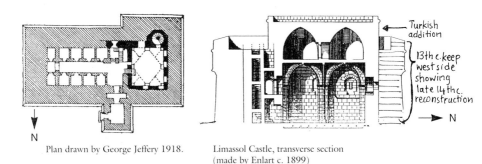

Plan of second castle, end 12th to mid-13th century (conjectural as no records have survived).

THE EXISTING BUILDING, ITS DESCRIPTION AND HISTORY.

Position: At the west end of the sea-front behind the old port.

Plan drawn by George Jeffery 1918.

Limassol Castle, transverse section (made by Enlart c. 1899)

Dating: 13th century with 14th century reconstructions, all encased in a 16th century wall.

The earliest present keep was begun in the mid-13th century. It replaced the Templars' fort, the east end of which may survive as part of the existing west wall. From inside, the original design can be perceived. There were two floors separated by wooden joists and boards. Note the holes to take the beam-ends and the remains of embrasures and stone seating above. The fine spiral staircase that connected the two levels and continued up to the battlements is of this period. The old entrance should be looked for on the upper floor, most likely where the open gallery is situated on the south side. Also at this time, the Byzantine chapel of St George was replaced by a much larger church built in the Gothic style and situated, like its predecessor, to the east of the keep.

Both buildings were damaged in 1294 as a result of Genoese occupation. The church roof collapsed and, during repairs ca. 1310, the church's windows were reduced to arrow-slits for defence. Examples of this conversion can be seen embedded in the walls of the cells.

96

Late 14th century reconstruction

Further devastation by the Genoese in 1370 necessitated considerable rebuilding. The new work was probably carried out by James I (1382-98). It involved a total restructuring of the interior. The keep became the single lofty hall we see today, being given a ribbed and vaulted roof carried on eight sturdy wall pilasters and a central column. The Gothic church was reduced to a shell, a strong curtain wall was built across the east end and in place of the nave a double range of small chambers on two levels faced each other across a narrow open courtyard: a wooden balcony ran round the upper level.

The keep had lacked a cellar; now an ample one was provided under the chambers. Visitors will note that it has three parallel galleries and no outside access and is similar to the cellarage at Kolossi Castle. Look for the foundations of a small apse – probably those of the 12th century Byzantine chapel. It is now that the space between keep and church may have been enclosed. Notice the window with a double splay on the south and, opposite, the upper portions of a much larger one – which may have lighted an earlier hall built out on the north.

The Venetian work

In 1538 the castle fell easy prey to Turkish raiders and the Venetians partly dismantled it. During the process, the central pillar in the great hall collapsed. Thirty years later, under imminent threat of the Turkish invasion, Limassol castle was not only repaired but immensely strengthened in order to withstand cannon-fire. In the keep, instead of replacing the central pillar, a clever alternative was followed which made use of the support given by the existing central ridge, the stress being wholly absorbed by the wall pilasters – leaving the great hall as it is today. A strong, fifteen to twenty foot thick wall was built round the entire complex.

The Turks and after

In 1595, the castle was put in order yet again and used by the military as a redoubt. The buildings on the roof belong to this period. At some time towards the end of the 16th century, the river Garyllis ceased to flow outside the walls and a new bed was constructed for it further west. The severe earthquakes of 1567 and 68 may have been responsible. From about 1800 the castle was also used as a prison; and so it continued under the British until 1940. From 1950 considerable maintenance work has been carried out and the thick walls have yielded some interesting finds.[1] The castle was opened as a Mediaeval Museum in 1987.

. One find was the skeleton of a man of 6' 4", buried Viking fashion, and thought to have died ghting off the Genoese in the 14th c.
nother was a cache of bones, every one of which was broken, and thought perhaps to be those of a ·aitor within the gates who let the Mamelukes in (1425/6).
·e Thurston: The Travellers' Guide to Cyprus 1967.

The Castle of Limasso.

LIMASSOL CASTLE MUSEUM

Exhibits date from 4th to 19th century.

Great Hall: round the walls are displayed carvings and tombstones of the 14th c. including a figure of Christ and a plastercast of foliage and figurine; from St Sophia Cathedral. Charts here and in the entrance hall show distribution and examples of mediaeval fortifications and of Early Christian and Byzantine churches.

Ground Floor: off the entrance hall, a long room with cells each side contains a collection of Frankish and Venetian tombstones. Each carries an incised representation of the deceased – monk, knight or noble lady – together with their attributes or emblems and inscriptions. Coats of arms of the most illustrious families brighten the walls above.

Upper Floor: similar lay-out. The main room contains armour; also finely carved stone and marble objects from early Christian basilicas. Displayed in cases are a collection of coins and one of oil lamps. In one of the cells is an exhibition of weapons; in another, gold, silver and bronze objects, including the famous 'David' plates from 7th century Lambousa; and in a third elegant Ottoman coffee-pots and such like. The remaining cells are devoted to pottery, carefully set out in chronological sequence, mostly from Cyprus but with some imports.

Outside: a growing assemblage of larger objects, mainly grindstones and presses, one of which has been reconstructed.

DJAMIR KEBIR MOSQUE

In daily use by the Moslem community of Limassol.

It lies less than a hundred yards north-east of the castle, opposite the market. It was probably built near the end of the 16th century at the same time that the Turks repaired the castle. Current excavations below the street immediately east of the mosque have exposed the imposing central and side apses of the 10th century cathedral of Ayia Ekaterina, composed of fine ashlar blocks.

History: *First church:* a palaeo-Christian three-aisled basilica, built 5th c. destroyed mid-7th; possibly the cathedral of the first bishops of Limassol.
Second church: a three aisled basilica built 10th c. from the ruins of the first, probably multi-domed and the cathedral of the city.
Third church: a Gothic building of the 13th century, thought to have been the Latin cathedral. When the mosque was rebuilt in 1906, Crusader coffins and tomb-stones were found below the floor-level; also the lower courses of the walls, carrying frescoes. (Jeffery page 370).

The Church of AYIOS ANDRONIKOS and AYIA ATHANASIA

Position: Behind the old Bishopric on the seafront (by the Continental Hotel).

Dating: Built between 1835 and 1850 (according to the inscription).

Description: The former Orthodox cathedral of Limassol and probably the oldest surviving church here. Like St. John's in Nicosia – which it resembles – it was kept deliberately small and was very well built in a Franco-Byzantine style. The bell-tower went up in 1850. It must once have had an arched portico on the west – also like St. John's – but it has been removed. The south entrance has a fine wooden door, carved and studded. Within is a chapel dedicated to St. Mamas which possesses an icon screen made in 1694. According to Gunnis, this screen is probably one of the best examples of its period surviving in Cyprus in an undamaged, unrepaired condition.

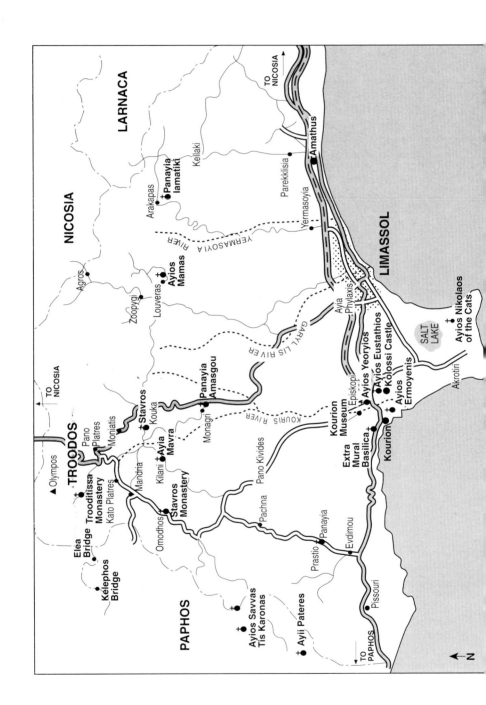

LIMASSOL DISTRICT

THE MONUMENTS

Note: * Indicates monuments of particular interest
        ** Indicates monuments of outstanding interest

AMATHUS

Position: Five-and-a-half miles east of Limassol along the coast road.

Description: Amathus falls into three parts: the acropolis, the lower town and the necropolis.

The Acropolis: the walls and main gate visible half-way down the hill slope date mainly from the 6th century AD. An early Christian basilica occupies the summit. (5)

The Lower Town: at the road junction stood the Church of the Port; now foundations only, it was a three-aisled basilica of the 5th to 7th century. The site of the much larger church of St. Tykhon is on the east above the river bed.

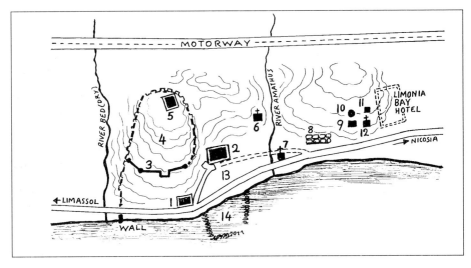

PLAN OF AMATHUS showing sites of the Christian period.

(1) Basilica (5th c.)	(6) Ayios Tykhonas Church	(10) Cistern
(2) Agora	(modern)	(11) Shrine of Ayia Varvara
(3) Walls	(7) Ayia Varvara	(12) Byantine funerary chapel
(4) Acropolis	(8) Tombs	(13) Site of inner harbour
(5) Basilica (early Christian)	(9) Mediaeval monastery	(14) Outer harbour (sunken)

The Necropolis: east of the river lies the city burial-ground, spread over the lower slopes of the hill. Above the road, about 150 metres along, are several built tombs of the Roman period. One of them is a stavrotholeum – adapted for Christian burial. At the far side of this area – and best approached by a path beside the Limonia Bay Hotel – are an early Byzantine funerary chapel, the shrine of Ayia Varvara (11) and the remains of a small mediaeval monastery. (12)

Centuries of looting has reduced the old city to grassed-over rubble. All available dressed stone was sold and shipped off for re-use in Larnaca, Alexandria, the Suez Canal and elsewhere.

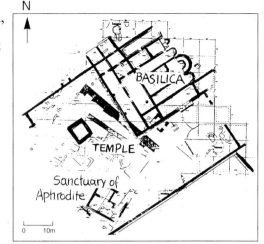

Early Christian Basilica, Acropolis

Dating: Built end 6th/beginning 7th century.

THE ACROPOLIS

Field plan of the Basilica, showing the Temple beneath.

(Taken from Kinyras, French archaeology in Cyprus)

Description: A very large complex which destroyed the Roman Temple and used the stone again. It fell into disuse within a hundred years – probably because of the Arab raids. The church is quite small yet has a vast L-shaped atrium which covers the pagan site almost entirely. The atrium had a portico along the west and north sides and a square water-tank in the centre of the west court. The church had three aisles, a narthex, an exo-narthex and flanking annexes – which differ from each other and may have had specific uses. In the south, for example, are indications of a large compartment built into the outer wall. The north is divided into two rooms, the east ending in a small apse and the west communicating directly with the church on one side and with a long, bench-lined room on the other. The exact role of this church is in doubt, there being no evidence to suggest that it was either a shrine to St. Tykhon or (lacking a baptistery)[1] the cathedral.

Decoration: Opus sectile in marble, limestone and terracotta was laid on the floor of the church. Many pieces have carving on the reverse in champlevé technique and come from an earlier building.

History: A church is known to have existed on this site in the 5th century and it is thought to have been in the shell of the Temple itself, which had already been abandoned by the middle of the 3rd century.

(Acknowledgements to the French Excavations at Amathus in Kinyras, pub. 1993, for plan and description.)

Ayia Varvara's shrine is in a rock-cut cave behind the Byzantine funerary chapel. In antiquity, it may have been a water-cistern similar to the one west of it. The wall paintings have been both white-washed and smoke-blackened and are irretrievably lost. St. Barbara is the guardian saint of pregnant women and of childbirth, as also was the Egyptian god Bes before her, popular in Amathus. (An Egyptian temple is thought to have stood over the cave in the Archaic period.)

---

1. Although according to the Oxford Dictionary of Byzantium, by the 6th century the detached baptistery was no longer provided: 'the font moved into the church, occupying a position in the narthex or in a room set aside for that purpose'.

The Mediaeval Monastery. The old funerary chapel seems likely to have remained in use as the monks' church: note the mosaic floors. Below the impressive rock-hewn cistern was their wine or olive press, the stone press-bed and marble separating pits still in situ. *The origin of this press goes back to the Roman period and has been described by Plinius. In Cyprus it was widely used not only in oil presses but also in wine presses even until recent times e.g. at Lania, Omodhos etc.* Extract from notice outside Limassol Castle. (For further information and complete restoration, see the Castle yard.)

Ayios Tykhonas Church. An important complex is currently being uncovered on the east. The Church of St. Tykhon stands on a spur above the river Amathus, just outside the walls of the upper town. Under the ruins of the mediaeval cathedral and later Frankish vaulting, the foundations of a very large early Byzantine basilica have been revealed. On the same level some of its columns of Proconnesian marble and pieces of Corinthian capitals were lying. A second building on the north side, closely connected with the basilica, has three apses in its north wall: burials found there suggest that it may have been an important shrine. Dating (by coins) has yet to be confirmed and excavations continue under the direction of Dr Procopiou, Department of Antiquities.

N.B. The site is open to the public when work is not being carried out. Access is by – drivable – track alongside the river-bed.

History: With the collapse of the city-states at the start of the Ptolemaic rule, the island was divided into four districts, and Amathus remained the capital of one right through Roman and Byzantine times. It became a Christian city early and the seat of a bishop. A tradition exists that St Paul preached here successfully. The first bishop whose name is known was Mnemonios, mid-4th century. He was succeeded by Tykhon who was consecrated in the late 4th century by one of the island's most famous archbishops Epiphanios: both men were later canonised. It would have been under Tykhon that the first cathedral was built in Amathus; and his memory is perpetuated in the village of St. Tykhonas, a mile inland. There is a tradition that he was martyred and that his relics were kept in a shrine in the cathedral.

The city's most famous son in the Christian era is St. John the Almoner who was born here ca. 560, his father being Governor of Cyprus then. In middle age, John was chosen to become Patriarch of Alexandria, where he restored the wavering Orthodox Church, mainly by his qualities of leadership and his unstinting efforts to help all in need. He also wrote a Life of St. Tykhon. He died in Amathus in 619. In his will, he stated that he had found the treasury of his church full and left it empty! Because of his charity towards the aged, poor and infirm, he was adopted, according to William of Tyre, as the patron saint of the Hospitallers.

Amathus survived the Arab raids better than Kourion, despite being overrun in the 7th and 8th centuries, and started to prosper again; but at some point Limassol expanded whereas Amathus declined. The cause may lie in the silting-up of the harbour. By 1191, when Coeur de Lion arrived, it was a beach he landed at, not a harbour – a beach blockaded by Isaac Comnenos with old hulks, boulders and bits of furniture.

Although the city struggled on into the 13th century, its death-blow was really administered by the English king when his troops stormed the main gate and destroyed the acropolis. Nevertheless, Amathus remained the seat of a bishop until the last days of Venetian rule. We are told that the last bishop actually in residence went mad and dismantled the church of St. Tykhon (the mediaeval cathedral) selling it stone by stone to the Franks and throwing the bones of the saint into the sea. (Gunnis, Historic Cyprus).

AYIOS NIKOLAOS TON GATON, *St. Nicholas of the Cats*

Possibly the first monastery in Cyprus and a 'must' for mediaeval travellers because of its battling cats.

Position: On Cape Gata near Limassol, south-east of Akrotiri Salt Lake.
Take the left-hand turn beyond Akrotiri village and continue on an earth road for two miles.

Dating: Founded ca. 325 AD. Present church probably late 14th century. Abandoned in late 16th century. Re-occupied by Orthodox nuns in early 1980's.

Description: New conventual buildings have been put up in the last decade incorporating much of the fallen stone, and the nuns have created new gardens. Seven arches of the west cloister, still standing earlier this century, bore witness to the high quality of the mediaeval masonry. The supporting marble pillars were spolia from Roman sites.

The church consists of a single nave and a pointed barrel vault. Its chief interest lies in the main doorway, on the north side, which has been incorporated from an earlier building. It has a pointed arch with a finial at its apex and the roughly carved figures of St. Peter and St. Paul at its ends. The white marble lintel is carved with a cross between four shields: the outer pair – a ciborium and a cross with four keys – are undoubtedly personal coats of arms; those either side of the cross are the well-known lion of the Lusignans and a second, much larger cross – implying high-ranking patronage.

St. Nicholas of the Cats

It might seem extraordinary that the remains of a complex with such a long history are so few; but the monastery on its flat plain was all too visible to raiders. Because of war, earthquake or just age, the monastery must have been rebuilt a number of times. The Latins were in possession from early in the 13th century, and they were obliged to replace the church which they had inherited not once but twice.

History &
Tradition:
According to the mediaeval historian Stephen Lusignan, after the return of St. Helena, Constantine the Great sent a governor to Cyprus called Calocaeros. The drought and run-down conditions had caused this area to be thickly infested with a particularly large and venomous species of snake. The governor dealt with this by giving the entire Cape to a community of Christian monks (later to be known as Basilians). He made it a condition that the brothers kept at least a hundred cats and fed them morning and evening *to the intent that they should not eat nothing but venom and that for the rest of the day and night they should go a-hunting for these serpents.* It is thought that the cats were a special breed fetched from Egypt or from Asia Minor. It became a custom, later on, for the monks to be given the entire catch of fish from the nearby salt lake on the feast day of St. Nicholas (December 6th) otherwise the fish farmers would not catch a single fish in the forthcoming year. (The Salt Lake was linked to the sea then.)

These arrangements continued for more than 1200 years. The spectacle of the cats streaming in from the fields for their supper at the ringing of a bell, tattered and torn from their encounters, astonished the mediaeval travellers who were brought to witness it. The monastery and its cats survived the Turkish invasion, but only by a few years; and a visitor[1] in 1589 recorded that the Muslims had slain or driven away the monks and the cats had all died for lack of food. A roll of martyrs[2] of the 1570 invasion was drawn up and to it was added the poor cats of Akrotiri.

KOLOSSI CASTLE
Commanderie of the Knights of St. John of Jerusalem (the Knights Hospitaller).

Position:
7½ miles west of Limassol. Best approach: drive south west through the Phasouri Citrus Plantation, turning right on reaching the main road to Akrotiri.

Dating:
Present castle built ca. 1454, restored 1933; original castle built 1210.

Armorial slab on Kolossi Castle (after Rey)

Description:
The castle is a massive square keep, standing 75' high with walls 9' thick, and built of medium-sized blocks of honey-coloured stone. It is enhanced by a tall, dark and shapely cypress which grows beside it, noisy with sparrows; behind is a fine tropical acacia. Note the well in the base of a tower on the east, being all that remains of the earlier structure.

---

1. Villamont Ex. Cypria.
2. Enlart note p. 349

Exterior: there are three storeys and the battlements. Once a ramp and drawbridge led up to the entrance: this has been replaced with steps now, but the pulleys can still be seen. Jutting directly over the threshold is a machicoulis through which deterrents could be dropped or poured onto the heads of attackers. The crenellated .parapet is provided with small ringed protrusions, fixings for hanging shuttering to prevent scaling of the walls and for platforms for extending the defenders' range. On the east face is a cruciform marble panel displaying the royal arms of Cyprus, flanked by those of Grandmasters Jean de Lastic and Jacques de Milli with, below, the fleur-de-lys of Louis de Magnac, Grand Commander of Cyprus from 1450 to 1468 and builder of the keep.

Interior: *the basement* contains three vaulted rooms: in two are cisterns for storing the rain-water brought by a conduit from the roof.

Kolossi Castle

Formerly this floor was reached only from an inside trapdoor.

The middle storey is divided into two vaulted rooms, 45' x 20'. To the east is the entrance hall, to the west the service room and possible kitchen (having a fireplace). Right of the entrance is a large contemporary mural of the Crucifixion. It is damaged, but the arms of de Magnac can be seen bottom left. The walls carry some 15th and 16th century graffiti: on the door-jambs at the entrance and in the window embrasures. In the south-east corner, a spiral stair leads to the third storey and thence to the roof. More modern steps descend to the basement.

The third storey was the residence of the Grand Commander. It is also divided into two large vaulted rooms, but at right angles to those beneath. Both chambers have splendid fireplaces bearing the fleur-de-lys; and that in the inner room is decorated with meanders and scrolls similar to those on monuments of the Knights in Rhodes. The closet in the north wall is a privy. The eight windows on this floor command an all-round view of the low-lying countryside. Stone seats in the embrasures are a step up from the hall floor and undercut for greater comfort.

Halfway up the walls on both floors is provision for cross-beams to support wooden floors. These extra rooms were lighted by two small windows and were probably sleeping quarters. A continuation of the spiral stair leads to the roof and battlements and a superb view: to the north as far as the Troodos foothills, to the south to Cape Gata and the Akrotiri Salt Lake.

The Sugar Factory is a barn-like structure consisting of four bays divided by transverse ribs under a barrel vault. The buttresses on the east were probably added in 1591 when the building was repaired after earthquake damage – vide the cartouche under the gable. On the north is the aqueduct which brought water from the river Kouris and which still functions. The ruins of the mill itself stand against the mill-race, and a force of water would have fallen through a trap over the north-west corner, turning a massive grindstone. Its size can be judged from that of the nether-stone, now lying behind the east wall. Two stone sinks remain, used for washing the sugar pots. The whole complex dates from the 14th century.

Pots for making sugar

History:

Byzantine. In 1191 a skirmish took place here between Richard the Lionheart and Isaac Comnenos – which may mean that some sort of stronghold existed then.

Latin. At first the overlordship was granted to a certain Garinus de Colos – from whom Kolossi derives its name. In 1210 Hugh I transferred the fiefdom to the Knights Hospitaller, and they built the first castle. After the fall of Acre in 1291, Le Colos became the Knights' main base for a few years; but an unsatisfactory liaison with the Templars spurred them to look for a more suitable H.Q: and in 1308 they seized Rhodes. Shortly afterwards the Templars were disbanded and the Hospitallers assumed sole control over the Cyprus estates of both orders, and of these Kolossi was the most remunerative.

In 1450, when Louis de Magnac became Grand Commander, the castle may have been in a poor condition. It had withstood attacks by the Genoese in 1373 and 1402 and by the Mameluke army in 1426. De Magnac built a new castle which was completed by 1454. It has been called a 'folly', as, because of the new cannon-fire, its design was already obsolete then.

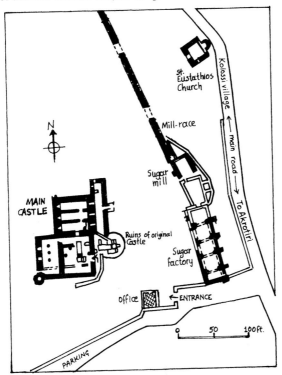

Plan of the
Castle, Sugar
Factory and
Mill and
St. Eustathios
Church

The Commanderie of Kolossi encompassed some forty villages and yielded a considerable revenue from the cultivation of cotton, olive trees, corn, sugar-cane and vines. By far the most profitable were the last two. The vineyards produced the grape from which the famous Commandaria wine was made, much appreciated by the Plantagenet kings of England.

Sugar. The cane, previously cultivated by the Knights in Syria, was grown in quantity and developed rapidly into an industry that provided the West with much of its sugar for three hundred years. 'Poudre de Chypre' was esteemed for its high quality. Essential for its growth was water; and this was readily available until the Cornaro family, who were rival growers on the east bank, contested the water-rights. There followed sixty years of acrimony until, finally, the Knights contrived to divert the river, thereby destroying their rivals' entire stock of cane.

It is ironic that, scarcely twenty years later, these powerful relations of Katerina Cornaro – the last Queen of Cyprus – were to acquire the whole Kolossi estate at the stroke of a pen: for then the Knights wound up their affairs in Cyprus and withdrew. Sugar production continued here into the early 17th century; but demand grew less as the West Indies trade expanded. Soon, all knowledge of the process was lost in the island. But Commandaria continues to be made to this day.

For more about the sugar industry see under Kouklia, Paphos.

109

AYIOS EUSTATHIOS CHURCH

The chapel of the Knights.

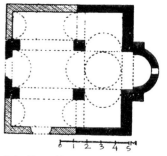

Position: A hundred yards north of the castle; the key is kept at the first cottage.

Dating: 12th century; reconstructed mid-15th.

Description: First built in a cruciform, domed style but with an extended western arm, the angles of which were later

Ayios Eustathios Church, Kolossi: ground plan
(From Kolossi Castle through the centuries by Dr. E. Aristidou)

enclosed, making the church rectangular: there is no narthex. Although not built for the purpose originally, it almost certainly served as the castle chapel. The dedication is appropriate, St. Eustace having been a high-ranking officer in the Roman army early in the 2nd century. He was converted to Christianity on seeing a vision of a stag bearing a shining cross between its antlers, and he was later martyred. Louis de Magnac's coat of arms could be seen emblazoned on the arch above the apse until recently. The old templon is carved attractively and symbolically with a vine carrying grapes, some birds and a pair of fish. In the south aisle are the remains of a marble tombstone.

Decoration: The church retains some wall-paintings, all of the 15th century. In the dome, the band between the Pantocrator and the Prophets is occupied not only by a Heavenly choir of angels converging on the Empty Throne but also by a row of Apostles seated in front of them in readiness for the Day of Judgement. The Virgin and John the Baptist stand as intercessors either side of the Throne which is in a mandorla and flanked by the symbols of the four Evangelists. On the seat is a Cross, bearing the nails, crown of thorns, spear and sponge on a reed. On the pendentives are the Evangelists themselves writing their Gospels. A large painting of St. Eustathios in an iconic position on horseback covers the north wall of the north arm: it is damaged.

Ayios Eustathios Church

110

EPISKOPI

I . THE SERAYIA. Seat of the Bishops of Kourion from mid-7th c.

Position: Off the Paphos/Limassol road. Turn south at village beside Mobil petrol station and go down a steep lane for 150 yards; site on left.

Dating: Basilica mid-7th c; chapel in use 12th c; sugar mill and outbuildings, mediaeval.

Description: Called 'Serayia' by the Turkish villagers – 'the place of the Palace.' Site of a three-aisled basilica, once colonnaded under a timber and tile roof. The opus sectile on the sanctuary floor matches that in the north aisle of Kourion basilica, and the marble (displaying the same low relief designs) comes from its walls: the large marble slab against the south wall was the altar table. When the Kourions abandoned their city early in the Arab raids, they rebuilt their cathedral here, but much reduced in size. At some later date the building was further curtailed, losing its colonnades and keeping only the nave and south aisle, which were divided by a wall having engaged piers – indicating vaulted ceilings. Two vaulted buildings flanking this belong to the 13th century, when the fiefdom of Episkopi belonged to Jean d'Ibelin. By the 14th century, sugar production had become a major industry here, and by the 15th century the estate was in the hands of the Cornaro family – the great rivals of the Knights of Kolossi across the river Kouris. In 1979, hundreds of the cone-shaped pots used in the process were unearthed immediately south of the chapel: the site of the sugar mill is on the north-east: the factory itself has not yet been found.

(Information derived from account by Susan Young in 'Ancient Kourion Area'.)

II. THE MUSEUM OF KOURION
(Open Mon. to Sat. 7.30 to 14.00)

From Ancient Kourion Area. ed. Swiny

The exhibits in this small museum include finds from the Roman House, the Early Christian Basilica and the Extra-mural Basilica; also early Christian pottery and coins from the area. They are exhibited in a lovely old Cypriot village house.

III. AYIOS YEORYIOS CHURCH
(Paintings being cleaned by the Dept. of Antiquities.)

In the village north of the crossroads is a 16th century church which the Turks converted into a mosque. It is a single-aisled, vaulted building with transverse ribs, and formerly decorated with a multiplicity of small scenes cp. Ayios Andronikos at Polis, where they were obliterated also. Here, the interior was covered with layers of plaster, the apse pulled down and an extension built on to the east end. The painting is less expert and more linear than at Polis and a lot more has been lost. Numbers of ancient stones went into the building of this church.

KOURION 1st to 7th century A.D. Roman House, House of Eustolios, Cathedral.

Romano – Christian ring from the Roman House, Kourion.

Position: On the Limassol/Paphos road, ten miles west of Limassol and four miles east of the Sovereign Base Area of Episkopi (not to be confused with Episkopi village). Enter by the Amathus Gate – second turning after the MI, under the escarpment.

At the time of Christ this was a populous city of some 20,000 people and a place of pilgrimage for worshippers of Apollo. Attracted here too were athletes, and in the 3rd century AD the Gladiatorial Games were held at Kourion theatre – an event commemorated in floor mosaics (see House of the Gladiators). The apocryphal Acts of Barnabas (5th c.) refer to the Apostles being refused entry to Kourion as they made their way back to Salamis; also declaring that they were shocked to encounter men and women stripped naked for a race – probably in the stadium, which they would have passed. That a Christian community was established here quite early is proven by the record of the fate of their Bishop Philoneides who threw

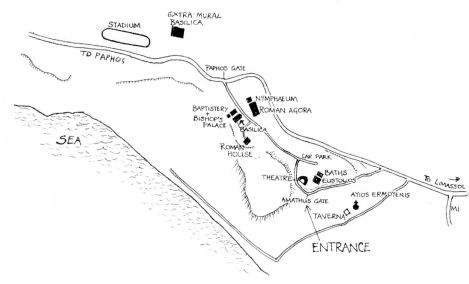

Kourion city and its environs   Acknowledgements to M. Dubin, Cyprus the Rough Guide

himself from the cliff rather than renounce his faith under Diocletian (284-305 AD).

The 4th century saw a general depopulation of the island, partly through the long years of drought that caused St. Helena such concern and partly because of a run-down Roman administration. There was much poverty and Kourion's population fell to possibly a tenth of its former level. In 365 came the last of a series of severe earthquakes, which had already damaged the city. It is now estimated to have been force 9 or 10 on the Mercalli scale – which is the level of total destruction. The dead and dying were buried under tons of masonry and rubble, trapped in their homes very early on a summer's morning; and to this day the time capsule of the south-west quarter of

Kourion has remained virtually undisturbed. The City was abandoned for about eighteen years. When the people did return, the new governors forsook the old gods and traditions and began preparations for mass conversion to Christianity, now the official religion.

By the beginning of the 5th century, two substantial buildings had been completed, the Cathedral and the House of Eustolios; the theatre and the Sanctuary of Apollo were not rebuilt. A name has come down to us from that distant time, that of Zeno, one of the early bishops of Kourion, who fought for the independence of the Church of Cyprus at the Council of Ephesus in 431. Kourion survived for a further two hundred and fifty years, but soon after the start of the Arab Raids in the 7th century the city was abandoned for good and the last bishop and his people moved inland to Episkopi.

THE ROMAN HOUSE (Earliest evidence of Christianity at Kourion.)

Position: Take first well-defined track before reaching the basilica, left of road. After two hundred yards, the red roof will be visible on left.

Dating: House built late 1st/early 2nd c; part-ruined by earthquake ca. 340; totally destroyed by earthquake 365 AD. Excavated in 1984-87 by Professor Soren, Arizona University.

Description: The original house was spacious and Greek in style, not Roman, in contrast to the patrician residences in the upper town; and the floors were of plain stone flags. The approach was through a narrow passage beside a monumental market hall, a gateway in the wall opening onto a courtyard. A colonnaded portico opposite ran along the front of the main building. That consisted of one very large room – the area now covered by Soren's museum – and a small one in front: outbuildings ranged along the back and the north-west. The house was already well over two hundred years old when the first earthquake struck and brought down the portico. A quarter of a century later, it had lost its comfortable urban look and was occupied by a poor family who had patched it up and sub-divided the rooms. Ovens appeared in the courtyard, and a mule was stabled under the propped-up portico; the alleyway was blocked off and simple two-storey housing backed onto the market hall. Now the entrance was from across the garden on the south-east.

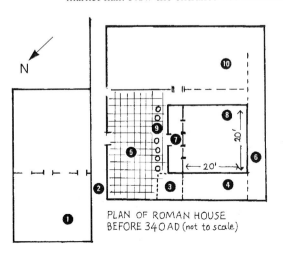

PLAN OF ROMAN HOUSE
BEFORE 340 AD (not to scale)

PLAN OF ROMAN HOUSE
before 340AD
(not to scale)

(1) Market hall
(2) Lane
(3) Water Tank
(4) Possibly service rooms
(5) Stone courtyard
(6) Additional rooms
(7) Tablinum
(8) Triclinium (now covered by museum)
(9) Portico with Doric columns
(10) Open area (possibly garden)

113

Finds: The house yielded no fewer than seven skeletons, all showing signs of sudden crushing death. Most tragic was the discovery of a young husband, wife and baby in close embrace. He was wearing a ring engraved with the Chi-Rho, symbol of Christ.

A horse trough weighing 800 lbs had been thrown across the yard, dragging the chained mule with it.

The Market Hall. So called from its monumental flamboyant facade, its public nature and the character of the finds. It was two storeys high, divided into a series of small rooms or shops and had a big forecourt. The collapse of this building caused the most damage, with its heavy blocks of limestone hurtling about. Finds here included a baker's oven and beside it the remains of a man – at 5.30 am probably the baker himself – an oil lamp in the shape of a duck, bronze vessels and tools. The discovery of a pile of lace bobbins made of bone has put the art of lace-making back centuries earlier than previously thought. The yard was full of animal, fish and fowl fragments. The walls had been plastered and garishly painted; drawings and graffiti were found.

The amazing little museum is now closed and the display transferred to the Kourion Museum at Episkopi.

THE HOUSE OF EUSTOLIOS Private house and bath complex presented to the city by the owner.

Position: At the eastern end of the city, by the theatre.

Dating: Late 4th to early 5th c. AD.

Description: The hospice is a complex of more than thirty rooms with public baths above. It is basically a peristyle house, having an internal courtyard surrounded by a colonnaded portico onto which the public rooms opened. It has lost its colonnade and its walls of finely-cut limestone blocks, and much of the south side has slipped down the cliff. Still in place, however, are a number of

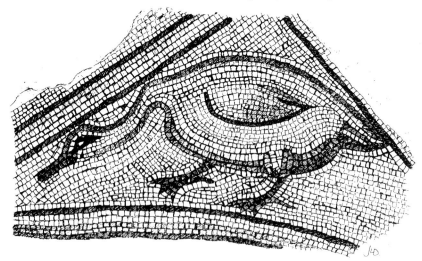

Grey goose mosaic, south-east portico, House of Eustolios

114

beautiful and interesting mosaics and inscriptions which show Kourion at the point of transition from paganism to Christianity. The best-preserved are in the east portico.

The approach to the hospice is through an open forecourt (2). (Note the remains of service and storage rooms on the north and, on the south, a series of small rooms on an earlier apsidal hall.) A vestibule (5) leads directly to the north portico of the inner court. This contains a small cistern which once held a fountain, and a rectangular fishpond. In the centre of the east portico, a doorway marks the entrance to the east hall (8), most probably a dining room, the door of which was designed to be folded back.

The Mosaics. In the vestibule is a wreath with a damaged inscription, *Enter for the good luck of the house*. The north portico has lost its floor and the west and south mosaics are badly damaged; but those on the east are well-preserved (7). There in the centre is a six-line inscription in verse, the letters black on a white ground, which in its restored state proclaims in Greek:

> *Eustolios, having seen that the Kourians, although previously very wealthy, were in abject misery, did not forget the city of his ancestors but having first presented the baths to our city, he was then taking care of Kourion as once did Phoebus (Apollo) and built this cool refuge sheltered from the winds.*

South of this, a second inscription has the following, in brown letters on a white ground:

> *Instead of big stones, instead of solid iron,*
> *Shining bronze and even adamant,*
> *This house is girdled with the much venerated symbols of Christ.*

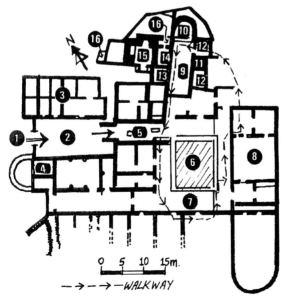

(1) Main entrance
(2) Forecourt
(3) Storage and service quarters
(4) Latrines
(5) Vestibule
(6) Peristyle courtyard
(7) Long porticoes
(8) East hall
(9) Rectangular hall
(10) Semicircular cold basin
(11) Rectangular cold basin
(12) Dressing rooms (apodyteria)
(13) Antechamber
(14) Tepidarium
(15) Caldarium
(16) Praefurnia

Plan of the House of Eustolios from the plan by Panos Ioannides in 'Kourion' by Demos Christou.

Four panels were set to illustrate it, but only two have survived in good condition. In one, fish and birds in a design formed out of four greek crosses have a guineafowl at the centre; in the other, ducks and geese are featured in a guilloch pattern. They all represent Christian qualities – the goose, for example, stands for Providence and Vigilance.

Beyond the panels, on the threshold of a large apsidal hall which has fallen away, is a third inscription:

> *The sisters Reverence, Temperance and Piety tend this exedra and fragrant hall.*

The mosaic carpet in the East Hall has a conservative, abstract design and has been less expertly laid.

THE BATHS

The Baths were planned round the rectangular hall of the frigidarium (9) and incorporated two disrobing chambers (12) and two small cold baths, each prefaced by a footbath (10 & 11) . Across the hall to the west, an antechamber (13) allowed a pause before proceeding to the tepidarium, which was warm and dry, and the caldarium, the hot bath (14 & 15 respectively). After completing the circuit, a return was made in reverse order. Water for both house and baths was brought to the head of the complex by the public aqueduct and collected in the stone cistern there: this ensured a continuous supply operating on the gravity system. The overflow was channelled through the hospice by two pipes, one leading to the courtyard and the other to the service quarters and thence out through the latrines.

The Bath Mosaics. The hall (9) was originally entirely set with mosaic work and three out of four panels have survived. In the centre of the northernmost is a bust of Ktisis, an allegorical figure personifying here the maker or founding spirit in a Hellenistic tradition, adopted by Christians to reflect God the creator of all things. Ktisis is displaying a builder's measure for the standard Late Roman foot. The panel below is an abstract key-and-square design. The third panel contains an exquisitely done emblem in the form of a partridge – which in Christian terms represents the Church, and also Truth.

History: The house had a different orientation originally, and was probably a late Hellenistic building (150-50 BC).[1] The palatial Roman peristyle house that belonged to the family of Eustolios was entirely destroyed in 365; but the hospice was partly, at least, built on its foundations. The work of rebuilding started in the late 4th century and was completed early in the 5th. According to the inscription, the Baths were restored first; understandably, because public baths had a social function in Roman city life and would do a lot to raise morale in Kourion. Nevertheless, a coin of Theodosios II (408-450), found in the mortar under the Ktisis mosaic, suggests a later date for the mosaics in the Bath hall at least.[2]

1. Prof. Rupp: Ancient Kourion Area ed. Swiny.
2. Megaw: Architecture and Decoration in Cyprus.

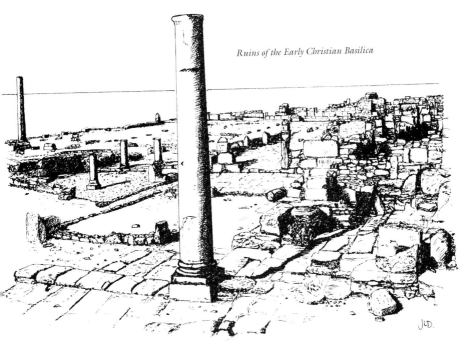

Ruins of the Early Christian Basilica

THE BASILICA – An Early Christian Cathedral

Position: On high ground to the north-west, opposite the Forum.

Dating: Early 5th century, renovated in the 6th c. Excavated 1934/5, resumed 1953, completed 1979.

Description: The complex comprises the remains of a large church, a baptistery and a bishop's palace. The cathedral has been reduced to its foundations mainly for the following reasons: the Arab raids, lime-kilns, and the Kourians themselves salvaging material for re-use at Episkopi. Now the site is almost robbed bare, but the ground-plan is intact. Much stone has come from earlier buildings and existing Roman foundations made use of. The structure followed a plan common to numbers of Early Christian churches throughout the empire: three aisles divided by colonnades, a clerestory, apse and narthex, and a wooden trussed roof. Economical to build and holding a large congregation, Kourion differs from Roman examples only in certain features at the east end, and these derive from Syria. From what was left of the fallen decoration, it is clear that the walls of the aisles were covered with thin whitish marble panels displaying animals and birds in scrolls and friezes in low relief. In the nave they were confined to the lower walls, the upper parts being mosaic. The flooring of the nave was mosaic and that of the aisles was opus sectile – of which a small part is left on the north-east.

In more detail

There were two main entrances: one through the atrium (6) and one through a portico at the east end (1). *The Portico* was created by blocking off the top end of a street which ran down a valley to the Amathus Gate. The pair of re-erected columns and bases are spolia from pre-earthquake buildings. From the portico, two vestibules (3) led into the north annex; attached to them was a *chapel for offerings* (2). A mosaic from the niche in the chapel's east wall included a wingless archangel carrying a wand – now in the Kourion Museum. Note the holy water stoup in a corner of the inner vestibule.

117

The annexes (4), also called the Catechumena, were where Christian converts not yet baptised waited during Communion: they would have had transverse arches and low roofs. Note provision for seating between the arcades, and the small side door into the church. The main traffic came and went through the *Narthex* (5) which had a dozen doors opening off it: one for each aisle of the church, one for each annexe, one at either end and a further five on the west side. Its formal use at this period would have been for processional purposes mainly.

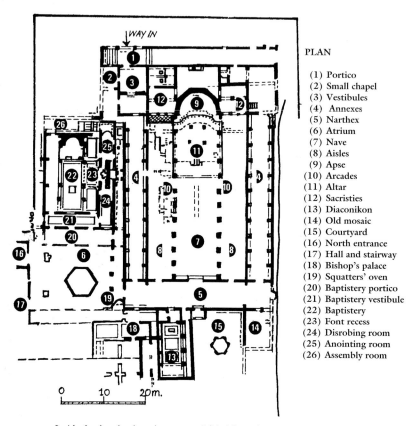

PLAN

(1) Portico
(2) Small chapel
(3) Vestibules
(4) Annexes
(5) Narthex
(6) Atrium
(7) Nave
(8) Aisles
(9) Apse
(10) Arcades
(11) Altar
(12) Sacristies
(13) Diaconikon
(14) Old mosaic
(15) Courtyard
(16) North entrance
(17) Hall and stairway
(18) Bishop's palace
(19) Squatters' oven
(20) Baptistery portico
(21) Baptistery vestibule
(22) Baptistery
(23) Font recess
(24) Disrobing room
(25) Anointing room
(26) Assembly room

Inside the church, a broad nave was divided from the two narrower aisles by granite columns, twelve each side. Now only one is in position, part of its white marble capital lying nearby. In front of the apse, a large *Sanctuary* (11) occupied a third of the central aisle, extending as far as the fifth column. The curb that carried the stone screen and posts may be seen; and nearly three pillars further west are the stub and socket of the ambo. On a line with the fifth column, a step would have raised the Sanctuary slightly higher than the nave; at the fourth column, four central steps brought the altar area markedly above it. Here the four bases of the baldacchino columns can be seen; also the level of the floor (where the pebble foundation for its mosaic still remains in situ). A masonry semi-circle behind the site of the altar was the eastern limit of the Sanctuary, and here would have stood the Bishop's throne. Over the centuries, liturgical practices changed and this area underwent several modifications: shallow steps raised it above the altar and seating for clergy was installed, for example. *The Apse* (9) is unusual for Cyprus at this date although common in Syria, being polygonal on the outside. Also in Syrian form are the *Sacristies* (12) which lack apses and open, not into the Sanctuary, but onto the side-aisles. Note the screen of three columns.

Outside the Cathedral at its west end and opening into the narthex is a *diakonicon* (13): a chapel where the church deacons received offerings. It was divided by transverse arches into

118

three bays and an end room, with a narrow corridor running the length: between the arches on the north were masonry benches, and all was richly decorated. The end room may have had an altar where the offerings could be dedicated and prayers said for the donors: it had an opus sectile floor. In the main room, the floors of each bay had different designs in mosaic.

Arrivals in the first bay were confronted with an inscription on the floor starting *Vow and pay to the Lord your God* (from Psalm 36), continuing *The voice of rejoicing and salvation is in the tabernacles of the righteous* (from Psalm 118) and ending *Comest thou peaceably?* (from I Samuel 4 in which his response was that he was come to sacrifice unto the Lord). This western chapel was built within the shell of an older building which also had a mosaic floor: it has been relaid in the small room across the courtyard (14). Note that the chapel and the offices north of it stand at a slight angle to the basilica, and that all may follow the lines of separate earlier structures.

Adjoining the chapel, but with no direct access, is a stone-paved *courtyard* (15) containing a six-sided water tank similar to those placed outside mosques. A fountain-head was found in it; and the six niches probably spouted water too. Entry was into the narthex through a porch. The suggestion that laden animals were brought to this point seems reasonable, the porch with its trap between two doors ensuring that no beast strayed further.

To find the *Atrium* (6) go through the north door of the narthex: there are the remains of a quite small peristyle court. Before the door is a large marble basin still in situ, and beyond is a squatters' bread oven of the 8th century – directly under the wall of the Bishop's palace (19). The atrium is to the side of the basilica because the approach road came in from the north through a broad passage (16); it had no choice because of the western cliff. In the centre of the court was another hexagonal water tank. One column from the peristyle has been re-erected. The smaller shafts come from the gallery that ran round above. On the north at (17) was an arcaded room with a stairway leading to the upper floor; it was possibly the place of reception for palace visitors. The complex of small rooms and passages on the west (18) would be the service rooms and offices of the palace, above which was undoubtedly the Bishop's residence. The discovery of hundreds of pieces of floor-mosaic among the debris fallen from the upper storey seems to bear this out.

The Baptistery
It was built on a cruciform plan with four subordinate bays and an apse, and it would probably have had a lantern roof over the central square. The reason for an apse in a baptistery is obscure: here it was not a later addition. Entrance was through the east portico of the atrium, which was enclosed and furnished with benches (20). Three doors admitted to a narthex-like vestibule floored with a mosaic carpet and possessing compound exits and entrances (21). In the main chamber (22) stood eight Corinthian columns, one at each corner of the lantern-space and two supporting the east and west arms respectively: their white marble capitals of acanthus leaves had been brought from an older place. The mosaic floors of the central area, south arm and bays were relaid in the 7th century and the north arm paved entirely with stone flags: but in the original flooring mosaic was used throughout.

The south arm (23) was enclosed on three sides and opened onto the font recess. Here, between pilasters, were three niches where the prelates stood during the baptismal ceremony. The font was small, cruciform and admitting of one candidate at a time: five steps down, five steps up. The recess had marble revetments and many small pilasters bearing gilded capitals, the conch being covered in mosaic tesserae of mother o' pearl and glass. Viewed through its original archway, it would have had, in the words of Megaw, *the appearance of a theatre stage in miniature*. At some later date the steps were blocked off, there being no longer any call for mass baptism. As with the pastophoria in the cathedral, so here with the font recess, its derivation is from Syria and Palestine rather than from Constantinople and Rome (where an open peristyle court and a central pool were preferred).

A long room west of the font (24), entered from the vestibule, was a disrobing room provided with benches. The converts were shedding their former lives with their clothes. Then, one by one, they entered the recess for triple immersion, stepping out on the far side to receive the chrism from the bishop before the free-standing small apse (25). Turning left into the east annex (26) where there were more benches, they would array themselves in new white robes and return down the north corridor to the vestibule and thence into the baptistery. When all were assembled, bearing candles and to chant of Psalm 31 and the

Traparion, the newly-baptised would go in procession through the atrium to the Cathedral and up the nave by the great west door to be welcomed into the Christian congregation for their first communion.

CHAPEL OF AYIOS ERMOYENIS (St. Hermogenes)

Position: On the plain below Kourion's Amathus Gate and first left after the M1.

Dating: Possibly Early Byzantine origin, a later rebuilding shows Frankish influence.

Description: A small church in a eucalyptus grove, it consists of a nave and a north aisle with buttresses on the south side. The nave is barrel-vaulted with pointed arches and an apsidal east end which is out of alignment, being inclined to the north-east. A single wide arch divides the aisle from the nave and a plain tomb, reputed to be the saint's, occupies the centre of the floor; in the north east corner is a holy water stoup. The chapel may have replaced a pagan shrine, being, as it is, in the centre of the Hellenistic and Roman necropolis.

A fair is held here annually on October 5th (the saint's feast-day) and lasts for several days, people coming from all over the Island to celebrate; but he is specially revered locally for his reputation for curing fevers.

Tradition: Born in Turkey of Christian parents, possibly in the 4th century. Studied in Egypt, Athens and Constantinople and finally became Bishop of Samos, where he was martyred.

Legend: His coffin floated ashore here and the chapel was built round it; healing and miracles ensued. St. Ermoyenis also looks after lovers.

Chapel of Ayios Ermoyenis

120

KOURION – Extra-mural Basilica

Position: Best reached from the north east corner of the Stadium where a short track runs north to join an earth road: turn right along this for the basilica.

Dating: Late 5th century AD. In use for about 150 years.

Description: It is a small basilica church of a standard plan but rather roughly built of re-used materials taken from the ruins of pagan Kourion: dressed stone from the stadium, spirally-fluted columns from the theatre, Doric and late Corinthian ones possibly from the forum and marble slabs from the nymphaeum. The two main entrances both admitted to the atrium: one through a vestibule on the north and the other (and present way in) up four steps from the old Roman road on the south.

The Atrium is a disproportionately large peristyle courtyard containing a large rectangular water-tank. (This proved a convenient later base for a squatters' lime kiln, which is the reason for the circular centre.) Like the road, the tank is probably an earlier structure and, with the atrium and adjoining rooms, appears to be slightly out of alignment with the rest of the complex. From the east portico three doors led into the narthex, and opposite doors opened into the church. Here, as in the cathedral, a clerestorey let in light above the colonnades, and low-roofed annexes abutted the side-aisles. Several steps raised the sanctuary above the body of the church; there, the site of the altar and of the synthronon (seating for clergy) can be identified.

A curious excrescence in the north-east wall of the north aisle is a hastily-contrived tomb-recess, highly unorthodox but presumably made after the start of the Arab raids when the church was no longer being used. Human

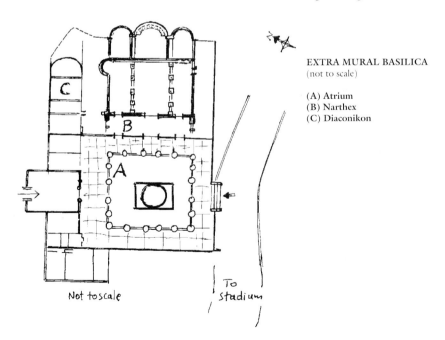

EXTRA MURAL BASILICA
(not to scale)

(A) Atrium
(B) Narthex
(C) Diaconikon

To Stadium

Not to scale

121

bones were found in the grave. The site of the diaconikon, or chapel for offerings, is also on the north-east and entered, as in the cathedral, from the north annex. On either side of the vestibule entrance are a number of small rooms, in one of which is the start of a stairway to an upper floor.

The church remained in use until the Arab raids. With a reduced population and a large cathedral, it is doubtful whether it had a separate congregation. It may have been a church with a special dedication, visited on feast days. Whatever its function, its position was lovely, in what would then have been a clearing in a greenwood, on the highest part, commanding a superb view across the bay.

Finds. Two of the marble slabs that paved the nave, sanctuary and diaconikon had scenes from mythology carved on their undersides: one of Anymone, Poseidon and the satyr (vide mosaic in the House of Dionysos in Paphos) and the other the head of a water nymph. Both may have been taken from the wrecked Nymphaeum. In 1895, a marble statue-base came to light. It bore a dedication to Demeter and Persephone in both Greek and Cypro-syllabic script. This led eventually (between 1971 & 74) to a search for their temple and the discovery instead of this basilica.

PANAYIA MONASTERY CHURCH, *Prastio near Evdimou*

Position: Three miles north of Evdimou. At first new houses, park on left and look for metal gates behind them; a path leads down to the church. For key, ask at the old coffee-shop in the village.

Dating: Foundation not known; new roof, 14th century; restored early 16th and early 18th.

Description: An old monastery church built over an ayiasma or sacred spring and considerably altered over the years. The present building consists of a single-aisled, barrel-vaulted church flanked by two chapels.

The church has outside walls three feet thick and its west entrance is framed by a deeply-moulded doorway with corbels and a hood with a rose finial, all in the Franco-Byzantine style of the 16th century. Within, it will be observed that the side walls consist of blocked, stone-built arcades, the arches slightly pointed, indicating that some time in the Lusignan period the church had three aisles. The north-east vault retains two scenes from the Festival cycle: the Washing of the Feet and the Last Supper; and in the conch of the apse is a well rendered Virgin Blachernitissa.

The south chapel is half the length of the main church. It has its own apse and remains of paintings at the east end: the Virgin between Archangels in the conch, overpainted, and St. Onoufrios on the south pier. Placed centrally before the sanctuary are a tap and small basin. Formerly, the holy water was brought from the spring through the rock-cut passage behind the main apse and flowed out of a fountain in the south wall into a large rectangular basin. Outside the west door, two more arches, half-buried now, show where an earlier water-course ran. Note the fine wooden door, 17th/18th c., cp. Ay. Andronikos' south door in Limassol. The shallow rectangular niche on the right under its ungainly pediment has lost its raison d'etre – presumably a plaque about the ayiasma.

122

The north chapel is a small mediaeval mausoleum with a large vestibule on its west side. Virtually a round, domed tower, it consists of four arched recesses over four benches, that on the north-west containing a broken coffin and some bones.

History: Little known. From the number of marble columns about (one forms the threshold of the main west entrance) the first building may have been a small, early basilica. According to local report, it lost its entire roof in the 14th c. – most likely through age and earthquake – and was re-covered only with great difficulty. It was restored in the early 16th century, when the arcades were filled in, and restored again in the 18th century. At some point it became a monastery church – note the metal gong and clapper; still suspended from the carob tree. The caves near the gate are Hellenistic tombs.

Legend: In the 14th century, a beautiful lady paid for the re-roofing of Panayia church. As Prastio was in the fiefdom of the Ibelin family, this could be true.

AYIOS MAMAS, *Louvaras*

Position: Eighteen miles north of Limassol via Ayia Phyla. At the Kalokhorio crossroads turn right at signpost and continue for 1½ miles. Ask for key in village.

Dating: Built 1455, painted 1495.

Description: This is a small, fully-painted chapel on the far side of Louvaras; it has a sloping protective roof and a later narthex. Inside, a detailed inscription between pairs of kneeling donors over the west door informs us that Constantine the priest had the church built and that,

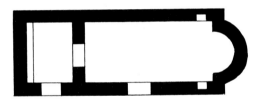

Ayios Mamas, Louvaras, Ground plan

forty years later, two councillors of the village and their wives paid for it to be decorated. The councillors are shown kneeling in supplication, soberly clad in their best clothes without adornment, and Christ blessing them at the edge of a mandorla. The wording ends, *And he who painted these is Philip who is named Goul.* This is the same man who decorated the monastery church of Stavros tou Ayiasmati near Platanistasa. The icon screen is of the simple templon sort, on which are some old icons brought from other churches; the architrave is painted. The original western exterior of Ayios Mamas, now enclosed, has the Deesis, St. Anna the Virgin's mother, and St. Irene painted on the wall; but the Baptist was destroyed when the narthex was built.

Decoration: It is in three tiers, the two upper ones illustrating the New Testament cycle in a series of small scenes plus some of the Miracles, and the bottom one displaying a range of saints. In the sanctuary, the programme is the conventional one except that the Communion of the Apostles is omitted in the apse for lack of space; and the conch has almost lost its Virgin – a pity because the Virgin at Ayiasmati is one of Goul's best works.

Style: Carried out in post-Byzantine local Cypriot style, the figures in the upper tiers are rather squat, as so often in such restricted space. The twenty-seven scenes are bright and lively in popular tradition with some Italian influence noticeable in the background buildings. Compared with his Ayiasmati commission, tou Goul's work here seems less innovative and painterly, always excepting the powerful portrait of the Baptist. But the monks of Ayiasmati probably demanded more of their man than did the counsellors. A & J Stylianou have studied both sets of paintings and found several scenes so

Ayios Mamas, Louveras

differently treated that it would be difficult to ascribe them to the same hand but for the common signature. Particularly unlike are the two Dormitions; but compare the Betrayal scenes and the Last Supper, too. Goul was, therefore, a versatile painter, with a variety of work-books or cards to choose from according to requirements.

Look especially for:

1. *St Mamas* on the north wall, east end. As patron saint of the church, given place of honour beside the Archangel Michael. Note the rainbow.
2. *John the Baptist* on the wall opposite by the screen. Here the touch of the Ayiasmati artist is unmistakeable: apart from the identical treatment of face and hair, he has captured the wild spiritual quality of the Saint.
3. *The Gadarene Swine*, west wall, south side, middle tier. A rarely-depicted miracle, in which Christ cures two men possessed of many devils, which then enter a herd of swine. (Matthew VIII 28) *See also Church of John the Baptist, Askas.*
4. Faith, Hope & Love, west wall, south side. Unusual personification of the virtues; their mother, Ayia Sophia (Holy Wisdom), is next to them on the south wall.

A glance at the main church of St. John the Baptist, which still keeps the massive walls of an old basilica, is enough to show that Louvaras is a village with a long history. In mediaeval Italian, Louvara means the place of banking and, according to local report, it was a financial centre in Venetian times. The big church was restored then, as the door mouldings show; it was renovated again in the 19th c.

MONASTERY OF PANAYIA AMASGOU, *Monagri*
(Our Lady of Damascus)

Position: In the Kouris valley, almost two miles below the village on the west bank. Look for signpost to Monagri about twelve miles after leaving the Limassol by-pass on the Polemidhia road – and just before reaching the Royal Oak.

Dating: Probably founded early 12th c. and rebuilt late 12th; reconstructed 16th c; restored 1960.

Description: A rectangular, vaulted church with arched recesses and two later transverse ribs which support the vault. The south door is blocked and the doorways on the west and north sides have moulded architraves of the 16th century: the pierced-stone round window in the apex of the west wall is also 16th c. Ruined walls of old monastic cells stand on the east and north; but on the west is a new wing, well-built in traditional style.

Decoration: Four periods may be discerned: early 12th c., late 12th, first half of the 14th (suggested); and mid 16th century.

First period, early 12th in the Sanctuary only.
Above the apse window, a bust of St. Spyridon; right of the apse, a deacon swinging a censer and, in the niche, St. Athanasios. The style is strongly reminiscent of painting of the same period in Asinou church; the same neo-classical look and plasticity.

Second period, late 12th: in the sanctuary and round the vaults is a cycle of the Life and Passion of Christ, starting on the south-east with the Nativity and ending in the bema with the Ascension (damaged) and Pentecost in the vault. A single gospel-writer, Mark, survives in the north-west recess. Also of this period are the busts of four hymn-writers above the north central recess and six Cypriot bishops on the north wall of the bema.

Style: The standard varies, implying that more than one painter was involved. The beautiful Presentation of the Christchild in the Temple, with its pastel colours, elegant, elongated figures and the Child reaching for its Mother, cramped for space as it is, brings to mind the master-painter of Lagoudera (1192) working here, perhaps, a few years previously. In contrast, to the left of this, the heavily-outlined, rigid figures in Christ's First Bath appear to have been copied from a Cappadocian Painter's Guide. In the south-west vault is part of the Baptism, wherein a shoal of gaily-coloured fish in a bright blue Jordan converge about Christ's feet as if in homage. In the words of the Convent's priest, *they recognise their Master.* Worth studying, too, is the composition of the Dormition.

Third period, circa first half 14th: some scattered figures in the west end. Over the north door are Mary of Egypt and Zosimos, St. Barbara stands by the west door and on the reveals of the south-west arch are the Apostles James, Philip and Thomas with the remains of two prophets above. (A & J

Stylianou point out that the placing of Apostles arbitrarily at the west end is degenerate, nor should they be mixed with prophets, but that it was common practice in the 14th century.)

Fourth period, mid 16th: all the rest – mainly in the apse and central recesses with some work at the west end. Below the Presentation of the Virgin, in the central recess, south side, is an inscription dating it to 1564. The scene has suffered from clumsy re-touching or cleaning; but among the surrounding saints is a powerful depiction of John the Baptist. Across the aisle, St. Peter is painted on a pier and in the recess north of that is a line of four Holy Fathers: Anthony, Theodosios the Cenobiarch, Sabas and Nicholas. Lastly, St. George and the Dragon, north-west recess, has been cut through by a doorway. The work in the apse is all 16th c: a demure Virgin with uplifted arms and the Christchild in a medallion, Blachernitissa style, attended by diminished, pretty Archangels in sprigged robes after the fashion of earlier, turn-of-the-century examples. Particularly successful are the officiating Fathers of the Church, their gentle solemn faces carefully built up and highlighted.

The iconostasis is of the same period. At the time of writing, many of the panels are away being cleaned; but the large, double-sided icon is in place showing, one side, the Virgin and Child and the other the Crucifixion. It was given in 1569 in memory of the lay-reader Philouris.

History: Panayia Amasgou is similar in form and period to Panayia Phorbiotissa at Asinou, and possibly was also built by one of the Byzantine lords on his retirement from public life. Unlike Asinou, the walls here bear few inscriptions that shed light on its history. It appears to have functioned as a monastery well into the 19th century before being abandoned. In 1992, a new monastic wing was built above the church on the west side, and in the December two nuns and five novices took up residence.

The ancient village of Monagri is on the old Troodos road, by the river. In the vicinity are two other churches worth visiting. St. George, the village church, contains some interesting late 15th century wall-paintings, including Daniel in the Lions' Den and a Last Judgement. The monastery church of the Archangel Michael, on the northern edge of Monagri, was rebuilt in the 18th century from earlier ruins and has a distinctive west porch supported by painted marble columns with Corinthian capitals.

AYIOS STAVROS CHURCH, *Kouka.* (Former monastery)

Position: From the Saittas crossroads, turn due west towards Perapedhi and Mandria. After two miles, a minor road leads left to the hamlet of Kouka (half-a-mile).

Dating: 12th century with later modifications and 15th century decoration.

Description: A simple cruciform church with arched recesses, later vaulted and dome removed. Other work includes a western extension and a small additional room at the east end, north side, which Gunnis suggests housed the monastery's holy relic – the wood-dust from the foot-piece of the True Cross. The diakonicon is missing. Still in the church is a large and ancient wooden cross with a central cavity; it is encased in silver. On the screen is an unusual icon of the Virgin and Child (17th c.), having in the centre a bronze medallion showing the same subject; round the sides are illustrations of the

Akathistos Hymn. Considerable remains of the monastic cells are evident round the courtyard.

Decoration: Some 15th century work exists in the south arm: scenes from the Passion and part of the Last Judgement in the vault and a St. George in a recess. In the north arm are traces of the Dormition, possibly from the 12th century. The paintings are now being cleaned and restored by the Department of Antiquities.

THE MONASTERY CHURCH OF AYIA MAVRA, *Kilani*

Position: Two and a half miles due west from the Saittas crossroads, take the left-hand turning through Perapedhi and continue south alongside the river Kryos towards Kilani (just over a mile). The church is on the approach to the village on the right.

Ayia Mavra   Sketch by Jeffery, 1918

Dating: Built 12th century, renovated and painted late 15th and extended on the west.

Description: A small church built over a spring which runs beneath the narthex and flows out above the road on the east wide. It is basically a single-aisled building, domed and vaulted, with arched recesses. The whole is protected by a steep, tiled roof. A path on the north side leads up to the rock-face above the church, where a further outflow of water is the source of local legend.

Decoration: Damaged, rustic and having a certain forceful character. Paintings are in the bema, dome and pendentives, east and west vaults; and a number of saints survive on the walls and piers. Observe that the Annunciation is in the pendentives with the Evangelists; that St. Timothy and St. Mavra are portrayed in the south central recess (with scenes from her martyrdom); that Barnabas is included (north-east recess); and that St. Augustine makes a rare appearance in the bema (north-east pier).

History, Tradition & Legend: The monk Barsky visited the monastery in 1735 and records that the skull of St. Mavra was kept in the church then.

Mavra is said to have been the niece of the Apostle Barnabas and to have been the wife of St. Timotheos. *Mavra and Timothy are generally mentioned together. Lusignan claims the village of Perapedi at the foot of Troodos as their birthplace, and says they were martyred on the banks of the Kurias near the town of Kilanion. According to his account, on the spot where their blood fell a stream of water gushed out.* Hackett, p. 397.

The local legend has it that Mavra beat upon the rock here just as her father and intended husband caught up with her. The Virgin heard her prayer, the cliff closed behind her and she was never seen again. The clear spring that

127

gushed forth then still flows today and either side are the marks of her hands on the rock wall.

KILANI ECCLESIASTICAL MUSEUM

Housed in the courtyard of the village church and opened in 1989 under the auspices of the Bishopric of Limassol together with the efforts of the local people, this is an excellent and representative collection, well worth seeing. Among the exhibits are sixty icons from the 13th century onwards, early printed books and examples of wood-carving and metalwork. Included are objects salvaged from some of the numerous ancient chapels in the area.

TIMEOS STAVROS MONASTERY, *Omodhos*

Monastery of the Holy Cross. In an attractive village famous for its lace-making.

Position:	Two miles south-west of Mandria, below Kato Platres. The monastery is in the heart of the village at the far end of a large cobbled square.
Dating:	Monastery founded probably 327AD and now disused. Church rebuilt 1816, renovated in 1858.
Description:	The former Byzantine church was completely rebuilt and enlarged early in the 19th century and is architecturally of scant interest. The best feature is the iconostasis (1817) which was specially commissioned by Bishop Khrysanthos of Paphos, according to an inscription in a niche on the screen.

128

Of the same date and workmanship are the pulpit, the icon-stand and the bishop's throne. The fine icons of Christ, the Virgin, John the Baptist and St. John the Divine show strong Russian influence. Outside, note the gravestone, built into the north wall, of an Englishman who died here in 1811, and its interesting inscription. The cells and offices of the vanished monastery cloister the church in a pleasing quadrangle of white-washed stone. They were restored in 1930. A series of arches support a first-floor balcony in a typical monastic lay-out. Two rooms at the west end can be entered: one is now a folk museum and the other is the former council chamber (Synod Hall) which displays EOKA relics and has a fine, intricately-carved wooden ceiling of 1812.

Omodhos is justly proud of its Holy Relics, kept within the church. A piece of the True Cross and a portion of the hempen rope which bound the hands of Christ, both contained in silver-gilt crosses, were certainly remarked upon by Rodinos in the 17th century; but they have probably been here since the foundation. The skull of Philip the Apostle was brought from the church of that name at Arsos for safe-keeping, and with it came the seals of four separate Byzantine Emperors to vouch for its authenticity!

History &
Tradition:
The foundation appears to be as old as that of Stavrovouni. Tradition tells us that this monastery was built over a cave, which became a small chapel for housing the relic – or relics – in the beginning, and that it soon became a shrine and place of pilgrimage for the Christians in Cyprus. It was not long before it became an important monastery, around which the village of Omodhos grew. As Kykko, so Omodhos monastery had connections later on with the Russian Church.

By the 11th and 12th centuries – the mid-Byzantine era – it was prestigious, and it continued to be so during the centuries of Latin rule. Because of its remoteness from the cities on the plains, and through the support of the people, Omodhos appears not to have been unduly disturbed – again like Kykko. It was in the fiefdom of the de Brie family then, and Frankish stone arches can still be seen around the village. The Turks left it unmolested too, until the massacres of 1821, that is. A special firman was issued from the Sultan in the year 1700 stating that the monastery was not to be touched. The monks were active in the community, their most noteworthy undertaking being the running of a Greek school from the end of the 18th century.

The abbot most remembered is Dositheos, who built the Synod Hall with its rococo ceiling, had the iconostasis painted and gilded, and in 1812 gave the church its bell. Along with other Cypriot leaders, he was hanged in Nicosia in 1821: Bishop Khrysanthos and the abbot of Kykko were of the number. A memorial to Dositheos stands outside the main entrance.

The village is delightful to wander in, with its narrow, winding cobbled ways, where the unexpected donkey is stabled and women crochet unself-consciously in doorways. The village wine-press, the mediaeval 'lenos', is still in working order and may be viewed; local wine and lace can be bought. Unlike the better-known drawn-thread and embroidery of Lefkara, Omodhos lace is proper lace, intricately worked and cobwebby, following traditional patterns. The time of greatest stir is on September 14th, the feast of the Holy Cross, when what is claimed to be the best village fair in the entire Island is held in the square.

129

PANAYIA IAMATIKI, *Arakapas*
Italo-Byzantine

Position: Thirty minutes drive from Limassol. Take the Yermasoyia or Parekklisia exits from the Limassol by-pass; the church is on the east outskirts of the village; ask at the coffee-shop for the key.

Dating: First built possibly early 16th c.; rebuilt 1727; restored 1974.

Description: The external walls of the church are of undressed stone and a wood and tile roof extends low over the side walls. The west and south doors are in the Franco-Byzantine style. In plan, the building is a slightly irregular rectangle, the length of the nave being approximately 42' on the north and 40' on the south and it is 30' in breadth. The 1727 shell conceals the remains of a substantial three-aisled Latin church with lofty internal walls. The broad central aisle is separated from the side aisles by arched colonnades which are plastered and painted. A single transverse arch spans the central aisle at the west end. The diamond-shaped floor-tiles are probably not original. A pair of unusual small chambers stand either side of the apse, entered from the nave through low pointed arches.

An extraordinary leather icon of the Virgin, discovered in the apse and now kept in the modern church across the road, has more resemblance to Spanish religious art than Italian. A second icon, of silver-gilt repoussé with the faces painted, is probably local work but shows considerable Catholic influence.[1]

Decoration: Remains of paintings of the early 16th century can be seen on the columns and soffits of the arcading, and in the spandrels between the arches. In the south-east spandrel, two of the Evangelists are writing their gospels; and on the wall adjacent to the north-west column, north side, are two well-preserved frescoes of St. Mamas and of Mary of Egypt and St. Zosimos. The soffits of all the arches are adorned with lines of angels in ornate medallions, the pillars with saints and the capitals with grotesque masks in acanthus leaves. The style is sophisticated and Italianate, and is among the most important surviving examples in Cyprus of the Italo-Byzantine School of painting. The delicate features of St. Mamas, the silky treatment of his robes, the lion's decorative mane and the overall vitality give an indication of this 16th century painter's quality.

Inscription: In the same area, below a painting of St. George – head missing – are five lines recording the repairs to the church by one George in 1727.

History: Nothing is known of the Latin church. Jeffery reports that a small monastery was still here in 1918; also a medicinal spring *much frequented by the sick*. The external walls and the roof underwent extensive rebuilding in 1727 as a huge pine tree had grown up in the west end.

Tradition: The special curative powers of the Virgin 'Iamatiki' were to stop haemorrhages; and the leaves of a particular tree which grows around here were used in treatment.

---

1. Three 16th century icons of Evangelists, formerly in the church, now hang in the Byzantine Museum, Nicosia.

TROODOS

History of Troodos

Troodos is not a separate district but the central mountain range, and it has a character of its own. Here are to be found many of the small, mid- and post-Byzantine painted churches, often in remote valleys and in the folds of the hills.

The four main areas are: the high Troodos, crowned by Mt. Olympos; the Marathasa and the Solea Valleys coming up from the north; and the wild Pitsilia region on the east.

For much in this section I am deeply indebted to Judith & Andreas Stylianou whose book, The Painted Churches of Cyprus, first opened my eyes to the beauty and significance of these places.

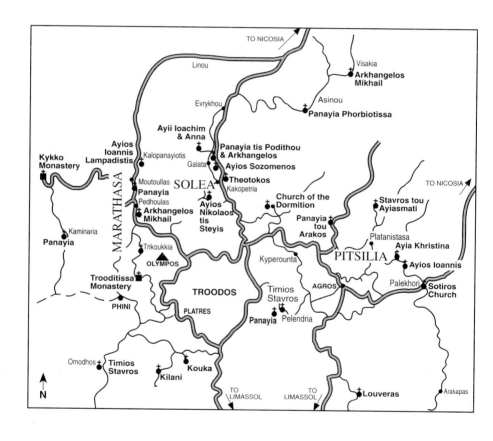

TO NICOSIA

Linou

Visakia

Arkhangelos Mikhail

Evrykhou

Asinou

Panayia Phorbiotissa

Ayii Ioachim & Anna

Ayios Ioannis Lampadistis

Kalopanayiotis

Panayia tis Podithou & Arkhangelos

Galata

Ayios Sozomenos

Kykko Monastery

Moutoullas

Theotokos

SOLEA

Kakopetria

TO NICOSIA

MARATHASA

Panayia

Pedhoulas

Church of the Dormition

Stavros tou Ayiasmati

Arkhangelos Mikhail

Ayios Nikolaos tis Steyis

Panayia tou Arakos

Platanistasa

Ayia Khristina

Kaminaria

Panayia

Trikoukkia

Kyperounta

PITSILIA

Ayios Ioannis

OLYMPOS

Palekhori

Sotiros Church

Trooditissa Monastery

TROODOS

Timios Stavros

AGROS

PHINI

PLATRES

Panayia

Pelendria

Omodhos

Timios Stavros

Kouka

Kilani

TO LIMASSOL

TO LIMASSOL

Louveras

Arakapas

N

THE MONUMENTS

Note: * Indicates monuments of particular interest
       ** Indicates monuments of outstanding interest

PITSILIA REGION

METAMORPHOSIS TOU SOTEROS, Church of the Transfiguration of the Saviour, *Palekhori*

Position: About twenty-eight miles from Nicosia and ten east of Agros in the east Troodos mountain range. Leave Nicosia by the Troodos road. After five miles, leave the turn-off to Kato Trimithia on the right and continue straight ahead (south-west) on a good road for twenty-one miles to Apliki. Palekhori is a mile and a half further on. Do not drive down to the village but keep left on an ascending road and very shortly the sign for tou Soteros will be seen (right). Call at the priest's house beside the church for the key.

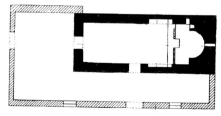

Plan of Church of Transfiguration, Palekhori

Dating: Early 16th century; enclosure early 17th.

Description: A small rectangular building of typical mountain type, it has a steep-pitched wooden roof and is enclosed on the south and west sides. It is fully painted. The dedication is on the right-hand surface of the north recess, but has lost the essential last line, giving the date; in addition, the name of the painter does not appear, nor is there a donor portrait.

Decoration: A straightforward N.T. cycle covers the upper walls of the nave in twenty-two scenes and on the lower walls are the saints. In the sanctuary is a full apse programme, the Old Testament scenes, saints and prophets. Over the niche in the prothesis on the left is the Sacrifice in which the Christchild is shown twice. The Annunciation and the Crucifixion are on the east and west pediments respectively – excellent positions for them. The Nativity is by the south recess, and then the cycle unfolds round the walls, ending with Pentecost by the north recess. The Western Resurrection is illustrated in preference to the eastern Anastasis. (Oddly, the Transfiguration, which took place before the Raising of Lazarus, here is put two scenes further on). The saints are mainly soldier-saints and monastics, but round the two recesses is a highly individual selection of saints and scenes.

On the outside wall of the west door are paintings dated by inscription on the lintel to 1612: they are a Deesis with John the Theologian with Christ as a Prelate in the niche above.

Style: This is a local post-Byzantine work by a good painter who has much in common with known local painters Philip tou Goul (Ayiasmati and Ayios Mamas, last decade 15th century) and Symeon Axenti (Ay. Sozomenos and Arkhangelos, Galata 1513 and 14): he was probably active somewhere between. There was a freemasonry of workbooks, and identical scenes can appear in these churches, differing only in style and technique; in the Betrayal and the Lamentation, for example. This particular painter's backgrounds vary according to his copy; sometimes Italianate, as in the Communion of the Apostles and Abraham Entertaining the Angels, sometimes Byzantine: where appropriate, the Byzantine formula for mountains is applied on a lavish scale. The colours used are almost entirely the warm earth and mineral pigments in which Cyprus is so rich. It is the treatment of faces that gives the work here its special quality: a technique not previously encountered, of breaking up the light by use of many white radiating lines. Attention was drawn to this by A & J Stylianou and is best seen in the face of the Virgin in the conch of the apse where it is applied over another technique – that of completely diffused light. The standard of decoration in the apse altogether is consistently high.

Look especially for:

Apse: The Virgin Orans, "Mistress of the Angels".
The Communion of the Apostles – all appear twice except for Judas.
The officiating Fathers. The two O.T. scenes on the side walls.

Nave: Sts. George & Demetrios, riding together like brothers (south recess).
Death of Mary of Egypt with Zosimos and a lion (left spandrel of south recess).
St. Mamas and his splendidly linear lion (right of west door).
Daniel in the Lion's Den (above north recess).
Vision of Pachomios, founder of communal monasticism (left spandrel, north recess).

History: Writing in 1918, Jeffery states: *As its name suggests, this is evidently one of the oldest villages in the island. It was known by this name as early as 1297, if this is the village belonging at that period to the Hospitallers.* (Historic Monuments of Cyprus.) At that time, the narrow cobbled lane winding steeply down from the church was the only approach to the village on this side. Palekhori formerly fell between two bishoprics but is now solely under Nicosia: it still has two mukhtars, however – one for each side of the river Peristerona. The church could have been monastic.

Tradition: Locally it is said that Palekhori derives from pale, hori, 'Come on in, there's still room!' and refers to the occasions when a huge number of people sheltered in the building during a great storm, and again when a plague swept through the district. Like a mother hen, the small church found room for them all.

AYIOS IOANNIS PRODHROMOS CHURCH, *Askas*
Church of John the Baptist

The paintings have not yet been cleaned.

Position: Proceed to Palekhori: Askas is one mile north-west and signposted. Key with Papandrea, the village priest.

Dating: 1560 (from inscription on board found in roof); extended at west end in 1763.

Description: A fairly small building under the customary protective wood and tile roof, it is divided into three aisles by low arcading which is supported by small columns with flat stone capitals. There are six decorated wooden cross-

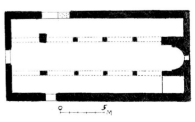

Ground plan of Prodhromos Church, Askas.

beams. The narthex may have been lost in the 18th century extension; but the west entrance was given a wide porch at that time. **The iconostasis** was made in 1887 and it carries the original icons from the 16th c. screen, namely St. Peter, St. Paul, the Virgin, Christ and John the Baptist: they are the best things here. The early Holy Doors can be seen at the west end. Observe that they show, not the Annunciation (usual) but the Death of John the Baptist and John baptising Christ.

The complete absence of paintings on the north and south and the modern windows suggest considerable restoration and repair to the outside walls over the years.

Decoration: Missing: the Life of Christ and the Crucifixion. These were presumably on the south, north and west walls of the church in its original form. What remains is an interesting and unusual series of compositions covering the arcades and the apse. The emphasis is on a) the life of the Baptist and b) the miracles, appearances and resurrection of Christ.

The south arcade shows the life of the Baptist in fifteen scenes beginning on the north side, east end. **The north arcade** is devoted to post-Crucifixion scenes interspersed with cures and miracles from Christ's ministry. This series begins on the south side with – disconcertingly – the Last Supper at the east end; but then comes Doubting Thomas and the sequence is clear. Over the west piers of both arcades can be found the Last Judgement. Within the apse we are on familiar ground: a Virgin Blachernitissa, a Communion of the Apostles and the officiating Fathers below.

Style: There is a consistency and attention to detail that is impressive, although the figures are somewhat limp and degenerate. To find a fresco painter working in the Byzantine tradition at such a late date is unusual. The paintings are dark with age and grime.

Look especially for:

South arcade, south side central pier:	Daniel in the Lion's Den.
North arcade, south side central pier:	Woman of Samaria.
North arcade, north side central pier:	Ascension, Pentecost and below, Parable of the Virgins.
North arcade, north side west pier:	The Gadarene Swine, Cure of the Lepers, Zacchaeus.
North arcade, soffit west pier:	Last Judgement: "Those who sleep on Sunday".
North arcade, north side east pier:	Dives & Lazarus (notice the dog).

CHURCH OF AYIA KHRISTINA, *Phterikoudi*
(Known locally as Ayia Paraskevi)

Position: Proceed according to directions for Askas, then follow the road for another two miles; the small chapel stands off the road, well before Phterikoudi.

Dating: 1518.

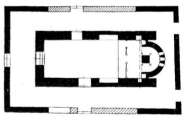

Ayia Khristina, Phterikoudi, Ground plan

Description: A small chapel with the usual mountain-type roof. It lost its west wall in 1901 when the building was extended; at the same time, the south entrance was moved further west and the original door converted into a window. An inscription there gives the date, dedication and names of the donors. They are Constantine Mardaki and his wife Madeleine, a Greek married, it seems, to a French lady. Her name is spelt Mandelena, and above the inscription is a painting of the Mandylion or Holy Towel imprinted with Christ's face.

Decoration: Of good quality and well-preserved, but limited by lack of wall surface to a single tier of saints in the nave. In a painting on the north wall the donors are kneeling, one each side of Saint Christina: the wife is fashionably dressed. The sanctuary has as complete a programme as space allows: the Annunciation in the pediment, flanked by Kings David and Solomon with Stephen, the first martyr, and St. Laurentios below; on the south wall is the Sacrifice of Isaac; the apse contains the Virgin Orans and Archangels above six officiating Fathers of the Church.

STAVROS TOU AYIASMATI, *Platanistasa, Monastery Church of the Holy Cross*

(One of the nine churches on UNESCO's World Heritage list.)

Position: In the eastern part of Troodos, under two-and-a-half miles north east of Lagoudhera as the crow flies – but the road is circuitous and the key (plus keeper) must be sought at the village. The church stands on a hillside above a remote valley, reached by a winding track (2 miles).

Stavros tou Ayiasmati, Platanistasa, Ground plan

Dating: Probably built early in the Venetian domination. Painted either in 1494 (A & J Stylianou) or around 1500 (Papageorgiou).

Description: A single-aisled stone building with one arched recess in each side wall, it stands within an enclosure of the same age, the whole structure being covered with a steeply pitched tiled roof. It is fully painted. The icon screen and decorated cross-beam are contemporary. The donors are depicted on the south external wall, offering the church to Christ, through the intercession of the Virgin. Inside, an inscription on the lintel of the south door records the painting of the church at the expense of the chief priest Lord Peter and Pepani his wife on Tuesday October 7th . . . (year lost). *The gift is God's and the hand that of Philippos the painter who is called tou Goul.* Goul also

139

decorated the church of St. Mamas at Louveras in 1495. A second inscription above the north door commemorates the foundation by the same pair, but no date is given.

Decoration: The finest and most complete cycle of the period in Cyprus. The paintings

Stavros tou Ayiasmati – Platanistasa

are in two tiers, having thirty scenes from the New Testament round the upper walls and more than thirty chosen saints ranged below. The Holy Cross of the church's dedication is painted on the wall of the north recess and miniature scenes relating to its discovery fill the angles and the soffit of the arch. The multiple surfaces of the typical Byzantine church are absent, therefore the artist has had to adapt to the flat walls. Both pediments are utilised, also the external surfaces of the south and west doorways.

The cycle begins on the south-east with the Birth of the Virgin, but the Annunciation is to be found on the east pediment; and the Anastasis has joined the Last Judgement outside above the west door. The painting scheme has been carefully planned; everything has been fitted in at or near its appointed place and no space wasted. Being a monastery church, the emphasis is upon monastic saints and hermits: they stand shoulder to shoulder on the lower walls, west end. Within the sanctuary there is a complete apse programme: the Virgin Blachernitissa between Archangels, the Communion of the Apostles with Christ full-face and eight officiating Fathers of the Church below. Five of these last are great Cypriots of the Early Church, with three more on the adjacent south wall. Observe that Barnabas is dressed as Prelate and Apostle.

The iconostasis is one remove from a templon, its lower part consisting of painted wooden boards; yet this supports an upper section delicately carved in foliage and chalice designs, all gilded on a blue ground: it carries icons of the Virgin, Christ and the Baptist, composing a Deesis. Above hangs the

140

board for suspending lamps, here embellished with medallions of early Bishops (including Popes).

Style: Post-Byzantine local Cypriot work with some Western infiltration. Tou Goul uses prototypes that appear to have come from various sources: work-books, guides, even transfers. They must have passed from hand to hand as some can be identified in other churches on Troodos; same iconography, different artist. The Latin influence is quite marked in certain details: in the background architecture in the Presentation of the Virgin; in the Washing of the Feet, done with naturalism and in true perspective, also Doubting Thomas. Yet the Birth of the Virgin, the Baptism, Crucifixion, Anastasis and Dormition are pure Byzantine. Iconographically, the scenes are very mixed. They are given unity by the consistency of the style, the use of warm, clear colours and a certain dramatic quality. Tou Goul is at his best with the saints, where he has a freer hand.

Look especially for:

1. John the Baptist by the screen, south wall. Fine portrait.
2. Onoufrios, south wall, west end. Note thick growth of hair and the bush tied on.
3. St. Mamas riding an anthropomorphic lion, by west door, also St. George and his small passenger.
4. The delightful Nativity and realistic milking-scene, lower right.
5. The Lamentation, above north door. (For its austerity, linear qualities and concentrated, contained grief.)
6. The Virgin in the apse. One of the most successful – but see Arkhangelos Mikhail Church, Pedhoulas for earlier version.

History: The founders of the monastery may have been refugees from Ayiasmati near Constantinople. As this church contains the earliest illustration of the Discovery of the Holy Cross known in Cyprus, they may have brought with them from Asia Minor a manuscript containing the scenes in miniature. The theme had been popularised by the Crusaders, but was not so common in the East.

PANAYIA TOU ARAKOS, *Lagoudera, Our Lady of the Wild Vetches*

(One of the nine churches on UNESCO's World Heritage list)

Outstanding series of paintings of the mid-Byzantine period.

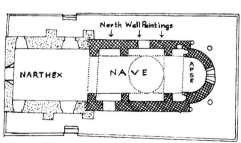

Plan of Panayia tou Arakos
(Acknowledgement to D.C. Winfield)

Position: High in the east Troodos mountains. Reached either by tarmac road from the Karvounas cross-roads, via Kyperounda and Khandria – about 10 miles – or via Spilia and Sarandi by broad earth-road through the forest – from Kakopetria about 11 miles. (Do not go down to the village as the church is about half a mile along the upper road).

141

Dating:	Built probably mid-12th c; decorated in 1192, with some earlier work; extended possibly late 17th c.
Description:	A rectangular building divided into three bays and an apse, it is vaulted and has a high central dome and lantern with twelve lights. A narthex was added in the 14th century; but this was removed and a new, enlarged narthex built, probably in the last quarter of the 17th century, and the west wall of the nave was demolished to create a more spacious church. The secondary protective roof which covers the entire structure probably dates from this period: both it and the monastic wing on the north side were restored in the recent past.

Panayia tou Arakos, Lagoudera

History:	Possibly first built in the mid-12th c. as a private chapel on the estate of the district overlord (the Authentis). According to an inscription over the north door, his son Leontios had it repainted late in 1192. It was not referred to as a monastery then. The turmoil of that year is well known: the rising against the Templars, the consequent massacre, and the arrival of the Lusignans as the new Latin rulers. The Byzantine lords were dispossessed of their estates. Perhaps Leontios gave his land to the Church and turned monk, a not uncommon practice. How a first-class artist, painting in the late Comnenian courtly style, came to be decorating a humble church in such a remote spot at such a time is not known. Nor is it known when the monastery ceased to function. In 1735, the redoubtable Barsky arrived and found only three monks here: his signature can be seen on St. Stephen in the sanctuary.
Decoration:	It is in true fresco. Inside, the eye is immediately drawn upwards to the colourful dome, where a meditative, rather sad Pantocrator presides. He is surrounded by a heavenly host in medallions; between the lights of the lantern, His prophets strike flamboyant poses. The western pendentives hold the gospel writers in pairs, leaving the eastern free for the Annunciation to span the sanctuary arch. Only seven large scenes follow on the walls and

vaults and, as their sequence is unusual, it is given here:
1) The Presentation of the Virgin: lunette, north central bay.
2) The Nativity: south-west vault.
3) The Presentation of Christ: east wall of central bay.
4) The Baptism: north-west bay.
5) The Anastasis or Harrowing of Hell: north-west vault.
6) The Ascension: east vault.
7) The Dormition: lunette, south central bay.
   (The Crucifixion would have been on the lost west wall.)

Notice in 1) the graceful, elongated figures and how, seen from below, they seem not so long; also the delicate embroidered finish to the tunics and the double appearance of the young Virgin – a convention quite acceptable in Byzantine art; in 3) that the Baptist has been brought in. (It has been pointed out[1] that the Arakiotissa on the wall opposite must be associated with this scene.) And notice in 5) the stance and force of the resurrected Christ, and the stigmata; also the broken gates and locks of Hell and the sarcophagi either side.

The Arakiotissa (south wall by the screen): Perhaps the most memorable figure is the beautiful Virgin of the Passion, standing in front of her throne with the Christchild in her arms. Above her, a pair of angels hold the instruments of the Crucifixion, and Mary shows in her face that she is aware of the grief to come. Leontios dedicates his church to her in verses either side of the throne.

All the individual portraits with their expressive faces are worth studying: all are grave – for those were dark days for Cyprus; some show deep compassion (old Symeon, for example, as he receives the infant Christ); and that of Christ on the Holy Tile over the north door reflects unrelieved suffering. In the bema, observe the Stylites on their pillars and, among others, St. Lazarus in the south-east recess, St. Onoufrios in the north-east recess and, opposite him, St. Stephen the first martyr.

Style: The work is some of the finest of the late 12th century; no examples remain in Constantinople itself. Colour, proportion and use of available space, all are masterly and all is carried out with meticulous care and an eye for detail. The feeling for pattern and rhythm, evident at Asinou at the beginning of the century, has been developed here into a real sense of movement, expressed in swirling robes and dramatic gestures: and it is contrasted with stillness – an obvious example being Gabriel and the Virgin in the Annunciation.

The possibility that this brilliant painter could have been Theodore Apseudes, who worked in the Enkleistra for St. Neopytos in 1183, cannot be proved, but it is likely.

Other work: **The Apse** was decorated by another hand some time previously: Winfield suggests a date in the mid-12th century. From earlier work discovered in the nave, it is thought that the entire church was painted then. The style is easy and flowing and larger brushes have been used: a competent artist who lacks the finer touches of the master. Included are the Virgin and Child enthroned between archangels, the prelates in medallions below and the Fathers of the Church. As at Asinou and Perakhorio, the altar is not represented and Barnabas and what may be Epiphanios stand in the place of honour.

---

1. A & J Stylianou

Narthex, east wall: some 14th century paintings in the corners; also restoration to work in the nave by the same hand e.g. on the Baptism.

External north wall: bust of Virgin orans over north door, 14th c. The remainder are naive 16th/17th century additions.

Significance of Lagoudera . . . *it provides a dated example of developments in the technique of wall-painting which were taken over and brought to fruition by Italian fresco painters of the 13th and 14th centuries.* David Winfield in his Guide.

STAVROS CHURCH, *Pelendria*

One of the nine churches on UNESCO's World Heritage list.

Arms of the prince of Antioch, Stavros Church.

Position: Off the Limassol/Kakopetria road. Between the Karvounas cross-roads and Trimiklini junction, on the old Troodos road. About half-a-mile below Kato Amiandos, the side-road for Pelendria goes off sharply to the left (signposted). Stop in the village and ask for the priest.

Dating: Church first built 13th century, north aisle added 14th, south aisle probably 16th. Painted mid-14th century (over 13th century decoration); some 16th century work.

Description: Originally a single-aisled domed church, barrel-vaulted and with arched recesses. The north aisle was built in a Franco-Byzantine style with a pointed vault; an arch cut through the central recess joined it with the nave: it was almost certainly a Latin Chapel. The latest addition was the south aisle. The whole was covered by a mountain type steep-pitched roof with projecting eaves, protection from the winter snows. A great part of both the north and

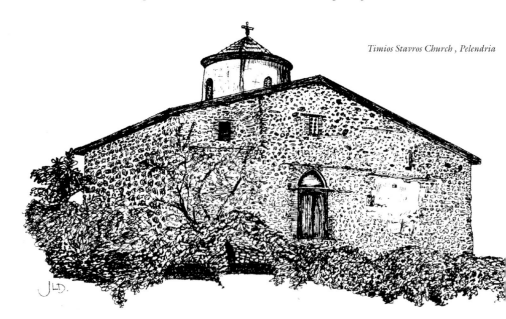

Timios Stavros Church , Pelendria

144

south aisles have had to be rebuilt; and the south has lost its apse.

Decoration: Completely redecorated in the third quarter of the 14th century, including the new Latin Chapel.

Main Church. An inscription over the west door records the renovation and repainting, but both donors' names and the date are missing. Many of the paintings are damaged. In the dome, the Heavenly Host round the Pantocrator includes the Evangelists in their symbolic form and in the drum below are no fewer than sixteen Prophets.

The Virgin in the conch of the apse is Blachernitissa (the Child in a medallion), the Communion of the Apostles is omitted and the eight officiating Fathers include three Cypriots – Tryfillios, Spyridon and Epiphanios.

The New Testament cycle suffered from the collapse of the old south wall. Now it begins with the Last Supper on the south-west, and it can be followed round to the Anastasis over the north central recess. It then moves into the bema with post-Crucifixion scenes, and it ends with the Ascension and Pentecost in the vault.

The Life of the Virgin is a cycle of fourteen scenes, beginning with Ioachim and Anna in the south-west vault and ending with the Dormition above the north-west recess.

On the lower walls Peter and Paul are, correctly, on the west piers. Among the mixture of saints are four commemorative portraits: i) north west recess, Basil, *son of the most noble archon Lord Olimites*, deceased; ii) by north arch, Nengomia, *wife of Basil the priest and lawyer of this place*, also deceased; iii) in niche over west door beside Baptist, a couple; iv) on north east, pier by screen, a couple with a child – donors. On the iconostasis is an unusual icon of the late 12th/early 13th century showing Christ, his hands bound, at the foot of the Cross; on the reverse is a modern painting of the Virgin.

The North Aisle. Because of the presence of the coat of arms of a person of high rank over the arch, it is sometimes referred to as the Seigneurial Chapel of Prince John, younger brother of King Peter I. Note the Lusignan lion and the bend for difference.

With the collapse of the north wall and the vault, most of the frescoes here were destroyed, and the decoration that remains is confined to the south and west walls with some 16th century work in the parabema. West of the arch is a large painting of Doubting Thomas with donors; the inscription is lost. West again are the Evangelists with, in the far corner, a portrait of an old man, Leon, deceased. On the west wall is a Tree of Jesse. Set in the iconostasis is a small shrine of old Coptic musharaby work against which is displayed a large cross encased in silver plates. Scenes from the Life of Christ are on the arms, but the centre has Constantine and Helena with the True Cross, and conceals a cavity holding a small cross of bronze.

The south aisle has a large painting of St. George on horseback with scenes from his life on the surrounds; 16th century.

Style. Two distinct styles are discernible, both relating to the 14th century period of redecoration: the conclusion is that two artists and their apprentices were employed here simultaneously. *Artist A* was trained in the Palaeologue tradition of Constantinople. The paintings in the dome, east pendentives, sanctuary vault and east lunette are his work; also what remains in the north aisle. It is distinguished by a mannered elegance and polish that is lacking in the other, soft delicate colours and a slightly Latin quality. *Artist B* was responsible for the apse programme and all else in the nave. His iconography is painstakingly correct, style conservative post-Byzantine and rustic; good of its kind. In contrast with A, his colours are strong, his figures bold and rather dumpy and look better when seated. A & J Stylianou have identified this painter as the one who redecorated the central bay of Asinou church.

Look especially for:

The Ascension (in the bema) and Doubting Thomas (in Latin Chapel), both by artist A.

From the Life of the Virgin by Artist B:

1. Blessing of the High Priests (south west vault last scene) for its composition and 'old' Virgin.
2. Prayer of the High Priest (north west vault scene 2) Mary's husband is chosen – a white dove settles on Joseph's rod.
3. Meeting of Mary and Elizabeth (north west vault, 2nd row last scene) the unborn Baptist bows before the unborn Jesus.
4. The donor and commemorative portraits. The couple in the north aisle are unlikely to be the Prince and his Lady – their dress is too plain – but, like Basil and Nengomia, members of the Royal household. All the men wear a white coif and Basil and the donor of Doubting Thomas have similar tunics and over-garments trimmed with rows of buttons; the latter's tunic also has a black fleur-de-lys embroidery. The ladies wear long red mantles that cover their heads and fall to their feet.

History: Pelendria was in the fiefdom of John, Prince of Antioch and Constable of Cyprus, from at least 1353 until his assassination in 1374/5. It remained in his family up to 1451/2, when it was given by King John II to his Queen, Helena Palaeologina. In more recent times, the Church of the Cross lay neglected for many years, and each winter the snow drifted in. Earlier this century it was repaired by the people of the village.

PANAYIA KATHOLIKI, *Pelendria*

Position: Centre of the village.

Dating: Beginning 16th century.

Description: This is the original village church, its steep, dark-tiled roof almost touching the hillside. The interior is divided into three aisles by wooden arcades, cp. the Church of the Dormition at Kourdali of the same period. A Last Judgement on the west wall belongs to the Italo-Byzantine school of painting. So do the icons on the contemporary iconostasis, again as at Kourdali – although here the panels have been unfortunately repainted and the glory lost. Nevertheless, both Gunnis and A & J Stylianou comment on the St. Mamas icon, which has a pronounced Italianate cast, the lion's head twisted to gaze up at the saint adoringly.

Observe the birds pecking the grapes on the screen itself, appropriate theme for a wine-producing village. Panayia possesses a collection of double-sided processional icons of various periods, doubtless from vanished churches of the neighbourhood; they have all been restored to some degree; the best is dated 1673. The special icon here is the Pelendria Panayia, painted in 1640 and one of the sacred rain-bringing icons of Cyprus. It stands in the nave surrounded by the same Coptic musharaby work as that in the nearby Church of the Holy Cross.

AGROS: good centre for visiting the Byzantine churches of the Pitsilia district.

Position: About twenty-five miles north of Limassol via Ayia Phyla and Kato Mylos.

Main Church: The large church of the Panayia is relatively modern and replaces a small 11th c. church which was pulled down last century. The original 18th century iconostasis has been retained with its excellent wood-carving. Two rare icons have also survived: they are the Panayia Agriotissa and Christ Pantocrator, both painted by a master in the second half of the 12th century and restored by one Dimitris in 1586. A replica of the old church is now being built in which they will be displayed.

History: The Monastery of Megalos Agros was founded in the 9th century when forty monks settled here with their holy icons, refugees from the iconoclasts of Asia Minor. It was still functioning in the 19th century. Sophocles Sophocleous, who cleaned the 12th c. icons, found underlying traces suggestive of earlier painting still.

SOLEA VALLEY

AYII JOACHIM and ANNA, *Kaliana*

Position: Mid-way between Tembria and Galata in the Solea Valley, a side road leading westwards off the old valley road is signposted (one mile).

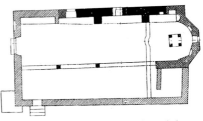

Ayios Sozomenos Church, Galata, Ground plan

Dating: Built early 12th century; reconstructed 14th c; belfry and extensions early 20th.

Description: A two-aisled building with a steep-pitched, tile and timber roof. The north wall has arched recesses and is a survival from the first church, which may have been domed. The rest was completely rebuilt in the 14th century. The south and west extensions, the two windows in the north wall and the belfry belong to the early 20th century.

The iconostasis is of the 17th century, well-made and carrying some 16th and 17th century icons, including one of the Virgin inscribed *Kalionitissa* which has round the edge the story of Ioachim and Anna in small scenes. On the central cross-beam are seventeen framed squares, each containing a painted coat-of-arms (mostly lions rampant, palm-trees and birds): similar decoration is found on the 14th century templon at Lampadistis Monastery.

Decoration: Confined to the arched recesses in the north wall. Best-preserved, and the painting that helped to date the wall, is the Forty Martyrs of Sebaste, west recess (cp. Asinou and St. Nicholas at Kakopetria of same period). Also early 12th century is the fragmentary Birth of the Virgin, east recess. Some painting of the 14th century remains in the central recess – note Mary of Egypt and St. Zosimos on the soffit.

History: In mediaeval times, Kaliana was an important administrative centre for the Solea Valley under Latin overlords; now it is a small charming village. In the 18th century, someone built an inn on the main road, a little below the Kaliana turn-off: officially designated Folk Art Architecture, it is worth seeing, so is its setting.

Ayii Joachim and Anna Church, Kaliana

AYIOS SOZOMENOS CHURCH, *Galata*
(Paintings yet to be cleaned)

Position: Centre of village and up the steep road behind the modern church. Ask for the key in the coffee-shop by the bridge.

Dating: Built and decorated in 1513. North side enclosed and roof extended after this.

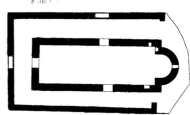

Description: It is a typical mountain church with a wood and tile sloping roof – but note the carved stone at the north-east corner. Ayios Sozomenos was erected

Ground plan of Ayios Sozomenos Church, Galata

by the villagers themselves, according to the inscription over the west entrance – unlike the numerous estate chapels which would be run up by the powerful landowners. Thirteen contributed, and the decoration was paid for by the lay-reader Ioannis, a lawyer from nearby Tembria. The painter's name is given as Symeon Axenti, who worked in the Arkhangelos chapel the following year. The inscription ends with a quotation from the patriarch of Constantinople, Germanos, writing in the 8th c:

> *Church is the earthly heaven in which the Heavenly God*
> *dwells and lives and walks, representing the Crucifixion*
> *and Burial and Resurrection of Christ.*

Decoration: It is fully painted with some external work on the north wall. On the upper part of the south wall and in the west pediment, the life and passion of Christ unfolds in more than a score of small scenes, starting with the Annunciation by the screen and ending with the Anastasis on the north-west wall: the Ascension occupies the east pediment. Less usual is the space on the north wall devoted to seven scenes from the apocryphal life of the Virgin. Lining the lower walls are the familiar rows of saints, extra space being given on the north wall to St. George and his martyrdom and, by the icon screen, the Dormition *and Assumption* of the Virgin. In the apse, the Virgin Orans is inscribed *Panhyperphotios* (see note below). The six Fathers of the Church include Epiphanios the Great and Spyridon, both Cypriot saints.

Look especially for:

South wall: Entry into Jerusalem; the Transfiguration (see note below).

North wall: The specially commissioned St. George, signed by Axenti.

Among the saints: Ayios Mamas, Ayia Paraskevi and Ayia Kyriaki on the south.

George & Demetrios, Nestore & Theodore the General (Strateliatis) on the north.

The external paintings: The niche above the north door contains the saint of the dedication, Sozomenos. A 5th c. recluse, he came to Cyprus from Syria and wrote prolifically on Church issues. Left of the door is the Last Judgement. The wall on the right displays in separate panels the Seven Councils of the Church (see Appendix) and the Triumph of Orthodoxy. This last commemorates the day in 843 when Iconoclasm was defeated, and anathema pronounced on all who thenceforward attacked Holy Icons. (Celebrated yearly on Orthodox Sunday, the first in Lent.)

Style: Some of Axenti's work is very good; and the period and the remoteness must be borne in mind. Vitality and freshness are apparent under the smoke-grimed surfaces; in the individual figures is proportion and grace and expressiveness.

Note: 'Panhyperphotios' means 'radiating extreme light'. Both the attribute of the Virgin and the Transfiguration are concerned here particularly with the mystical nature of Divine Light as perceived by the Hesychasts in the 14th c. and which caused widespread controversy. The transfigured Christ on the south wall is in a mandorla and is radiating light. The eight-pointed star is formed by two overlapping squares and was a 14th c. symbol of Divine essence and energy. (See also the Palaea Enkleistra nr. Kouklia.)

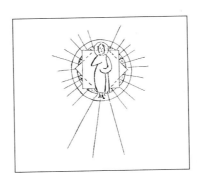

Ayios Sozomenos, Galata

149

PANAYIA THEOTOKOS CHAPEL (now known as Arkhangelos), *Galata*.

Position: See directions for Panayia tis Podithou; it is near the lane, left of the track.

Dating: Beginning of 1514.

Description: A family chapel, it is a small, simple structure with decorated transverse beams at head height (watch out). Originally it had three doors and the south is now blocked. It is fully decorated. The icon screen is contemporary, and on either side of the holy doors is the de Coron coat of arms.

Decoration: By Symeon Axenti who had completed the painting of St. Sozomenos church in the village four months previously. The distribution of scenes is similar, the choice of saints on the lower walls slightly different: St. Peter and St. Paul are missing, but the hermit St. Sozomenos is included, standing next to the female saints on the south west. Either side of the donor painting on the north wall are scenes from the Life of the Virgin cycle: left, Ioachim's Prayer and Ioachim and Anna; right, the Virgin's Presentation in the Temple and the Dormition. A similar but more extended cycle is on the north wall of the village church.

Panayia Theotokos Chapel, Galata

In the N.T. cycle (south wall, east) Axenti has painted a particularly attractive Nativity: the Infant and the midwife both appear to be testing the bathwater in one corner while, in the other, Joseph is in earnest conversation with an old shepherd who is wearing an enormous sheepskin coat. The paintings in the apse are considered the best work, but the Church Fathers, although the same six as appear in St. Sozomenos, are not so finely drawn. The Virgin Orans is a slender and lovely young girl – c.f. Palekhori where the same iconography has been used.

The donor painting is over the north door and in good condition. It shows a Deesis with the Virgin and the Baptist either side of Christ Enthroned interceding for the donor, his wife and children, who kneel below. An inscription on the panel explains that the chapel was erected by Stephanos Zacharia and his wife Luisa, but that the painting was paid for by Polos Zacharia and his wife Madelena and their children. *Their painting was completed on the 17th January 1514 of Christ. Hand of Symeon Axenti.* Therefore, it must be the Polos family whose portraits are rendered here. This donor painting is particularly interesting: not only does it show the capability of a good artist to paint in two styles – formal Byzantine and straight from life – but it also casts light on aristocratic society in this remote district in the early 16th century.

Polos is soberly clad in a long dark-blue gown and matching hat with upswept brim; his hair is grey and he has a neat white beard. He is offering the chapel to his Lord, and a key dangles from one finger. Madelena kneels in prayer opposite holding a rosary. Her robes are richly trimmed, her very wide dark-blue sleeves with white fur and pearls, her red skirt with gold embroidery; her hair is half-concealed under a long silk veil, secured with more pearls. Behind her kneels the eldest daughter carrying an open Greek hymnal; she is also fashionably and expensively dressed. The Lusignan lion on their coat of arms reveals the fact that Madelena was French of Royal lineage. The Zacharias family she had married into was Venetian and long-established in Cyprus. Her rosary implies that she remained a Catholic; but from his conformity with the Byzantine ethos, Polos was Greek Orthodox, despite his Latin forbears; and the children likewise.

PANAYIA TIS PODITHOU, *Galata. A monastery church.*

Italo-Byzantine.
(One of nine churches on UNESCO'S World Heritage list.)

Position: Both this church and the chapel of Arkhangelos lie a quarter of a mile to the north of Galata on the east bank of the river Karyotis. From the centre of the village, cross the bridge and immediately turn left down a lane. After about 300 yards, you will see the roof of the church down a track to your left.

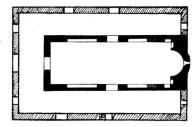

Panayia tis Podithou, Galata, ground plan

N.B. First obtain the key from the central coffee-shop.

Dating: Built and decorated 1502.

Description: This mountain church is larger than most and is covered by a steep-pitched wood and tile roof. The roof extends almost to ground-level in order to include the portico which encloses the church on three sides. To admit more light, four dormer windows were opened in the roof about thirty years ago: as well as being ineffective, they are totally out of character. On the external west wall over the door is an inscription recording the building of the church in 1502 by Dimitri de Coron and his wife Helen.

Something is known of his life, for forty years previously he was a military commander in the service of King James II. He was not a Cypriot knight but a Greek from the Peloponnese. In the donor painting above he is shown as an old man; his coat of arms, far right, is three stars on an azure field. Within the church, the gilded icon screen is a good example of contemporary Cypriot wood carving: it was repaired in 1783. At the centre of the cross-beam is the Venetian symbol, the lion of St. Mark, and at each end a Byzantine double-headed eagle.

Decoration: Only the Sanctuary, the east and west pediments and the external face of the west wall carry paintings: the church was never completely decorated. In the pediment above the donor painting is a large composition in praise of the Virgin, who is surrounded by O.T. prophets. (See also in Kourdali church and Ayiasmati, same period.) The subject is illustrated in the Painters' Guide, a late 14th century compilation. Over the west entrance into the church is the Anastasis, and either side of the door stand the Virgin and Christ.

Panayia tis Podithou – Galata

152

The bema: it contains the majority of the paintings. They are, perhaps, the most successful Italo-Byzantine blend to be found in Cyprus. Dominating the Sanctuary are the Virgin and Child in the conch of the apse. Strong Italian influence has produced their sweet, tranquil expressions and the distracting prettiness of the Archangels; in the throne can be seen an attempt to give depth to an otherwise two-dimensional painting. Yet the iconography is entirely Byzantine. *Unusual:* the Archangels bear ceremonial candles in elegant holders in their left hands. The striking figure of Gabriel in the Annunciation (apse wall, left) is more conventionally robed but has the robust, heavy-limbed look shared by the Apostles in the apse – another Italianate feature. In the Communion of the Apostles, every face is carefully distinguished and the significance of the moment is heightened by each look and posture. Both Judas and Paul are shown.

On the side walls, in place of the usual sanctuary O.T. scenes, are the story of Joachim and Anna, the Virgin's parents, in six panels. In the east pediment are two scenes that also appear in relatively similar positions in the Latin chapel at Lampadistis: Moses receiving the Ten Commandments, and Moses and the Burning Bush. A&J Stylianou make the interesting suggestion that the traditional name of the monastery, 'Podithou', could have derived from God's command to Moses to take off his sandals in front of the vision of the Virgin in the fire.

The nave: it has only one wall-painting – the Crucifixion in the west pediment. By Byzantine standards, it is an extraordinary scene, lacking all restraint and lasting spiritual meaning. From a humanist point of view, it is masterly in the portrayal of shock, distress and outrage. In both iconography and style, it is Italian. Now the central figure beneath the Cross is Mary Magdalene, her long hair unbraided over a bright pink cloak. Left, the Virgin is collapsing into the arms of her friends, St. John cringes on the right, and behind each is a host of soldiery. In one triangular corner, Christ's cloak is being fought over, and in the other an old monk leans on a stick and looks intently up at his Lord on the Cross: he is most likely the donor of the painting.

History:　When the Russian monk Barsky came to the monastery in 1735, only two desperately poor monks were living here. They told him how Turkish soldiers rode through periodically, stealing and despoiling all their produce. In the mid-thirties, Rupert Gunnis observed that the ruined monastic buildings were still standing. Now, only the church, chapel and some of the monks' olive trees remain.

PANAYIA THEOTOKOS, *Kakopetria*

Position:　North of the village on the boundary with Galata, diagonally across the road from the Rialto Hotel. The key is kept at the first house beyond the petrol station.

Dating:　1520 (by inscription).

Description:　An estate chapel, simply constructed of mud-bricks on a stone base and having the usual steep-pitched mountain roof of timber and tile. It has doors on the north and west sides. Notice the nematom or girdle composed of loosely twisted threads: it is often put round a church in times of illness as a protection from evil spirits. Inside, an interesting dedicatory panel over the north door is inscribed:

Supplication of the servant of God Leontios, lay-reader and chief clerk and of his wife Lucretia, founder and heir of the holy monastery of the most holy Mother of God, Amen. In the year 1520 of Christ.

The couple are portrayed kneeling before Christ with their small daughter Maria (in her best dress and a necklace of gold coins). Leontios has a deeply lined face and seems a lot older than his wife – and is she a Venetian lady married to a Cypriot? If Leontios is the heir, the unnamed man in front, with a grizzled beard, is possibly his father, installed here in his declining years.

An old-style templon divides the sanctuary from the nave: it consists of wooden panels and uprights painted with formal flower and leaf designs, and one misplaced panel showing a kneeling woman. The two icons were painted in 1638.

Decoration: On the north wall and in the sanctuary only, the rest having been lost. As usual in these small 16th century chapels, the paintings on the side wall are in two tiers. Here we see the final stages of the N.T. cycle in five scenes. Beneath is a row of six saints, among them the Cyprus-born John the Almoner and Rheginos, archbishop in the 5th century. On the jambs of the door, St. Zosimos gives the sacraments to St. Mary of Egypt. To the right is a large Dormition which includes three attendant bishops and an angel who is severing the hands of the impious Jew. In the bema (sanctuary), the Virgin Orans has Christ in a medallion on her chest, Blachernitissa style; and below the Communion of the Apostles are six Fathers of the Church, including the

Theotokos – Kakopetria, by Jeffery

Cypriots Spyridon and Epiphanios. To the right of the apse is yet another Cypriot bishop – Tykhon of Amathus. On the walls are the Sacrifice of Isaac and the Entertainment of the Angels.

Style: A very competent artist with ability to paint from life, offering a good example of conservative post-Byzantine work on the island.

154

Look especially for:
The donor portraits
A fine St. Zosimos, left door-jamb
The Entertainment of the Angels – note the cow bellowing for its calf
The Dormition – note the Apostles arriving in clouds above the Gothic buildings

AYIOS NIKOLAOS TIS STEGIS, *St. Nicholas of the Roof*

On its walls, 600 years of Byzantine art.
One of the nine churches on UNESCO's World Heritage List.

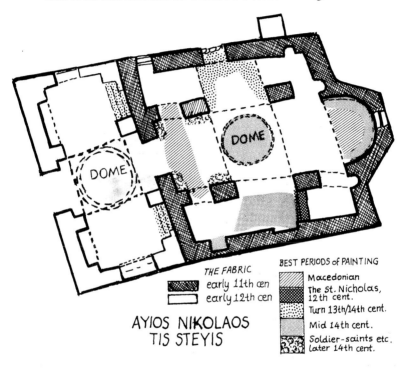

THE FABRIC
▨ early 11th cen
☐ early 12th cen

AYIOS NIKOLAOS
TIS STEYIS

BEST PERIODS of PAINTING
▨ Macedonian
▦ The St. Nicholas, 12th cent.
▦ Turn 13th/14th cent.
▦ Mid 14th cent.
▨ Soldier-saints etc. later 14th cent.

Position: About 2½ miles north west of Kakopetria beside the river Klarios. It is off the old Troodos road. Go through the village and turn right at the sign. (The road deteriorates but is well signposted.)

Dating: Built and painted early 11th century. Narthex added early 12th. Further painting early 12th, turn 13th/14th, mid and later 14th and in 1633.

Description: The building is an inscribed cross-in-square with four pillars supporting a central dome; it is asymmetrical. The narthex consists of a north and south bay and a central dome. The construction is of roughly-cut stone with rubble stone walls built up to carry the steeply-tiled roof – which protects the original roof of the church.

History:	This was a monastery church founded in time of peace and prosperity: the Arabs had been quelled and the Turks were not yet a threat. Although the monastery was occupied until the mid-19th century, no other of its buildings has survived; nor have any records. The monks owned and cultivated considerable land in the district, including the famous mill by the stream in Kakopetria. Marauding bands of Turks were probably responsible for the closure of the monastery.
Decoration:	**In the main church**

Plan. Despite a confusion of saints, martyrs and medallions and a variety of styles, it can be followed. The risen Christ, the Pantocrator, presides over all high in the dome encircled by angels and prophets; the evangelists are writing their gospels in the squinches below; and then the whole story spreads out over the vaults, beginning with the Birth of Christ in the south-east, continuing round the west end, up the north side and ending in the Sanctuary vaults with Christ's Ascension.

Ayios Nikolaos tis Steyis – Kakopetria

Periods of painting.

I. Early 11th c. (Apse and west vaults). Macedonian and rare.

This work was done by a master, and each scene is presented in a deceptively simple manner but with great effect. (*The illiterate must read on the walls of the churches that which they cannot read in books,* wrote Gregory the Great. And few people could read in those days.) Especially remarkable is the double scene of the Transfiguration and the Raising of Lazarus: note the threefold symbolism and the air of miracle and destiny that is conveyed. In the conch of the apse, the Mother of God is the Queen of Heaven and the two Archangels are guards carrying spears, an imperialistic rather than a spiritual concept. (The 14th c. frescoes that covered this, the Ascension and Pentecost until recently are now in the Byzantine Museum in Nicosia).

156

II. Early 12th c. (south-west corner and narthex). Same period as Asinou but not in the same class. Most successful is The Forty Martyrs. (See page 278 for history.)

But study the 12th c. masterpiece, the St. Nicholas, on the blocked-up door of the diakonikon, south of the icon screen, a contribution by a visiting master probably.

III. Late 13th/early 14th c. (north-west vault). Characterised by pale faces and gentleness. Note especially the poignant Crucifixion, its economy and balance and its controlled, elongated figures.

IV. Mid 14th c. (Sanctuary, dome and south vault). To this period belong all the bright, rosy-cheeked, somewhat rustic scenes, including a particularly engaging Nativity. *Unusual:* the Babe at the breast is a Coptic, not a Byzantine, feature cp. the young Harpocrates.

V. 14th c. second half. (On piers and beside door at west end.) Saints and over-life-size military saints George and Theodore, also Onoufrios and John the Almoner.

VI. 1633 (East piers) St. Peter and St. Paul. The inscription of the donor monk below St. Peter records the only definite date in the entire church. By Peter's left foot, the travelling Russian monk Barsky has placed his neat cartouche.

Decoration of the Narthex

In the north vault and above the entrance to the main church are remnants of a rather rigid Last Judgement, early 12th century. In the north-east and south-east recesses are the Archangels and assorted saints, done by the same hand that rendered the Crucifixion (turn 13th/14th c.). The paintings were paid for by the husband and wife seen kneeling in the north-east recess. The inscription dedicates a workshop to the monastery along with the curse of St. Nicholas and those of the 318 Church Fathers upon any who interfere with it!

CHURCH OF THE DORMITION OF THE VIRGIN, *Kourdhali.*

Italo-Byzantine. Former Monastery.

Position: South-east of Kakopetria in the Troodos area. Take the main road out of Kakopetria towards the Karvounas cross-roads. After 2½ miles, turn right onto a small side-road marked 'Spilia', which is a village two miles on. Drive through and shortly reach the hamlet of Kourdhali. Ask for key at house before church.

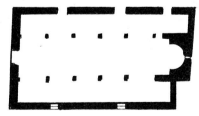

Ground plan of the Church of the Dormition

Dating: Church and decoration early 16th century.

Description: A rectangular building with a generous tiled roof, steep-pitched, mountain-style. North-west is a small humped bridge built of tiles and thought to be as old as the church. (It reminded Gunnis of the Chinese bridge on a willow-pattern plate.) The holy spring in the forecourt is used for the Blessing of the Waters and Whitsun ceremonies. Inside, the nave of the church is divided into three aisles by painted wooden arcades. Both these and the roof are replacements put up in 1969 by the Dept. of Antiquities, the originals having been destroyed in the renovation of 1921. Still here are the wooden pews, their delightful ends carved to resemble heraldic beasts. The Sanctuary is unusual in that the side-chapels (parabema) are separated from it by a pair of solid walls. Damp is a problem here, especially at the west end, which may account for the loss of all the paintings on the south wall and of most on the north.

The Iconostasis is beautiful and further enhanced by its icons, which are mostly contemporary and examples of Italo-Byzantine art at its best. The Enthroned Christ, right of the royal doors, has been repainted, and St. Mamas and his lion is a later work. Notice that Sts. Anna and Ioachim have special places of honour as parents of the Virgin, either side of the twelve Feasts of the Church, middle row. The Great Deesis above is particularly fine.

Decoration: In the Sanctuary and north chamber and on the west wall.

The donor portraits are right of the west entrance below the Dormition – appropriately, as this is the church's dedication. Two couples kneel either side of a model of the church, but a band of plaster has fallen away, taking with it most of the heads. An inscription behind the left hand pair begins, *Supplication of the servant of God, deacon Kourdhalis and of his wife and children, founders of this monastery.* The deacon is an old man dressed in vestments, the cuffs of his tunic showing, trimmed with lace. He alone is proffering the model, which looks different in that the domed apse stands clear of the roof. Opposite him is Leon the priest, a much younger man; his mauve tunic has a pair of crosses embroidered on it and the cuffs are also lace-trimmed. The wives are identically dressed in dark blue gowns laced at the bodice, silk aprons and silk veils. On the left of the entrance are St. Mamas, without the lion, strangely paired with St. Paul (who seems to be tonsured).

Across the west wall, above door height, are ten small scenes, all that remain of the N.T. cycle. Six of them have post-Crucifixion subjects, including both the Western and Byzantine versions of the Resurrection. Of interest in the Empty Tomb scene is the un-Byzantine look of the women with their unbound hair and long thin Italian noses. The last four panels are scenes from Christ's ministry: they appeared at the Church of St. Mamas, Louvaras, in the same iconography a few years previously.

Inevitably, the **the Crucifixion** in the pediment shows the greatest Western influence: a useless St. John has his back to the Cross, the Virgin is in disarray and the middle ground is crowded with foot-soldiers and prancing horses. As a dramatic event, it is successful _ a well-presented three-dimensional scene, dominated by the Cross – but the spiritual content has disappeared. More traditional is **the Dormition:** note the eloquent face of Christ and the rather disastrous profile of St. Paul at the foot of the bier. **The Ascension** and **Pentecost** have been placed on the west walls of the south and north aisles; below them are the Virgin and Child Enthroned surrounded by Prophets, and a Tree of Jesse respectively. The surviving painting on the north wall is of St. George (by the icon screen).

Much of the best work is at the east end: in the splendid figure of St. Barnabas, for example, who is wearing the robes of an Apostle and over them a bishop's omophorion; and in the six officiating Fathers of the Church, all wearing the polystavrion yet all strongly differentiated. The Communion of the Apostles has been omitted.

The Virgin Orans in the conch is attended by Archangels be-jewelled and pearled like heavenly Byzantine courtiers. Notice that the Annunciation occupies the pediment above. Over the niche in the prothesis is an interesting example of The Sacrifice, wherein the Christchild is in both chalice and paten, with a third face gazing down from the aer above. (Unique to Cyprus in this form, see also at Ayia Solomoni, Paphos, Ayiasmati, Platanistasa and Metamorphasis tou Soteros at Palekhori.)

Style: This is an artist of considerable talent, but his Italo-Byzantine style is inconsistent and not totally assimilated.

History: The hamlet has clearly taken its name from the founder of the monastery who is said locally to have come from Kurdestan. This may be more than speculation, for the church possesses several early 15th century manuscripts; and bound up in one are several leaves written in Arabic.

MARATHASA REGION

THE MONASTERY OF THE VIRGIN OF TRIKOUKKIA (THEOTOKOS)

Derivation: lit. three seeds but may refer to the giant oak trees of the region called Kokkous cp. Kykko.

Position: One mile south of Prodhromos down the old Platres road, 4,400' above sea level and two miles above Troodhitissa.

Dating: Foundation unknown; in existence 13th century; rebuilt 1761.

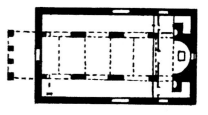

Trikoukkia Monastery Church, ground plan

Description: A three-aisled church under a steep mountain-type roof and with a tiled portico on the west; now surrounded by a fruit-growing research station. Look specially for the beautifully carved window shutters. Behind the parabema are two identical L-shaped cells, functions unknown. The church has a much-venerated early 17th century icon of the Virgin which is resorted to in times of drought. Jeffery states: *It seems to have been the original rain-compelling icon of the Theotokos afterwards associated with the monastery of Kykko.* The monk Barsky, who saw the place in 1735, some years before it was completely rebuilt, described it as poor, old and falling to pieces due to heavy taxation by the Turks. It was quite large then. The monastery was disbanded in the 19th c.

Trikoukkia Monastery Church

Tradition: That the church was built by St. Luke – which makes it even more probable that this was the first repository of the Holy Icon of Kykko.

MONASTERY OF TROODHITISSA PANAYIA

Position: Halfway between Platres (3½ miles) and Prodhromos (3 miles) on the old, twisting Troodos road. At 4,675' above sea level, situated higher than any other monastery in Cyprus.

Dating: Founded in 1250; present church built 1731; monastic buildings mainly 19th c.

Description: The monastery stands immediately below the main road, sheltered by the escarpment. Its buildings are unremarkable, and the visitor should go straight through the central gateway to the church at the further end of the quadrangle. Extensive renovations were carried out in 1967-68, including replacing the church's corrugated iron roof with one of locally-made tiles. Under them is a typical, fairly large, three-aisled building with an open timber roof.

On the iconostasis is the monastery's chief treasure, the holy icon of the Troodhitissa Virgin. Since 1799, it has been covered with silver-gilt repoussé work; but a copy shows the Virgin crowned, with the Child sitting upright on her right arm, both dressed in richly-patterned cloth – her mantle especially betraying considerable oriental influence. Above hangs a belt – the ayia zoni – with silver buckles, which has the reputation of curing barrenness in women once they've put it on! (As at Kykko, this icon is the first object brought to safety in a forest fire.) Also to be seen are several well-painted, though Latinised, icons of the 16th century.

Outside, a path in the grounds leads to the sacred cave wherein the icon lay hidden after iconoclasm. A short distance further down are the ruins of the smaller monastery of Ayii Anargyri of the 15th century – thought to be haunted!

160

Troodhitissa Monastery

**History &
Tradition:** The tradition is that, in the 8th century, an unnamed monk smuggled the Holy Icon out of Asia Minor to save it from destruction by the Iconoclasts, Cyprus being a more tolerant place. For twenty-five years, the icon remained at the Monastery of the Cats, near Limassol. Then the same monk brought it up to the safety of the high mountains – this was in the days of the Arab coastal raids – and he and a fellow monk passed the rest of their lives as hermits in the sacred cave. The icon was discovered there in 990. This monastery was founded in 1250 and built purposely to house the icon – so there is a gap of 250 years if the tradition be true.

Some facts: it has been burnt down twice; Barsky, here in 1735, called it a paradise; and during the Turkish massacres of 1821, Troodhitissa became the refuge of numbers of high-ranking clergy, having been granted protection on orders from Istanbul.

Legend: (In the old days, a son, born through the agency of the girdle, was promised to the monastery; now, an alternative suitable gift is accepted in lieu.)

There are several variations of the following story. Once, a woman came up from Paphos and tried to snatch her child back. They were pursued and a large stone thrown after them which would have killed the boy had not the Holy Icon moved and caught the stone. Part of it is still wedged in the back of the icon.

Troodhitissa is a popular place for Cypriot family excursions in summer, and the annual fair which takes place on August 15th causes traffic problems on the narrow roads because the concourse is so great.

161

PANAYIA CHURCH, *Kaminaria*

Position: Remote. Six miles south-west of Prodhromos, but best approached from Phini by way of Ayios Dhimitrios and Lemithou – a tortuous route but tarmacked: driving time about forty minutes. Key with village priest (ask at first coffee-shop).

Dating: First quarter of 16th century.

Description: A tiny chapel, restored in mid-70's by the Department of Antiquities; some damage to the paintings through loss of plaster. It stands on a track overlooking the village.

Decoration: Lack of space precluded a festival cycle, and the single row of paintings in the nave is limited to saints, a donor panel and the Crucifixion in the west pediment. St. George and St. Demetrios, splendidly accoutred, pace across the north wall on noble mounts – note St. George's small passenger, wearing an embroidered turban. Behind them comes St. Mamas on the west wall, his shepherd's crook borne like a spear; he is riding a majestic lion with a human face. Only in the Crucifixion does some untraditional iconography appear in that the Virgin here crouches on the ground, her two friends standing behind – a Western touch.

The **bema** manages to contain the Sacrifice of Isaac, saints and deacons and, in the apse (all of 6' high), an abbreviated Virgin Blachernitissa between Archangels above the officiating Fathers of the Church. All the Fathers wear the polystavrion. Observe that three out of the six are Cypriots and two more Cypriots stand one each side of the apse – St. John the Almoner and St. John Lampadistis.

The **donor painting,** east end of the north wall, portrays a lady and her three sons kneeling in attitudes of prayer in a hilly landscape. She is fashionably dressed in a blue and red brocaded gown, long silk veil and apron. Her sons have thick, almost shoulder-length hair under wide, low-crowned hats with upturned brims ornamented with buttons: they appear to be almost identical in apparel, although only the first son survives to any degree; and he wears a blue robe with a scarlet collar and has a purse at his waist. Under the few remaining letters of the inscription are cabalistic signs, formerly more extensive.

Style: The painter was an artist skilled in the traditional Byzantine style and with a miniaturist's concern for detail and ornament: vide the horse-trappings, the armour and cloaks of the soldier-saints, the hair of St. Eleutherios (in the bema) and the heads of the Church Fathers. His use of a light background for the donors sets them apart from the religious panels they have sponsored.

KYKKO MONASTERY

The name Kykko is a corruption of *'Kokkous'*, meaning the acorn of a huge local oak (quercus coccifera) which once covered this area but is now scarce.

Full title: **The Holy Royal Stavropegiac Monastery of Kykko, Founded with a Cross.**

Position: Twelve miles west of Pedhoulas, following a ridge of the Troodos range; tarmacked road. The route from Paphos via Pano Panayia and the ensuing fifteen miles of earth-road to the monastery should be ventured on with caution.

162

Dating: Founded end 11th century. Destroyed by fire in 1365,1541,1751 and 1813.

Description: The monastery is famous throughout the Orthodox world, and the Abbot of Kykko is of equal rank with the bishops. It lies on the western edge of the Troodos mountains, overlooking the vast Paphos Forest, and is 3,800' above sea level. It is composed of a jumble of buildings put up in the 18th, 19th and 20th centuries; and the lay-out is erratic because the site is almost triangular. Nevertheless, central to it are two quadrangles with the church at the far end. One building remains from earlier days: it goes back to 1592 and stands opposite the main entrance to the church. The new and large guest-block reflects the monastery's reputation for hospitality.

The Church: rebuilt 1754; part of the apse is from the earlier period (1592); bell-tower added after 1882.

It is a small, domed church of three aisles, each of which has a separate dedication, namely: the central to the Panayia, the north to the Archangels and the south to All Saints. Over the south entrance is a marble panel with a Byzantine cross and two birds carved in relief: Gunnis thinks it may be a relic from the original 11th century church.

The iconostasis was completed in 1755 together with much of the other wood-carving – although the northern screen is later, being renewed after the fire of 1813. Note the row of ostrich eggs, symbols of resurrection. To western eyes, the interior of Kykko's church is suffocatingly over-decorated. No surface is left unadorned and the air itself is invaded by a line of glittering Russian chandeliers; (the latest and biggest, though, is Greek and a gift from an earlier abbot). The large frescoes in the vaults – one to each section – conform strictly to the Byzantine ethos but lack spiritual force entirely, being almost schematic.

The Icons

The renowned holy icon of the Virgin of Kykko stands in a shrine in front of the iconostasis. The painting is attributed to St. Luke and is one of only three recognised by the Orthodox Church. If, as is claimed, the work is in encaustic (colours mixed with melted wax and mastic) it is indeed very old. The icon has been completely encased in silver gilt since the 16th century, the present cover being made in 1795: it has a representation of the painting stamped upon it. This shows it to be the Virgin of Mercy or Eleousa, and later Byzantine paintings of the type are called 'Kykkiotissa'. Examples can be seen in the Byzantine Museum, Nicosia.

To the right of the icon hang two relics: a bronze arm and a swordfish's saw. The first is said to belong to an infidel negro whose arm withered when he profaned the icon; the second was the gift of a sailor in 1718 who, when his ship was pierced by the great fish, prayed to the Virgin of Kykko and was saved.

The holy icon was always the first object brought out when fire threatened the Monastery. In 1821, the Turks looted the place but they did not find the Icon. It is considered to be the most powerful agent for making rain to fall; and in times of severe drought the Virgin of Kykko is taken in procession and placed on a stand at Throni amid a great concourse of people. She has also been carried thus all round the island. It is the most sacred icon in Cyprus.

Among other icons, the earliest is a Crucifixion of 1520, the rigid figures contrasting markedly with the excellent portrait of the kneeling donor priest. John Kornaros, the famous Cretan master, was in Cyprus at the end of the 18th century, painting some rather westernised icons, several examples of which can be seen here, including a Virgin and Child in silver frame, left of the bishop's throne, dated 1801, and St. Luke painting his Virgin Eleousa, left of the original.

The Belfry (post 1882) contains six bells. The largest weighs a ton, but the second largest is the one in daily use, hung at a lower level. The other five sound only on Sundays and holy days and are rung by one man, using one foot for the great bell and both hands for the other four.

The Museum, in a room in the inner courtyard, has a display of Gospels, crosses, chalices, vestments etc.

Throni tis Panayia. Just under two miles up the road to the south-west and on the highest peak, it commands a wonderful view over the seemingly unending Paphos Forest. Throni has become a place of pilgrimage to the grave of Archbishop Makarios III, who was a novice at Kykko and chose to be buried here.

History: **Foundation.** In 1092, in the time of Alexios I Comnenos, a detachment of the Imperial Army was landed in Cyprus to deal with a corrupt Governor, the general in charge, one Manuel Butumites, apparently taking over as governor himself for a time. When a hermit from the Troodos area called Esaias cured him of sciatica, Butumites sent him to Constantinople to treat the Emperor's daughter, who had the same painful complaint. She too was cured, and the grateful Emperor gave Esaias this very special icon from the Palace as a reward; furthermore, he sent over an abbot and funds for building and endowing the monastery to keep it in. The Royal foundation was

164

confirmed by an Imperial charter, but the document was burnt in the fire of 1365.

The first monastery was made of wood and was totally destroyed in that same fire. The rebuilding was paid for by Queen Eleanor, wife of Peter I. It was in her dhomaine, but the gesture reveals a surprising concern for an Orthodox monastery by the Latin overlords at that date. Again, wood was the chief material; and in 1541 the entire place was burnt to the ground once more. It was the new third structure that the Russian monk Barsky described in 1727. He found the monastery *perfect from every point of view* and praised Abbot Sofronios and the monks highly for their devotion and their hospitality (which he enjoyed to the full).

Over the centuries, Kykko acquired considerable property both in Cyprus and abroad, and had close connections with the Russian Church. Many pilgrims came, especially from Russia, and bestowed valuable gifts. Kykko grew rich and powerful above all other monasteries in the island. After the rise of the USSR, the Russian link was broken, other interests were disposed of, and now Kykko's revenue comes wholly from within Cyprus. Much of this money is poured out again in religious, educational and charitable work.

> *The monastery, throughout its history, has been a place of refuge for the people of Cyprus whenever they were oppressed or threatened by an invader. The abbots and monks of the monastery, through their life, actions and prestige, offered much to the island. The history of the monastery is interwoven with that of Cyprus . . .*

Abbot Dionysios: A Brief History of Kykko Monastery, 1979.

CHURCH OF ARKHANGELOS MIKHAIL, *Pedhoulas*

One of the nine churches on UNESCO's World Heritage list

Position: At the head of the Marathasa Valley, 1½ miles above Moutoullas. At the village, leave the main road and negotiate narrow lanes to a large domed church below. The Archangel chapel is in a cul-de-sac further on. Key kept at nearby house.

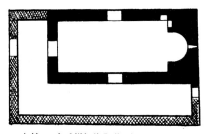

Arkhangelos Mikhail, Pedhoulas, ground plan

Dating: Built and decorated 1474. Roof renewed in 1969.

Description: A very small building under the usual sloping mountain roof. It has three doors, and a vestibule was added on the south and west later. The templon is contemporary, intact and an excellent example of its kind. Among the coats of arms painted on its cross-beam is the Lusignan coat of arms, centrally over the holy doors. This indicates that the chapel was within the boundary of a royal fiefdom; but observe that the double-headed eagle of the Byzantine emperors is also honoured further along the board.

Decoration: An inscription on the west wall reads: *All you who resort to this church, remember . . . and me the humble . . . painter . . . from Myrianthousa.* His name has gone but, as the last word refers to the Marathasa Valley, we know he was a local man. (Transl. and information A&J Stylianou.)

165

Arkangelos Mikhail Church, Pedhoulas

The chapel is completely decorated on two levels: eleven compositions from the Festival Cycle above, saints below, with the Crucifixion and the Ascension in the pediments. In the bema, St. Athanasios replaces the usual scene on the south wall of Abraham Entertaining the Angels, and a boldly-executed Virgin Blachernitissa presides in the conch of the apse[1]. Outside the south door stand Christ and the Virgin & Child with the Archangel Michael in the niche above.

The Donor painting is inside, over the north door. The inscription on the lintel records that the church was built *at the expense and great labour of the most honourable priest Vasilios son of Hamados . . . and it was painted in AD 1474, 6983 from Adam*. Vasilios, an elderly anxious-looking man in vestments, is portrayed from above. Vasilios's wife and two daughters stand behind in a row in attitudes of prayer. They each wear a long cloak covering the head, but whereas the wife's is a heavy and sober affair, both the daughters' are much jollier, being of creamy linen with the traditional bright bands of embroidery that are still familiar today. The girls wear dresses of stunning elegance – no doubt made for the occasion – and scarlet slippers.

Style: An example of local post-Byzantine painting fifteen years before Venetian rule. There is no Italian influence; the iconography is strictly Byzantine and conservative. The painted architecture and furnishings show reverse perspective (see Dormition) or on occasion float (Annunciation). Although the figures lack subtlety, are flat with unfocussed gaze and with faces that

---

1. A&J Stylianou point out that the same model was used twenty years later by tou Goul at Ayiasmati church.

166

bear a marked resemblance to each other, the overall effect is one of unity and charm.

Do not miss the splendid Archangel Michael left of the templon (his cross-gartering, his headband, his cloak); or Constantine and Helen and St. Barbara in the north-west corner being among the painter's best work.

Other points of interest:

1. The old, simple symbols denoting mountains have disintegrated into complete chaos (see Nativity, Entry into Jerusalem, Baptism).
2. The Lamentation, north wall, includes features of the Deposition and the Entombment, giving us three scenes in one – good where space is limited.
3. The Betrayal, west wall, has a formality like an ancient Greek tragedy in mediaeval terms.

PANAYIA TOU MOUTOULLA, *Moutoullas*

One of the nine churches on UNESCO's World Heritage List.

Panayia tou Moutoulla Plan

Position: In the Marathasa valley, a mile south of Kalopanayiotis. Look out for narrow paved road on right after bend. It ends in a parking area and thence it is only a short walk up to the chapel. The key is kept at the last house.

Dating: Built and decorated 1280 with 15th century additions.

Description: Earliest dated example of a church having a protective wooden roof; it is steeply pitched with hooked flat titles: note the well-carved doors. The north-west extension is a later addition. Within, the sanctuary is screened by a templon on which is displayed an icon of the Virgin & Child dated 1659 and which is protected by an elaborate frame of musharaby work.

Inscription: Three to note: one above the donor painting recording the foundation of the church by John of Moutoullas and his wife Irene in 1280; one on St. George calling him *the Cappadocian;* and another on the St. Christopher painting, *supplication of Christopher the Councillor and his wife.*

Decoration: The Sanctuary or Bema has all its original painting: the Virgin Blachernitissa flanked by Archangels; and below the Church Fathers converging in Liturgical procession. On the north wall is a large, pale portrait of the donors who are holding a model of the church between them.

In the nave, Christ and the Virgin are on the piers facing the worshippers: together with John the Baptist (north wall) they form a Deesis – most powerful vehicle of prayer. The decoration here is damaged and several scenes have been lost; but the cycle can be seen to follow the accepted sequence, starting with the Annunciation on either side of the apse wall and continuing on the south with the Nativity and the Presentation in the Temple (this last is 15th century work). The Raising of Lazarus, Entry into Jerusalem and the Crucifixion occupy their customary positions west, and the cycle ends with the Harrowing of Hell and the Dormition on the north side.

The lower register has the usual line-up of saints – with women well represented – and includes George slaying an anthropomorphic dragon (female and crowned) and, opposite, a mounted St. Christopher. On the outside wall are further 15th century paintings: the Last Judgement and Christ and another St. George.

Style: These paintings have an oriental slant with stiff, flat and linear figures and all embellishment omitted: the artist's workbook could have been a 13th century copy of a much earlier Cappadocian manuscript. The colours are vivid, each scene and saint having a scarlet and blue-green ground, except for Christ and the Virgin, who have blue. The figures are somewhat dwarf-like, having large heads and squat bodies, the faces without expression and eyes unfocussed. Yet, seen against the richly-coloured grounds, the overall effect is one of unusual charm.

Look especially for:

The donor picture.
The Annunciation: a snake-headed fountain.
St. George's Dragon: human and female above the waist and all serpent below; she wears a crown.
The Crucifixion: Cappadocian derivation most clearly seen here despite Crusader-style Centurion.
The Nativity: Joseph sits on a wooden donkey saddle, the kind still in use today.
The Last Judgement: note the triple aura of Christ, the murderer tied to a board and attacked by demons, the striped tent in which is 'the person who sleeps on Sundays'.

AYIOS IOANNIS LAMPADISTIS MONASTERY

One of the nine churches on UNESCO's World Heritage list.

Position: In the large village of Kalopanayiotis in the Marathasa valley. The priest's house (for key) is on the north side of the village, the monastery below and across the stream to the east. Continue on high road to village centre for narrow road down. Refreshments available.

The Monastery consists of a complex of three churches which share a single enormous pitched roof: Ayios Herakleidios, Ioannis Lampadistis and a Latin Chapel. The cells and workrooms range round a courtyard on the south. Outside, a steep path winds down to the stream and the traditional spot where Barnabas and Saul baptised Herakleidios (who later became the first bishop in Cyprus).

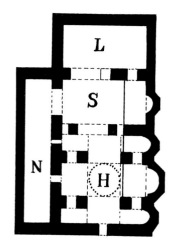

L = Latin Chapel
S = St. John Lampadistis
H = St. Heracleidios
N = Narthex

Ayios Ioannis Lampadistis Monastery
Ground plan

A. THE CHURCH OF AYIOS HERAKLEIDIOS

Dating: Built 11th c., decorated first half 13th c. and again ca. 1400.

Description: An inscribed cross-in-square building with four piers supporting a central dome, cp. Ayios Nikolaos tis Steyis. Alterations in the 18th century blocked the original entrances, a new doorway being cut on the south side and a broad arched opening made through the north wall, destroying the wall-paintings. **The Templon** is of more than usual interest and is probably 13th century work. It is covered with heraldic-looking beasts, including the Lusignan lion and the Byzantine eagle; also the arms of various Latin knights. The icons beside the royal doors are Herakleidios with donor, on the right, inscribed *Supplication of the servant of God George the priest and of his wife and children, Amen. November 24th 1543 from Christ,* and on the left, Archangel Michael, late 15th c.

Decoration: The two periods are quite distinct: the earlier has a few large, rather exotic scenes in rich colours, whereas the later covers every other available space in a multiplicity of small bright scenes and in a naive, rustic manner. On the lower register is an unconventional mingling of saints, prelates and prophets, put wherever space allowed.

Earliest work: only visible in the apse on a stretch of patterned 11th c. plaster, where a pair of praying monks of the 12th century have been uncovered.

13th century (first half). These paintings cover the dome, the south vault (Ascension) and the central vaults and lunette at the west end. The bright colours are faded and patchy now, the best preserved being the Entry into Jerusalem.

Note especially: the Ascension, for its use of space and colour; the Entry, the eastern appearance of the citizens at the gate and the black gloves of the youths cutting palm; the Sacrifice of Isaac, normally found in the Sanctuary as prefiguring the Crucifixion.

Below on the west piers almost all the saints are 13th century depictions, also Christ and the Virgin on the east. Notice particularly the female saints Marina(?), Paraskevi and a resplendent Kyriaki, with the days of the week in medallions down her front.

Style: Characteristics of the late 12th/early 13th century manner appear here in the strong warm reds and ochres, rosy cheeks and rather staring eyes, stiff postures and pervading eastern influence. The abrupt severing of all Byzantine links in 1191 made for increasing conservatism in art. Here the painter is drawing on the previous Late Comnenian age. We are witnessing an art in transition, a time when the style might be becoming rigid and derivative but has not yet hardened – and the spirit that informed the old masters is still alive.

Circa 1400. The later period of decoration encompasses a complete N.T. cycle in blocks of small scenes. It starts over the altar with the Annunciation, continues in the south-west compartment, crosses over to the north vault and ends in the north-west compartment. The emphasis is on the Passion. The lower register includes a number of obscure religious figures among the more familiar saints. (The Dormition and the Tree of Jesse were cut through in 1731.)

Look especially for:

The row of prelates in the bema for the style at its best – all are wearing the polystavrion.
The Entry into Jerusalem, left of the altar, for the lively ass.
Baalam and his talking ass, by the south door.
Via Crucis, north vault, for the Crusader influence.
The Denial of Peter, south west compartment.
St. Herakleidios and St. Mamas (minus lion), north west compartment.

Style: There is little variation in faces and gestures and the figures no longer integrate with their backgrounds but stand in front as if on a stage. The iconography is tenaciously Byzantine, the style is folk-art. Most successful are the individual saints on the lower walls.

THE NARTHEX

Built mid-15th c., it is an extended annexe and serves both churches. At some time, the vault collapsed together with its decoration, and it was replaced by a wooden roof. The remaining paintings extend over three walls and contain quotations from the Gospel, often lengthy. In a damaged inscription on the south wall, the painter claims to have come from Constantinople, although his work is decidedly provincial. A second inscription nearby, at the end of the east wall, accompanies the donor portraits and refers to Michael, lay-preacher and choirmaster 'of this Catholic church', his wife and children, *the weekly priests.* Michael is wearing a white coife, his wife has a long cloak-veil and both their sons are dressed in Orthodox vestments. The sons are tonsured like Latin monks. The theme of the paintings is Christ's healing, miracles and appearances, reassuring for the sick who waited here. On the far right is a large Last Judgement. An exquisitely painted epistyle is displayed on the west west wall, brought here from nearby Panayia Theoskepastos Church. It contains twenty-three miniature illustrations of the Feasts of the Church in their order of celebration through the year: it is the best thing in the narthex. (14th/15th century).

Ayios Ioannis Lampadistis

B. CHURCH OF ST. JOHN LAMPADISTIS, *the church in the middle*

Lampadistis was an obscure 11th c. monk who died young, and by the 12th century his grave had been forgotten. Then an epileptic touched it by chance and was miraculously cured. Others came to be healed, a church was built, and gradually the young monk's fame spread far and wide, eclipsing St. Herakleidios.

The present church was probably built in 1731, which was when the archway was cut through the north wall of the older building. Preserved from the 12th century is the north-east pier and narrow arch, where stands the saint's tomb. A niche in front contains his skull in a reliquiary; and, above, the plaster is crowded with the signatures of 18th century pilgrims from overseas, including Barsky's comment enclosed in a cartouche. The icon of Lampadistis on the icon screen was probably painted in 1543.

C. THE LATIN CHAPEL

No records exist regarding its history. It contains the most complete series of Italo-Byzantine paintings in Cyprus; other examples are to be found at the Church of the Dormition, Kourdali and at Panayia Podithou, Galata. This artist could paint in either tradition, but the style is not so well assimilated as at Podithou: the Virgin and Child Enthroned in the apse has the most successful blend, whereas the Old Testament scenes above are straight from Florence.

The vaulting is Italianate too, painted imitation ribbing dividing it into sections in which are busts of the twelve Apostles in quatrefoil frames and, along the central 'rib', twelve saints in medallions. Covering the walls north

171

and south are illustrations of the twenty-four stanzas of the Akathistos Hymn to the Virgin, one for every letter of the Greek alphabet. It has been attributed to the Patriarch of Constantinople in thanksgiving for Our Lady having saved the city from the Slavs and Avars in 626. In these scenes, the Italian influence varies according to the subject – generally, the more traditional are completely Byzantine both in iconography and style. (See the Monastery church of St. Neophytos for another, slightly later, example.)

A Tree of Jesse takes up the west wall, under it an original door with fine carving. For the Byzantine mode, study the Nativity, stanza 7; for the Florentine, Abraham Entertaining the Angels on the east lunette; for excellence, the Magi, stanza 8; Note also the last stanza (north wall) where the Virgin and Child appear to reject the Orthodox in favour of the Latin prelates.

As A&J Stylianou conclude, this talented and versatile artist must have been painting in Italy for some time to achieve such landscapes and such refinement.

KALOPANAYIOTIS

As well as the Monastery of St. John Lampadistis, several of the many small churches scattered through this large village are worth visiting. Suggested are:

a) Panayia Theoskepastos (The epistyle is now kept in the narthex at the monastery.) It lies a short walk east up the earth road behind Lampadistis, almost wholly concealed by an enormous tree – hence its name meaning 'concealed by God'. 14th/15th c.

b) Ayios Andronikos. Small, early 16th century chapel a little upstream on the east side of the village: it lies behind houses opposite the second fountain. The walls are rubble-built with infill of broken brick and it has a later narthex. The decoration has gone from the south wall, but the west and north still retain a complement of a dozen assorted saints. In the apse is the Virgin Orans between archangels. The Crucifixion on the west pediment, although incomplete, contains the Virgin on the lower left, fainting in simple dignity in the arms of her friends. Overall, the style is simplified, bold and linear, the faces look alike.
N.B. This church is known locally as Ayios Dhmitrianos, and there is still indignation over the original icon of that saint which, it is claimed, was stolen by the French early this century and is now in the Louvre.

c) Chapel of St. George. In the village. Contains an exceptionally fine icon of Christ Pantokrator with its donor, a tonsured priest, painted around 1500.

NICOSIA

History of Nicosia

Nicosia is a labyrinth of lanes and alleys, bounded by a ring of stone.
W. Hepworth-Dixon.

Ancient: Ledra or Lefkotheon; *Greek:* Lefkosia

NICOSIA

History

The archaic settlement of Ledra lies beneath the southern half of the modern city. The precise location is not known, but its northern and western boundaries are probably indicated by the original course of the river Pedheios (where Paphos Street and Hermes Street now run). Its alternative name, Lefkotheon, is thought to have been bestowed on the city by Lefkon, son of Ptolemy Soter, in 280 BC. This ultimately became 'Lefkosia', and by the 7th century seems to have superseded the more ancient Ledra. The third name, Nicosia, is subject to various theories; but it arrived late – probably with the Crusaders – and is mainly used by Western Europeans.

THE RIVER PEDHEIOS

'Pedheios' means simply the river of the plains. It rises near Makheras Monastery at the eastern edge of the Troodos mountains and flows across the central plain, through ancient Tamassos and through Nicosia and enters the sea near Salamis. When Cyprus was thickly forested, it must have been a true river: Homer writes of ships sailing to Temese with a cargo of iron. In historic times, it has always been a seasonal torrent, sometimes violently so, and a dry bed for the rest of the year.

An Italian visitor to Nicosia in December 1394 commented:[1] *Through its midst flows a brook which a man can cross on stones when it does not rain. When it is rainy weather, a great quantity of water runs down, and so there are several bridges over the stream, some of stone and some of wood, by which men cross during rain.* Until the Venetians diverted the river in 1567, it flowed through the centre of the city, from west to east: Paphos St. and Hermes St. and the three roads leading to the Garaffi bastion adjoining the Famagusta Gate follow its course almost exactly, even to the branching of the stream into three channels on its way out. In those days, the bed was a receptacle for the town waste, which soon (one hopes) shrivelled in the sun while awaiting the civic cleanser, the first torrent of the winter, to carry all away.

On occasion, the rush of water was terrifying, behaving like a bore, giving little warning, and leaving in its wake carcasses of men and animals, and wreckage. The worst flood recorded was on the night of November 10th 1330, when three thousand citizens were drowned. Every church opened its doors to the homeless and the Archbishop turned his palace into a hospice.

THE MIDDLE AGES

Early Christian period

The town was sufficiently important to be made the seat of a bishop. The most famous is St. Trifyllios who, as Bishop of Ledra, attended the Church Council of Sardica in 343 AD. He was both friend and pupil of St. Spyridon, then the bishop of Tremithousa, but today more famous as the patron saint of Corfu. Trifyllios is the likely author of a Life of Spyridon in verse, which was used as source-material for 7th century vitae. Evidence has been found for three basilicas in the area, one of which may well be the Paleo-Christian Cathedral – possibly sited near St. Sophia, where the Bedestan is now.

---

1. Martoni Ex. Cyp.

Mid-Byzantine period

In the mid-tenth century, after the Arab raids had ceased, Lefkosia was chosen to become the new centre of administration for the whole of Cyprus, and a governor with the title of Duke was appointed from Constantinople. Both the Government and the Archbishopric were transferred here from the former capital, Constantia (Salamis), which had silted up. Although the city had neither port nor navigable river, its inland position made it relatively safe from sudden attack, and it enjoyed a healthy climate. No records or plans exist of the Byzantine city. The Governor's castle is thought to have been somewhere in the triangle made by Omeriyeh Mosque, Ayios Antonios Church and the modern Archbishopric. In 1191 it became the stronghold of the Knights Templar during their short rule over the Island. They were excessively harsh masters and, because they were few in number – scarcely more than a hundred men and fourteen horses – on Easter Day 1192 the citizens of Lefkosia attempted their massacre. But the Knights barricaded themselves inside the castle and at dawn next day began a slaughter on a different scale, and blood ran in the streets. For a long time afterwards, a great stone was pointed out marking the point the flow had reached.

The Lusignan Period 1192-1489

Although Nicosia had suffered in the last decades of the 12th century from weak government and from piracy, in 1192 the Lusignans succeeded to a fair city, full of small fields, orchards and gardens. It had no walls then. An account by a distinguished pilgrim in 1211 reads: *This is the king's capital city, situated almost in the middle of the plain; it has no fortifications. A strong castle has just now been built in it. It has inhabitants without number, all very rich, whose houses in their interior adornment and paintings closely resemble the houses of Antioch. In this city is the seat of the archbishop. Also the court and palace of the king, where I first saw an ostrich.*[1] The city was quite obviously prosperous once more and the rich and luxurious life of the Franks in their feudal regime well and truly established.

From hence forward everything that enhanced Nicosia would be Latin, not Byzantine; and the way of life, the dress and the language were, and were to remain, French. High-ranking prelates took office, bringing their own architects and craftsmen with them to build the cathedral and churches in splendid Gothic; and younger sons of noble houses in France were sent over for knightly service. After the fall of Acre in 1291, the city's population was swollen by the addition of the dispossessed knights crossing over from Syria with their entire households. Monasteries and nunneries of most western orders were established, the most illustrious being the royal monastery of St. Dominic, which was founded in 1226. In its grounds rose a great abbey church and a new royal palace. The site, thought to be in the area of Paphos Gate, was cleared by the Venetians, who swept away at the same time all the kings and queens that lay buried there, at least sixteen illustrious prelates and many noble knights and their ladies.

The finest remaining monuments of the period are the Gothic buildings that went up in the 13th and 14th centuries: St. Sophia Cathedral and the Church of St. Catherine in particular – now both mosques in the occupied zone. Omeriyeh Mosque, formerly the Church of St. Mary of the Augustinians, is still accessible, but is rather shorn of its majesty having lost all its vaulting.

By the last quarter of the 14th century, the power of the Lusignans was weakening, its

---

1. von Oldenberg Ex. Cyp.

heyday past. After the sack of Nicosia by the Genoese in 1373, in the reign of King Peter II, Nicosia was walled for the first time. The perimeter was four miles and the area enclosed roughly the same as the old city of today, although more extended on the south, south-west and east. Much of the city remained outside the new walls. In 1382 they were reinforced, fortified and surrounded by a ditch. Half a century later, these defences failed to keep out the Mamelukes, no doubt because the men who should have commanded and manned them were dead in the field at Khirokitia. Once inside, the Egyptian soldiers broke into every building, killing, smashing and looting in the manner of victorious armies then: the royal palace was burnt to the ground but the abbey miraculously escaped; and thousands of prisoners were taken to Alexandria and sold into slavery. In 1427, a year after King Janus' ransom from captivity in Cairo, a third palace was ready for him near the present Kyrenia Gate. It was still standing in 1904.

Nevertheless as the 15th century progressed, the Frankish dominance became increasingly enfeebled. The Greek Orthodox Church was once again established in the capital, Gothic architecture and carving grew degenerate and derivative, and Nicosia filled with a mongrel crowd of adventurers of every nationality. Even in court circles, French was hardly heard, and Greek supplanted it as the spoken language. At the same time, behind the scenes, Venetian diplomats were doing some forward planning.

1472 saw James II, the last Frankish king, married to the Venetian Katerina Cornaro. Within two years, she was acknowledged Queen of Cyprus, both James and their infant son being dead. She surrounded herself with Venetian courtiers and diplomats in the Lusignan palace, and Cyprus became, in all but title, a dependency of the Republic.

THE VENETIAN PERIOD 1489-1570

In 1489, fearing the rise of the Ottoman Empire and therefore in need of a forward naval station, the Venetian Republic openly took control of the Island. The Queen was persuaded to abdicate and a Military Governor, a Providetore, was installed in the palace. The new rulers found a city already in decline, and their increasingly corrupt administration did nothing to prevent further decay. It soon became clear that they were interested in Cyprus only for its strategic position and for the revenue they got from it. The Cypriots, who resented both the Lusignans and the Venetians, began to emigrate in large numbers.

A severe earthquake in 1491 hit Nicosia badly, and a lot of rebuilding and repairs were needed. The west end and upper parts of St. Sophia Cathedral sustained massive damage but were superbly restored by Venetian masons, the art of the Renaissance blending with the French Gothic. One may still observe, here and there in the old city, particularly in the Omeriyeh quarter, decorated Venetian doorways, perhaps in situ, perhaps preserved in a younger building, perhaps even an 18th century imitation. Fresh heraldic insignia were added to those of the Lusignans, and everywhere, on banners and in stone, was that distinctive emblem of the Republic, the Lion of St. Mark.

Another severe earthquake shook Nicosia in 1547: yet nothing was done over the years to repair the city's fortifications. Therefore, when in 1563 an Ottoman attack seemed only a matter of time, and reports were called for on the condition of the walls, they were found to be, not only totally inadequate for the new cannon-fire, but half in ruins. Two years later, Guilo Savorgnano, the Republic's most distinguished engineer, submitted plans for new defences. The Senate approved them and he was dispatched to Nicosia forthwith to implement them. The plans involved: pulling down the Lusignan walls, constructing a circular wall of smaller circumference, diverting the Pedheios river from its course through the city and into an encircling moat and levelling every single building, mound and tree beyond; all to be accomplished in the shortest possible time. The levelling started in 1567. That was when St. Dominic was pulled down and when eighty more churches and monasteries disappeared. When the Turks did arrive in 1570, the walls were not quite completed, still wanting their stone facing in the upper parts, and the moat was a fosse and too shallow; but all else had been done.

The Turkish army landed at Larnaca on July 1st and the local Cypriots welcomed them and brought food. The Turks marched to Nicosia without meeting any opposition. After a siege of forty-five days, the city fell. The previous day, amid the terrible roar of battle and with the enemy thundering at the gates, the brave Bishop of Paphos – a Latin – preached the very last sermon to a packed congregation in St. Sophia Cathedral.

A week later, Mustafa Pasha, the Turkish General, gave thanks to Allah in St. Sophia for his victory: the great Gothic Cathedral had become a mosque. There had been three days of unrestrained butchery and desecration – the customary reward of the common soldiery, but particularly savage here. Subsequently, any Frank or Venetian who was still at liberty went in fear of discovery; and all Latin property remained in Turkish hands. A Turkish Governor took up residence in the Palace and his officers occupied the fine stone houses of the Venetians; the Gothic churches were converted into mosques, markets and storehouses. Greek Cypriots and their property were treated better, and a church was allowed for the Orthodox ritual. Nicosia began to take on an Eastern look once more: balconies were enclosed and their windows latticed to conceal the Moslem women behind them; minarets dominated the skyline and the voice of the muezzin sounded over the streets, calling the faithful to prayer.

Hall in a private house

An old private house,
steel engraving by R.V. Waldheim

177

Siege of Nicosia – old engraving

THE MONUMENTS

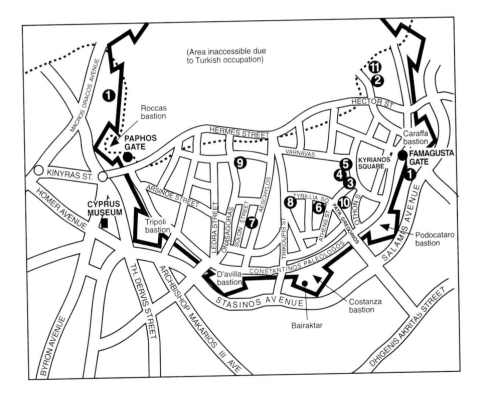

Note: * Indicates monuments of particular interest
        ** Indicates monuments of outstanding interest

179

THE MONUMENTS

THE VENETIAN WALLS

Old Nicosia is considered one of the best examples of a fortified city of the late 16th century, surpassed only by Palmanova in Italy (another, later, work by Savorgnano), and its walls are still virtually intact. The moat has been filled in to some extent, and several roads carry traffic across at new points. The walls are forty-foot high earth ramparts, eighteen feet thick. They have a circumference of two miles with eleven heart-shaped bastions at regular intervals, and the encircling moat is one hundred feet wide. The bastions are not all the same size, and each one is named after a Cypriot nobleman or a high-ranking Venetian official: Barbaro bastion on the north, for example, honours Francesco Barbaro who was the engineer who completed Savorgnano's design.

The Kyrenia Gate was formerly known as Porta del Proveditore or Gate of the Military Governor, and it led to the Palace. By-passed in 1931, it is now an island with a road on either side. A commemorative stone over the outer entrance records the Venetian foundation and on the reverse have been added verses from the Koran. The inner face of the gateway carries the monogram of Sultan Mahmoud II, put up after the restoration work of 1821.

The Paphos Gate was formerly known as Porta di San Domenico, being the nearest to that famous Monastery, which was sacrificed in the interests of defence. In 1879 a cut was made through the wall on its north and the gate closed: it has recently been re-opened for pedestrian use. Note the monogram of Sultan Mahmoud on the inner face. Now Turkish soldiers look down from the Rocca bastion beside the cut, which adjoins the Green Line. The stretch of battered buildings above the Gate was the HQ of the Cyprus Police until 1958.

Constanza Bastion with Bairaktar Mosque

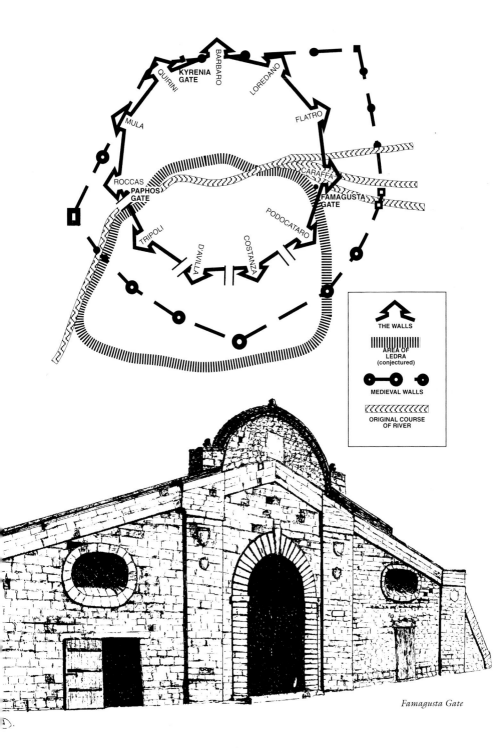

KYRENIA GATE

BARBARO

QUIRINI

LOREDANO

MULA

FLATRO

ROCCAS

CARAFFA

PAPHOS GATE

FAMAGUSTA GATE

TRIPOLI

PODOCATARO

D'AVILA

COSTANZA

THE WALLS

AREA OF LEDRA (conjectured)

MEDIEVAL WALLS

ORIGINAL COURSE OF RIVER

Famagusta Gate

The Famagusta Gate is the chief monument of the Venetian period remaining in Nicosia and was formerly known as Porta Guiliana after Savorgnano, the engineer who designed the walls. This gate, however, is a copy of the Lazaretto Gate constructed in 1565 in Candia, Crete, by another Venetian – Michele Sanmicheli. It was popularly called the Lower Gate. The wooden latticed doors are probably original. They lead into a barrel-vaulted passage, fifty yards long. Halfway down is a circular space under a dome reminiscent of a small Pantheon, open at the top to admit light. The halls either side of the passage were guardrooms. The whole structure is impressive. The Gate has only been restored and made accessible to the public in recent years and it is now used as a cultural centre, where exhibitions, lectures and performances are put on. Note the six coats of arms on the facade of the building, also the Sultan's monogram on an extraneous piece of stonework above the pediment. In the Municipal House on top of the wall the poor and aged folk of the city are cared for.

The Moat is a place of recreation now, and the various uses can be descried as one walks along the ramparts: in one place, tennis courts, in others a green and shady public garden, a cafe, or a games pitch.

THE CHURCH OF PANAYIA KHRYSALINIOTISSA:
Our Lady of the Golden Flax

It stands on the street of that name on the east side of the old city, and the dedication refers to the finding of a sacred icon in the field of flax which once was growing there. Queen Helen Palaeologina is said to have been the founder in 1450 of a Greek Monastery on the site, and this was its church. (It could also mark the position of the mid-tenth century cathedral, thought to have been in the vicinity, built when the archbishop transferred from Salamis together with the Government.)

The oldest Byzantine church remaining in Nicosia, Khrysaliniotissa kept its monastery walls into the present century. It has survived a number of rebuildings and repairs.

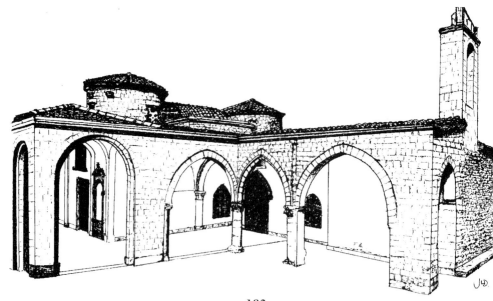

Gunnis considers that Venetian remodelling is responsible for the strangely elongated south transept – vide the marble plaque on the wall, bearing a coat of arms of the period. Further extensive alterations took place between 1735 and 1740. The icon screen is a patchwork of styles and periods. The church was a repository for a valuable collection of icons, now in the Byzantine Museum, some of which are thought to have been rescued at the time of the Turkish invasion from the Greek Orthodox Cathedral (now the Bedestan).

Khrysaliniotissa is also the name of the surrounding district. Being close to the Green Line, its mediaeval streets and alleys have a deserted look. Recently, the municipality has undertaken a programme of repair and rehabilitation, with the aim of bringing family life back to an area that modern developers have not harmed. Elegant 18th century houses, half-buried under years of patching and decay, are revealing their original lines: here the sweep of a staircase, there a colonnaded courtyard. Once this was a select neighbourhood, and echoes must still have lingered as late as 1882, when Lord Kitchener chose to take up residence near St. Kassianos Church while he was carrying out his survey of the Island.

THE BYZANTINE MUSEUM[1], *Archbishopric, Nicosia*

Icons from the 8th to the 18th century; a collection begun by Archbishop Makarios III more than twenty years ago to save icons from being snapped up at low prices by dealers and sold abroad. Now expanded into a valuable and comprehensive display in which the development and variety of style and subject can be appreciated.

Examples

12th century: Cyprus was full of high-powered officials from Constantinople. They brought over Court painters with consequent enormous advances in skills: see panels of Christ and of the Virgin from Laghoudera, first central stand.

13th century: Changes in painting reflected social and political upheavals.

a) The Byzantine style continued: see the Dormition from the Church of the Holy Cross, Pedhoulas.
b) There was a reversion to eastern elements: see Elijah from the Monastery of Ioannis Lampadistis.
c) Through the Crusaders came a western influence: see the Anastasis, also from Lampadistis.

14th century: The diversity went on, but contact with Constantinople became closer again and the Palaeologue style came to Cyprus: see the panels of St. Peter and the Archangel Michael from the church of Khrysaliniotissa, Nicosia.

15th century: The fall of Constantinople in 1543 and the presence of Helen Palaeologina led to an upsurge of Byzantine painting in Cyprus – often betraying some Italian influence: see the two-sided processional icon depicting the Virgin and, on the reverse, the Deposition, from the church of St. Marina, Kalopanayiotis, free-standing.

---

1. See also Supplement: Icons and the Iconostasis

16th century: The trends of the previous fifty years led to the emergence of a distinct Cypriot school of painting, which developed alongside the Cretan school: see the Virgin Hodegetria with donors and large church, 1529, from St. Kassianos Church. At the same time, the close contact with Venice brought increasing Western influence: see the Anastasis of 1563 from Khrysaliniotissa Church, Nicosia.

N.B. Through the centuries of Latin rule, local, rustic painting persisted: see St. Mamas ca. 1500, from Khrysaliniotissa Church, Nicosia – on right wall.

Under Turkish Rule: Output stopped abruptly in 1570 at the Turkish invasion. 17th and 18th century icons show a marked decline: e.g. the Dormition of the Virgin from Trypiotis Church, Nicosia. Good quality panels came mostly from Venice: the Annunciation from St. Anthony's Church, Nicosia. Cretan painters, coming to the Island in the second half of the 17th c., helped improve local standards; and the icon of St. Luke from the Church of St. Luke, Nicosia, is a remarkable example of the benefit.

DO NOT MISS

1. The two large panels by the entrance, the Virgin Enthroned and St. Nicholas. Both come from the end of the 13th century and are similar in style and technique, but in the first the inscription is in Latin and in the second in Greek. The Virgin panel is reputed to have stood in St. Sophia Cathedral, and the donors are Dominican monks, whereas the St. Nicholas comes from St. Nicholas of the Roof near Kakopetria: but they are both probably by the same artist. The implication is that a sought-after Byzantine painter would accept commissions from both Latins and Greeks at that time.

2. The three long narrow panels on the left wall, mid-14th century and in the Palaeologue style. The first one is possibly the most exquisite thing in the entire collection.[1] Christ is above two angels who are conveying to Him the prayers of Manuel the lay preacher and his wife Eupheia for the soul of the princess Maria. She merits close study: notice the jewellery, and the gold fish patterning her gown. These and many other 14th century icons were discovered stored in nearby Khrysoliniotissa Church, but did not necessarily originate there.

3. The 15th and 16th centuries were times when western merchants packed the cities of Famagusta and Nicosia; so now look closely at the foot of each panel where donors may be kneeling: they display a variety of costume, from sombre Flemish to ostentatious Latin, from rich Cypriot to humble monk or priest; and seeing them we can people the mediaeval streets again.

4. At the far end of the room is a replica of an apse. It carries 14th century post-Byzantine wall-paintings which formerly decorated the apse of the Church of St. Nicholas of the Roof. It was necessary to remove them to prevent further damage from damp. The operation became specially delicate when rare frescoes of the 11th century were revealed underneath. It took six months to separate the two.

5. The Kanakaria Mosaics. These are the chief exhibits in the recently opened second room and date from the 6th century AD. Kanakaria is in occupied Cyprus on the Karpas peninsula. Stolen from the church and sold, they were the subject of a court case in the United States concerning right of ownership. As unique as that other 6th century mosaic in Angeloktisti Church, Kiti, but with an Eastern cast and

---

1. See front cover.

damaged, they consist of the Virgin Enthroned, the Christchild in her lap facing outwards, the head only of one Archangel (Gabriel) and ten of the Apostles in medallions: Peter and John missing.

AYIOS IOANNIS CHURCH, THE CATHEDRAL
Dedicated to St. John the Divine

Fine example of an Orthodox church still strong in the Byzantine tradition in the eighteenth century.

Position: Beside the old archbishopric in Archbishop Kyprianos Square.

Dating: Built 1662, decorated 1736, bell-tower added in 1858.

Description: Small, single-aisled and barrel-vaulted in the Franco-Byzantine style, with external buttresses and a west portico. Inside it is fully painted.

Exterior features: Built in to the wall above the west entrance are pieces of carved stonework dating from the 14th or 15th century and almost certainly relics from the Benedictine church which stood here then. The most striking is a rectangular panel, probably one side of a sarcophagus, showing the Crucifixion with the Virgin and St. John flanked by a knight in plate armour and his lady kneeling in prayer. Below, another panel displays three Lusignan coats of arms, and a fourth has been fitted over the door. Above the south entrance is another coat of arms in a marble block, Italianate but defaced.

The Interior: After the purposely modest exterior necessary under the Turks, the gilded woodwork and bright paintings illuminated by crystal chandeliers can astonish an unsuspecting visitor: so much put in to so small a space – and put in obviously with such devotion. The wood-carving is in the best tradition of Cypriot craftsmanship of the 18th century, covered with gold leaf, and intricate. The four large icons on the screen are by the Cretan master John Kornaris, painted between 1795 and 97. Below the pulpit is an icon by an earlier master, Theodore Pulakis; it is of St. John the Divine and is dated 1672.

A small icon of St. Barnabas hangs on the episcopal throne; and suspended from the canopy is a pomegranite symbolising the unity of the Church. The other thrones are for the President, the Greek Ambassador and visiting prelates. In the centre of the floor by the low screen is a roundel of pierced marble: it is the Byzantine double-headed eagle, and all new bishops and archbishops take their oath of loyalty at their consecration standing thereon. Lastly, note the inscription over the west door which begins: *The Church rises like a sky full of lights, illuminating all the faithful.*

Decoration: Although first painted under Archbishop Sylvestros, the present work was carried out in the time of his successor, Archbishop Philotheos. Begun in the bema in 1736, it was still being completed twenty years later. In the sanctuary and the main body of the church, the decorative scheme has been scrupulously followed in the post-Byzantine manner. The Christological cycle covers the central vaults with a sequence of small scenes in four tiers, beginning with the Annunciation at the top on the south-east and ending with a large, crowded Crucifixion also on the south wall. In the apse, Philotheos has included St. Sylvester – Bishop of Rome in the reign of Constantine – among the officiating Fathers of the Church, himself appearing as donor. He may be seen again by the north door, praying to Christ through St. John.

185

*Ayios Ioannis
Cathedral*

The painting becomes noticeably less good as the work progresses towards the west end. Here above the north door and in the vault are Christ's Miracles and Appearances; and on the wall, beneath an elaborate scene of the Creation, the Seven Councils of the Church are depicted.[1] Opposite on the south are a Last Judgement and the Tree of Jesse; and on the jambs of the west door stand Mary of Egypt and St. Zosimos.

N.B. On the south wall by the episcopal throne are four panels illustrating for the first time the discovery of the tomb of the Apostle Barnabas in 478 AD and the consequent recognition of the Church of Cyprus as an independent Apostolic foundation:

i)   Barnabas appears to Anthemios the Archbishop in a dream and points to his tomb.

ii)   The Apostle's remains are discovered, also his own copy of St. Matthew's gospel.

iii)   Cypriot prelates present the gospel to the Emperor Zeno in Constantinople.

iv)   Zeno grants independence to the Church of Cyprus and confers privileges upon its archbishops in perpetuity.

---

1. See Appendix and Ayios Sozomenos Church, Galata.

History: Erected on the site of the 14th century chapel of the Benedictine Abbey of St. John the Evangelist of Bibi. In its Treasury was preserved a finger of John the Baptist, and the first dedication must have been to that St. John. After the desecrations of the Mamelukes, all Benedictines left Cyprus and the Abbey was deserted. Subsequently it became an Orthodox monastery. According to an inscription on the west wall, the monastery chapel was rebuilt from its foundations by Archbishop Nikephoros in 1662. It was redesignated a cathedral in 1720 when Archbishop Sylvestros transferred the episcopal seat from Arkhangelos Monastery at Lakatamia to the centre of Nicosia.

THE OLD ARCHBISHOPRIC stands alongside on the north. It was built about 1730 and incorporates one wing of the old abbey. The ground floor has been turned into a Museum of Folk Art containing a valuable collection of costumes, embroidery and hand-made objects from bygone days. On the upper floor by an external staircase is a slab showing three stylised palm trees and a lamb carved in high relief: its iconography is early Christian. In the library of the Gymnasium opposite is a statue of Christ, which probably came from the Benedictine chapel.

THE HOUSE OF THE DRAGOMAN

Only surviving example of an 18th c. mansion – or Konak – in the island, giving an idea of life for a leading Cypriot family under Turkish rule.

The House of the Dragoman

187

Position: Between Ayios Antonios Church and the Archbishopric, on Patriarch Gregory Street.

Title: The word 'Dragoman' is translated as 'interpreter', and there were a number of these minor officials attached to consulates. However, the Grand Dragoman was appointed by the Archbishop to represent the people in secular affairs. It was the most important civil office a Cypriot could hold and all state business went through his hands. He had to be both liaison officer and diplomat and the benefits and dangers of such a post were considerable. Hadjigeorghakis Kornessios was Grand Dragoman from 1779 to 1809 and became the wealthiest and most powerful Cypriot of his day. He held office for thirty years. His enemies finally overthrew him and he was beheaded in Constantinople after charges of corruption. For an example of an earlier dragoman, see the Church of St. George in Arpera.

THE HOUSE

Dating: 1793. Expanded from a smaller, possibly Venetian house, residence of a noble Cypriot family called Podocataros. In or after 1830, modified and divided into two dwellings. Restored and opened to the public in 1987.

Description: The front of the house stands directly on the street, facing north. It has two wings extending southwards and a central arcaded courtyard, which gives onto a large, walled garden.

The external aspect is fortress-like, with a single entrance and barred windows. Projecting above the doorway is a closed wooden kiosk, and under it a marble plaque – possibly from the earlier building – which displays a high-relief carving of the Lion of St. Mark above a Byzantine double-headed eagle in a shield surrounded by pomegranite and foliage. The second door was added later when the house was divided and is probably from another place. Traces of patterned bands of red-ochre and green, observed by Enlart under the eaves, suggests that the walls were once decorated on the street side.

Inside the house there is a second marble plaque above the main door. It bears the monogram of the Dragoman and three crosses (defaced). All the ground floor rooms open onto the portico, and the surrounding columns and arches give an impression of substance and grandeur. The two wings differ, though: the western continues the golden sandstone of which the house is built up to the eaves, whereas the upper floor on the east wing is much lighter in construction, incorporating a lot of wood in the Turkish manner. The ground-floor rooms were used for domestic offices, servants' quarters and stores, and the heart of the house is to be found on the upper storey.

A covered wooden staircase leads up to a spacious hall: around it are the main rooms. Overlooking the street is a raised platform, the interior of the kiosk from which the women could look out to the street without being observed, Moslem-style. The Dragoman possessed fragments of the True Cross which were kept in the large room to the east of the kiosk: it is still referred to as the Room of the Holy Cross. But the purpose of this house – and its glory – is revealed when one comes to the 'oda' or reception room. Its ornately carved and gilded ceiling, the oriental luxury of its low, cushioned divan which occupies three sides of the room, the long, draped windows and the once richly painted panelling, all were designed to impress.

Here would come the Archbishop and prelates of the Orthodox Church, foreign consuls and all who desired more private discourse than could be achieved in the official suite at the Seray. The cupboard built into the recess conceals the start of a stairway, an escape-route which leads to the roof – such was the tension and danger that was never far away.

Descending again to the courtyard, one comes to a stone fountain bearing the date 1803, its water flowing into an ancient sarcophagus. Set apart on the east side of the house, and now accessible only from the garden, are the kitchen and laundry. Down the garden stands the Konak's own small bath-house. A Turkish hamam, it consists of three interconnecting rooms, the last under a glass-lit dome being the hot one with underfloor heating.

Marble slab with the winged lion of Venice – Dragoman's House

TRYPIOTIS CHURCH *dedicated to the Archangel Michael*

Position: On Solon Street, two hundred yards behind Laiki Yitonia.

Dating: 1695, according to inscription beside south porch, but incorporating earlier material.

Description: **Exterior:** here is the greater interest, lying chiefly in the lintels of the three doors. The west consists of a block of white marble and clearly comes from elsewhere. It is finely carved 14th/15th century work, a canopy of miniature gables, pinnacles and wild roses. The north lintel has a renaissance coat of arms. The most curious piece is on the south side, being a solid sculpture in low relief of two lions flanking a Romanesque figure supporting a vine with, below, an inhabited frieze of palmettes: it has the appearance of great age and may be part of an earlier building left in situ. *(Enlart)*.

Interior: although not outstanding, it contains a fine iconostasis of the 18th century, which is of unusual length – necessarily so, because the church is as wide as it is long. It was carved by Taliadoros, who also made the screen in St. Lazaros Church, Larnaca. Among the icons, note that of the Archangel, painted in 1634: 'Tripiotis' means 'maker of the hole', and refers to the story of a torrent being diverted down a hole, thanks to the Archangel Michael (as illustrated).

OMERIYEH MOSQUE
former Church of St. Mary of the Augustinians

One of the three most important monasteries in the Lusignan city, and the largest church after St. Sophia.

The rose window
(Sketch by Enlart).

Position: Due west of the Dragoman's House, in Tyrillias Square. (Good view over the old city from the minaret.)

Dating: Church built in first half 14th century, chapel probably mid-14th, west-end porch, end 14th; 1570 severely damaged; repaired and converted into a mosque 1571.

Description: Once lofty and elegant, its decoration confined mainly to the ribbed vaults, the capitals and west porch, this monastery church has lost its original roof and upper walls. The collapse was due to cannon-fire – signs of this may still be seen on the walls – and, no doubt, the effect of subsequent earthquake on the damaged superstructure. Of the existing roof, the less said the better.

The church has a single aisle divided into three bays, and it is buttressed. On the north-east, a chapel has been attached. This has a turret in the west corner, ready-made base in 1571 for the Turkish minaret. Also in the west wall is a small rose window, its tracery still intact. On the south-east are remnants of a two-storeyed Venetian building. The enclosing walls, cloisters and conventual buildings have disappeared, with one exception: across the square on the north-west side are the remains of the Monastery's Chapter House, now functioning as a Turkish Bath!

History: The Monastery covered about six acres, part gardens, part farm, with orchards, at least one field of wheat and barley and a plantation of sugar cane. That the place was held in high esteem by the Lusignans is apparent from the large number of noble names inscribed upon the gravestones that used to crowd the church floor. In 1469 the retiring Latin Archbishop chose St. Mary's for his remaining years and built an adjacent hospice for poor pilgrims going to the Holy Land. (The Venetian house is probably a later part of this charity.)

Many pilgrims came to the church to visit the Shrine of Sir John de Montfort, because this shrine had made the Augustinian Monastery famous in the West. Sir John had died in Cyprus in 1248 during the Fourth Crusade and had been buried with much honour in Nicosia, because he was a great and good man. Cures and miracles occurred, and it is believed that the shrine was set up in the chapel here which was built specially to house it. Felix Faber writing in 1480, says of it: *In the church on the left hand is a stately and*

190

gilded tomb . . . the body lies whole but the flesh, muscles and skin are shrivelled. So it looks as though Sir John had been embalmed.

The Monastery became Turkish property in 1570 and St. Mary's was possibly the first church to be adapted for Moslem worship, the Turkish General, Mustafa Pasha himself, being responsible. The reason was his firm belief in the legend that it was on this spot that a relative of the Prophet, the Khalif Omer stayed while visiting Nicosia in the 7th century, and a mosque it has remained ever since.

In 1935 Rupert Gunnis obtained permission to remove the Lusignan gravestones and store them in the Bedestan. First seeing the light of day after 350 years, they had become a piece of vanished history.

PANAYIA PHANEROMENI
(The Holy icon of the Virgin found by revelation)
Phaneromeni Church is the largest within the walls and stands at the top of Onasagoras Street. It was built in 1871 during the last years of Turkish rule on the site of a ruined Byzantine nunnery of the same name, but was probably first founded as an abbey for Cistercian nuns in 1222. It incorporates fragments from the old church – notably the gargoyles on the roof; but the main fabric is composed of stones brought from the remains of La Cava, the Lusignan castle at Athalassa. There is a fine 17th c. iconostasis, an ancient carved cross encased in gilt filigree work holding in its centre a fragment, it is claimed, of the True Cross, and some interesting icons, including the miracle-working Virgin of Phaneromeni. A poignant mausoleum in the courtyard east of the apse bears continued witness to the murders in the 1821 massacre of Archbishop Kyprianos, and the bishops of Paphos, Kition and Larnaca, whose remains are buried here. The monument was erected in 1930 to mark the centenary of Greek Independence. Perhaps more than any other, this church gives the western visitor the full atmosphere of an Orthodox city church and its close ties with the community.

AYIOS KASSIANOS CHURCH *(Feast day 29th February)*
A minute's walk from Panayia Khrysaliniotissa and close to the barrier, it has its own very supportive parishioners, whose forebears, in 1854, paid and provided the labour to get their church rebuilt. The original church was probably Latin and 15th century and had been burnt out during the siege of 1570. Parts have been incorporated into the newer building: the small bas-relief of the Virgin and Child over the west door, for example; but Jeffery considers that the central arcade supporting the vaulting of its two aisles may also be original. Another superb collection of icons has gone from here to the Byzantine Museum, but some treasures remain: an exquisite panel painting of the Panayia in a case in the nave dated 1400, a (restored) Panayia Eleousa on the iconostasis.

St. Kassianos was one of the German saints who came to Cyprus in the 4th century, thought to be buried in a ruined church of the same name at Alekhtora. The helmet in which he was supposedly martyred is preserved on the altar here – and is donned by sufferers from severe headaches!

AYIOS ANTONIOS CHURCH

At the juncture of Ayios Antonios Street and Patriarch Gregorios, it lies about three feet below street level. Rebuilt in 1743 on older foundations, the church is of slight antiquarian interest, although it has a most elegant bell tower. In the narthex is a Latin-style tombstone showing a lady in 16th century dress; and mention must be made of the famous long-case clock in the nave, which has a ship on its pendulum.

Ayios Antonios Church

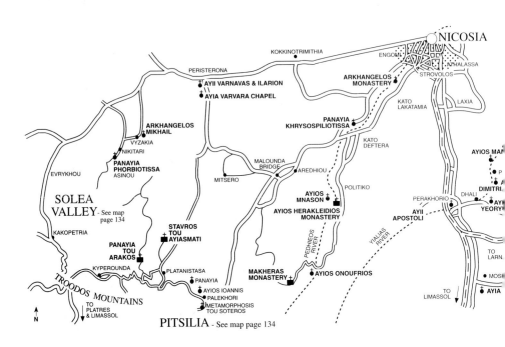

NICOSIA DISTRICT

THE MONUMENTS

Note: * Indicates monuments of particular interest
      ** Indicates monuments of outstanding interest

194

SOUTH WEST

ARKHANGELOS MONASTERY, *Kato Lakatamia*

Franco-Byzantine

Dedicated to the Archangel Michael but often referred to as Archangel Gabriel Monastery. Seat of the Archbishops during the earlier period of Ottoman rule.

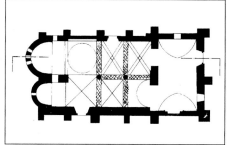

Position: Best reached via Hilon Street and the Lakatamia by-pass. Continue past new housing development. The monastery will then be visible among trees below the road, left.

Ground plan of Arkhangelos Monastery Church – with acknowledgements to the Holy Monastery of Kykko

Dating: Church built end 15th and mid 16th centuries; narthex 1660.

Description: Some of the monastic buildings that formerly enclosed the courtyard have been lost, but those on the east and south have been sensitively restored. The church itself has been superbly built of fine ashlar masonry. It is two-aisled, having a high-vaulted nave with a dome, and a narrower but also lofty northern aisle, separated by three columns (one engaged). A large narthex serves both. Gothic features are immediately apparent in the external

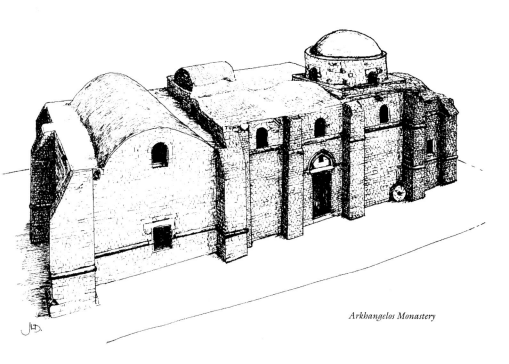

Arkhangelos Monastery

buttresses, the style of the three entrances and the vaulting within. The west door has a wide and imposing pointed arch and a broad band of shallow moulding, the lateral doorways have pointed carved hood-moulds over square lintels, and all are of a very late period in Gothic design.

The interior reveals alterations and additions of several periods. The *south aisle* is thought to incorporate the walls of the original church. That was a small, rectangular building with an apse, barrel-vault, central dome and side recesses built, according to report, in the late 11th or early 12th century. Towards the end of the 15th century it seems to have been largely rebuilt and extended. (The severe earthquake of 1491 brought widespread damage to this area.) The Gothic ribbed cross-vaulting replaced the round Byzantine barrel-vault then.

The *north aisle* was attached some time between 1547 and 1570. It has its own apse and was probably a Latin Chapel but, with the dividing wall replaced by an arcade, so closely integrated with the Orthodox church as to imply a close Veneto-Cypriot alliance. It is from that time that the confusion over the dedication began; and that of the new chapel may well have been to the Archangel Gabriel.

The narthex was built by Archbishop Nikephoros in 1660 and a commemorative stone can be seen on the east wall. It has a plain pointed vault with a north-south orientation. The Archbishop is buried here and his tomb stands against the north wall under an elaborate moulded arch. Right of the north door are graffiti recording the years of drought when the famous rain-bringing icon, the Virgin of Kykko was brought here.

Decoration: In the niche south of the iconostasis is a colossal Archangel Michael: painted in the 16th or 17th century, it covered up earlier work of which a small part – heads of saints – is visible; (insufficient for firm dating, but possibly Comnenian, and therefore on an original wall). The iconostasis was carved at the time of Nikephoros and he is shown on two of the icons dressed in rich ceremonial robes: beside the Virgin and Child and below the Archangel Michael. These, the royal doors and several of the other icons were painted by one Paul in 1650. St. John the Theologian is a later icon, painted in 1783, and it depicts as donor a wellknown abbot of Kykko Monastery, Meletios III, who was responsible for Arkhangelos then.

History: In the 16th century, Arkhangelos was a centre for mss and bibliography; and from about that time a school of painting was established here under the auspices of Kykko. In the 17th century, the monastery became the seat of the Archbishop and the church was therefore the Orthodox Cathedral until the move to St. John's in Nicosia in 1720. Meanwhile, in 1713, Kykko had taken over the administration of Arkhangelos. The sketch of the monastery done by Barsky, the Russian monk, in 1735 shows the church much as it is today but still enclosed on all four sides.

In more recent times Arkhangelos ceased to function as a monastery and the buildings decayed. Then in 1986, another Nikephoros, the abbot of Kykko Monastery, restored the existing wings and founded the Kykko Study Centre for research into the history of Cyprus and the Church, a much-needed project that has already proved itself invaluable.

196

PANAYIA KHRYSOSPILIOTISSA, *Kato Dheftera*
Our Lady of the Golden Cave

Position: On the east bank of the river Pedheios, halfway up a cliff, eight miles from Nicosia off the Kato Dheftera road. On approaching the village, turn right at sign.

Dating: Possibly early Christian origin.

Description: A natural sandstone cave enlarged to form an apse, nave, narthex and vestries, and lovingly tended by women from the village. Once completely decorated, all the plaster has fallen away except in the sanctuary – and that has been defaced by 17th and 18th century graffiti and blackened by oil-lamps. The church contains a rain-inducing icon of the Virgin which is resorted to in times of drought by all the surrounding villages, especially by the farmers. The site may have begun as a Christian refuge and until recently access could be cut off by a drawbridge. *This cave church is a very interesting and picturesque example of a type of Levantine monastery or hermitage uncommon in Cyprus, but very characteristic of ancient Levantine Christianity.* Jeffery, Historic Monuments of Cyprus.

AYIOS HERAKLEIDIOS MONASTERY, *Politiko*
An historic place of great charm, now a convent.

Position: 12 miles south west of Nicosia. Drive down Byron Avenue and continue through Strovolos and Lakatamia, keeping on the east side of the river Pedhieos. At Pano Deftera, take left fork and proceed along by-pass to Pera, where the turn-off for the monastery is signposted. It stands on high ground immediately south of Politiko.

Dating: Mausoleum 14th c.; church 15th and early 17th c. on 5th c. foundations; mon. buildings 1773. Abandoned after the 1821 persecution; restored by Archbishop Makarios in 1960's for nuns.

Description: **The Church:** Two aisles separated by three arches and with two dedications: the south aisle (15th c.) is to St. Herakleidios and the north (early 17th) is to the Holy Trinity. The narthex is an extension of the nave cp. St. John's cathedral. The whole rests within the now-demolished nave of a vanished three-aisled, possibly 9th century basilica, and the present south wall incorporates pillars from that building's 5th c. predecessor. Part of the 5th c. mosaic floor is open to view by the north-east pillar. On a table under the eastern arch lie two reliquary boxes, one containing a bone of the saint, the other his skull. On the west and south sides of the church is a portico.

Ayia Trias Chapel: At the east end of the south portico – which was the south aisle of the old basilica – stands this very unusual *mausoleum*. The interior is cruciform under a steep dome and the opus sectile floor includes hexagonal marble tiles of the 6th century. The elevated, four-panelled, pierced-stone screen is of an early type, displaying the chi-rho symbol, and was probably the sanctuary screen from the old basilica; but it is largely covered in plaster. The two great sarcophagi below on either side are said to be those of St. Herakleidios and St. Mnason, the first Cyprus bishop and his friend and successor. Four lesser sarcophagi are those of other very early Christian saints of Tamassos. A trapdoor conceals steps leading to an underground Roman tomb, deemed to be Herakleidios' original burial-place; but it is best reached by a door and steps on the other side of the church (beyond the apse).

197

The Monastic buildings: completely renovated in 1773 by Archbishop Khrysanthos. A wide path, neatly patterned with pebbles, runs beside the north range. There is a profusion of flowers and shrubs.

Barsky, the Russian monk, came here in 1735 and a 20' high rock in a nearby field is known as Barsky's Rock. Ayios Mnason's monastery was half-a-mile north-west: small ruins and a poor chapel are all that remains.

Decoration: Few wall-paintings. Two of the 10th/11th c. on the columns in the south wall are of Christ (east of entrance) and a prophet (behind the icon screen). A striking row of Church Fathers (south wall, west end) was painted by Philaretos, an 18th c. monk. He also illustrated the baptism and consecration of Herakleidios (soffit of eastern arch).[1] The monastery was a centre of icon painting in the 17th and 18th centuries and of those displayed note especially the 1611 Baptist (left of south screen). Even the two icon screens are of different periods: the north was carved in 1774 and the south early in the 17th century; they make an interesting comparison. The pulpit, too, is finely crafted.

Ayios Herakleidios Monastery – the mausoleum

History: The ancient city of Tamassos owed its importance to its prolific copper mines. It was densely populated at the time of Christ and well provided with altars to pagan gods. Herod the Great had leased the mines and sent Jews from Palestine over to work them; and it was from this community that Herakleidios made most of his converts. Understandably, there was hostility and incidents occurred. Nevertheless, Tamassos was the earliest centre of Christianity in Cyprus and Herakleidios the first bishop. Politiko was the

1. Philaretos also painted at Ayios Minas Monastery and at Ayios Yeoryios, Arpera.

administrative centre of the city. Remains of a fine 4th c. mosaic floor east of the mausoleum are probably part of an earlier building put over the shrine.

At the beginning of the 5th century a three-aisled basilica was erected, its south aisle being on the site of the present portico. It had a mosaic floor, was colonnaded and contained the 4th c. mausoleum. In the year 806 it was destroyed by the Arabs and later in the century a new basilica was built and decorated; it had an opus sectile floor. It fell into ruins about the end of the 13th century. The mausoleum was restored first in the 14th c. but it took a further three hundred years for the church to reach its present, much modified form. Nilos, Bishop of Tamassos in the last quarter of the 12th c., founded the Monastery here in 1180. It was called Blachernitissa.

Tradition: Herakleidios, native of Tamassos and son of a priest of Apollo, acted as guide to Barnabas, Paul and John Mark on their way through the Troodos mountains. They converted him to Christianity and he was baptised in the river at Kalopanayotis. Four or five years later, he was consecrated first Bishop of Paphos by Barnabas. He ministered first in a cave and later from a small cell and was joined quite soon by Mnason, an historically accredited figure (Acts XXI.16) and *an old disciple* – who may have been one of the seventy Apostles.

St. Herakleidios was martyred at the age of sixty, killed by pagan fanatics, and Mnason succeeded him as bishop. It is said that Mnason was responsible for the destruction of the Temple of Asklepios in the city.

MAKHERAS MONASTERY (The Monastery of the Knife)

Position: On the eastern edge of the Troodos mountains below Kionia peak. Drive to Kambia by way of Strovolos and Kato Dheftera: Makheras is nine miles further, along a climbing, twisting forest road (tarmacked). Refreshments available in summer.

Makheras Monastery

199

Dating:	Founded mid-12th c.; burnt down 1530 and 1892; present buildings completed 1902.
Description:	Beautifully situated in the forest looking north across the central plain. The curious name 'Makheras' is thought to refer to the discovery of the Monastery's holy icon of the Virgin in a cave guarded by a sword; but it could simply mean the keen winds experienced up here in winter. The cloistered courtyard shelters behind a massive buttressed building resembling a fortress. In the centre stands a spacious church and the legend of the icon is illustrated in mosaic round its west doorway. The icon itself hangs on the iconostasis, covered in silver-gilt and guarded symbolically by a tiny knife; it is the first thing to be saved when a forest fire threatens. In the Treasury is kept a 1756 copy of the first abbot's Ritual Ordinance, printed in Venice. Next to the souvenir shop in the west cloister is a cell devoted to the memory of Gregorios Afxentiou, Grivas's lieutenant, who died heroically in 1957; he was a monk here. The cave in which he died is just below and now a shrine.
History:	In the mid-12th century, two hermits from Syria made a new Retreat for themselves up here beside the well. After three years, Neophytos the older man died, and it fell to the other, Ignatios, to make the arduous journey to Constantinople to plead for funds to found a monastery. He and his companion spoke to the Emperor, Manual Comnenos, who supported the project by granting a charter of independence, an annual grant of money and ownership of much of the surrounding land. The monastery was completed in 1190 by Nilos, one of the outstanding men of the time. Nilos had joined Ignatios eighteen years previously; he became the first abbot of Makheras, went on to be Bishop of Tamassos and eventually Archbishop of Cyprus. The monastery had good relations with the Lusignans; and gave shelter to King James I and his court in 1393, when the great plague was raging in Nicosia.
Tradition:	In the time of the Iconoclasts, in the 8th century, an icon of the Virgin was hidden in a cave near the holy well and a naked sword buried before it. Four centuries later, Neophytos found it and built his cell on the spot. In the time of the Lusignans, the imperious wife of Hugh IV, Queen Alix, forced her way into the church sanctuary – a place where no woman is allowed in the Orthodox Church – and was promptly struck dumb. She remained thus for three years, when the miracle at Tokhni restored her speech.[1]

ST. ONOUFRIOS CHURCH

Two miles before reaching the Monastery is a chapel dedicated to this Egyptian hermit. It may indicate a link with the origins of the founders of Makheras. Onoufrios was a young monk at Hermopolis near Thebes, about 400AD. He went to the desert to seek complete solitude, and remained there, according to legend, for sixty years, communing only with God. When he was found, he was naked and covered with thick white hair. A popular saint, he is always depicted with a long white beard and behind a bush. There has been a church on this site since the 13th or 14th century, and traces of the monastery that was attached later can be made out. The present building dates only from 1967 and replaces one destroyed by fire; it was decorated in 1975. The life of the saint is recorded by the entrance.

---

1. See Ayios Stavros, Tokhni

WEST

PERISTERONA Church of Ayii Varnavas and Ilarion

Position: 18 miles west of Nicosia on the Troodos road. Turn left after the Akaki turn-off, then almost immediately right and continue downhill to the river bridge. The Church is opposite.

Dating: Early 10th c. with later narthex.

Description: It is a five-domed basilica with three aisles. Three of the domes are in line over the nave and one spans the middle of each side-aisle to make the arms of a cross. This and the example at Yeroskipos are the only five-domed churches in Cyprus and unique for the type of building. The walls between the aisles are of thick masonry pierced by arches, unlike the airy colonnades of the early Christian basilicas. The wall-paintings have been lost all but two: a fine King David on the north west central pier, early 16th c.; and a Virgin and Child of the 12th century. The icon screen, although restored, dates from 1549 and holds some good icons. Note particularly the Presentation of Christ in the Temple (ca. 1520) with kneeling donor, and, on the north side, examples in the Italo-Byzantine style. The patron saints can be seen in a rare painting which stands against the north-east centre pier. Other good icons are hung in the north aisle, including a large one of St. Barnabas the Apostle.

The doors at the west end may be original in their frame, although much repaired, and are a good example of Byzantine craftsmanship. They lead into the late narthex, the facade of which looks contemporary with the 19th century bell-tower. In the narthex against the wall are two Latin tombstones removed from the floor of the church, and pieces of the early Christian screen and ambo. Two mediaeval pewter plates, a Bible of 1604 printed in Venice and a 16th century chest are also on view. The chest's lid is open to show a painted scene of a castle under attack – said to be the siege of Rhodes in 1522.

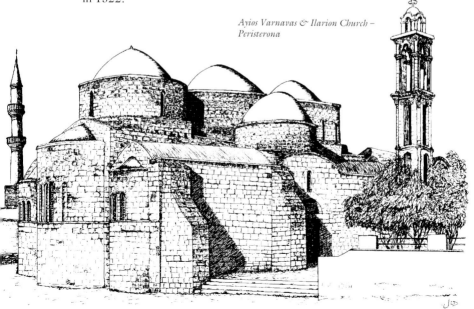

Ayios Varnavas & Ilarion Church – Peristerona

History: Saint Barnabas and Saint Hilarion here are not the Apostle and the Hermit of Paphos, but two high-ranking officers of the Roman army in the 5th century who subsequently renounced the world to follow Christ in poverty and good works. There may well have been an early Christian basilica here – vide the stone screen found during excavation – rebuilt in the resurgence after the devastations of the Arab raids.

CHAPEL OF AYIA VARVARA, *Peristerona*

Tiny 16th century restored building on the western outskirts of the village which has kept a good portion of its decoration, including two donor paintings. On the south wall is St. George and the Dragon with three donors: the two men are dressed in belted blue tunics, the lady wears a white tunic-dress over a blue shirt. On the west wall is St. Luke and a single male donor; also on that wall is St. Paraskevi holding an icon of Christ. In the apse are the Virgin Orans with Archangels. Below, four Fathers of the Church bend towards a painted altar, Gregory and John Chrysostom on one side, Basil and Cyprus's own Epiphanios on the other: all are wearing the polystavron. On the architrave of the iconostasis is a row of saints in roundels, and on the screen itself a 16th century icon of the Virgin. The paintings are damaged but the quality is good.

PANAYIA PHORBIOTISSA, *Asinou*
Our Lady of the Pastures

The most famous of the painted churches. One of the nine churches on UNESCO's World Heritage list.

Position: Eastern foothills of Troodos. Off the Nicosia to Kakopetria road. Before the fork to Kykko, take minor road to Nikitari village but bypass the village and proceed up the valley for three miles where the church will be seen on the right. If shut, return to Nikitari for the priest.

Dating: Built and painted 1105/6. Narthex added ca. 1200. Further painting: centre bay 14th c., narthex 14th c., plus earlier work.

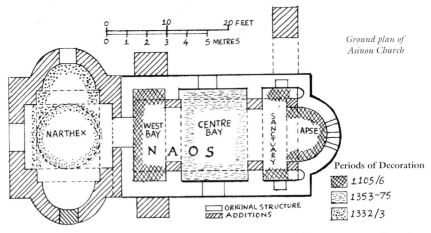

Ground plan of Asinou Church

Periods of Decoration
▓ 1105/6
▒ 1353-75
▓ 1332/3

Description: The building is a type common throughout the Byzantine Empire: rectangular, with flattened barrel vault, a semi-dome over the apse and arched recesses. It is constructed of roughly-cut stone blocks using a simple

202

mud-based mortar, and there is evidence of frequent repair and buttressing, including a flying buttress on the north-east. The narthex is of well-cut sandstone and neat design and incorporates a central dome flanked by semi-domes on the north and south. The whole is covered with a secondary steep-pitched wooden roof.

History: First occupied by Greek settlers from Asine in the Peloponnese in 11th century BC. A small village was still here in mediaeval times, and the monastery survived into the 17th century. Otherwise, no records exist, apart from inscriptions inside the church itself. From these we are informed that a certain Nicephorus founded it and paid for the decoration and that he held the title of Magistros – which makes him a high-ranking noble of the Byzantine court. He was, almost certainly, the son of the then governor of Cyprus and married to the Emperor's younger daughter.

Decoration: **In the main church**
The cycle starts in the Sanctuary (bema) with the Birth of the Virgin in the north east recess and the Presentation of the Virgin opposite; then in the south vault the Nativity takes up the N.T. story and the scenes unfold, ending with the Crucifixion and related scenes on the north side. Two styles are apparent: that of a master of the early 12th century and that of a provincial two-and-a-half centuries later.

Early 12th c. Two-thirds of the original 1105/6 decoration remains and it is all in the Sanctuary and the west end. The style reflects that of Constantinople: neo-classical and rhythmic, with finely differentiated faces and bold use of line. This is early Comnenian and retains the sternly spiritual look that derived from the East, a look that was to soften as the century progressed – compare with the Lagoudera master of 1192.

In the Bema: The Liturgical theme of the Sanctuary programme is almost fully developed by this period. But observe that the *Fathers of the Church* are not yet converging upon the altar in participation, and that there is no altar depicted yet, the space being occupied by the great Cypriot saints *Barnabas and Epiphanios*. The outstanding painting here is the *Communion of the Apostles* (which did not move into the Apse until the mid-11th century). In it, Christ is shown twice, in the accepted Byzantine convention. Only the southern part is intact, but it has all the qualities of a momentous occasion; a graceful, solemn composition, and Christ looking to the end of the line at Judas's departing back. On either side of this – and hard to see behind columns – are Gabriel and the Virgin in the original *Annunciation* scene. (The 14th century Annunciation is on the later, reinforcing transverse arch in front.) Also obscured by the columns are the strong portraits of an emaciated *Mary of Egypt* and of *Bishop Zosimos* offering her Communion.

The West Bay: *The Dormition of the Virgin Mary,* representing her death and assumption, extends across the whole of the west wall over the door. Above are the *Entry into Jerusalem* and the *Last Supper,* but it is the Dormition that holds one's gaze. Gunnis has described it as *a stately minuet of grief.* Dominating the scene are the still figures of the Virgin on her bier and of an inscrutable Christ, who stands behind: He holds up a swaddled babe which is her innocent soul. Symmetrically on either side are the swaying, mourning Apostles. (Here the expressive use of drapery is very effective.) In the vault are the remains of *Pentecost,* the *Raising of Lazarus* and the *Washing of the Feet.* The entire north-west recess is taken up by an arresting illustration of the *Forty Martyrs* shivering half-naked on the ice. Opposite stand the Emperor Constantine and Empress Helena holding up the discovered True Cross; and beneath them is the vital inscription which gives the firm dates 1105/1106 for the decoration of the church.

14th century: Most of the central bay was redecorated in the third quarter of the 14th century by the same painter who worked in Ayios Stavros Church at Pelendria in a dazzle of bright, meticulous scenes across the vaults, with lavish use of blues, reds and gold. On the lower register, where the life-size saints are, earlier versions show through damaged plaster. We owe this painter thanks for saving the original donor painting and inscription above the south door by rendering it again.

Decoration in the narthex

Except for the south apse, all the upper parts of the narthex depict scenes of the Last Judgement and were painted in 1332/3, according to inscription. The scheme has been well planned and carried out in a conservative style. (Observe the little devils tipping in their favour the scales full of souls – left of west door.) The rest of the space is covered with saints and donors of varying periods, the earliest being the magnificent St. George on the blocked south door – probably early 13th century. St. George's shield displays the Byzantine cross-in-crescent emblem; the gold leaf has fallen from his armour, but the work is still rich in colour and has almost miniaturist detail. The donor was another Nicephoras, a self-styled 'tamer of horses', and it is from his inscription that we learn for the first time that this was a monastery church. Above is a mid-14th century westernised Mother of God and Child with donors, rather mannered in a style brought in by the Crusaders. Below on the left is St. Mamas on a delightful lion and on the right stands Anastasia, the curer of poisons, with her namesake beside her as donor, dressed in silk – a fine rendering by the artist responsible for the repainting of the Virgin on the conch of the apse. Either side of the Virgin Phorbiotissa is a supplicant monk and, very unusual, to the right a couple of hunting dogs tied to a spear.

Methods of painting *(taken from 'Asinou, a Guide' by David Winfield)*

Byzantine painters worked fast, and quite large scenes could be completed before the plaster dried out. Pigments combined with the lime in crystallised form as the lime dried, making for a much more enduring painting than if done on dry plaster. The artist himself did the preliminary plastering area by area as needed. A limit was set by the red borders – example: left edge of St. George shows the join. Then a red or yellow sketch was made on the still damp plaster – example: Christ-child over St. George. Then came the colour build-up – *not* mixed on the wall – and the preliminary sketch was lost under the paint. As a guide, therefore, the sketch lines were often incised – example: Anastasia's dress. Faces, on the other hand, were blended on the wall, over-dry plaster being scraped away and fresh added. Cyprus is rich in minerals and could provide most of the basic colours a painter would need: umber and haematite and red and yellow ochre, for example; but gold-leaf is another matter, use of which implies a rich donor.

Church of Panayia Phorbiotissa, Asinou

CHURCH OF ARKHANGELOS MIKHAIL, *Vizakia*

Position: A mile east of Nikitari – the village for Asinou – and just out of Vizakia, right of the road. Key from priest in village.

Dating: Built and decorated in 1502.

Description: Roughly-built small chapel of uncut stone and mud-brick; the narthex is open on the south and is later in date. The whole is under a wood and tile protective roof. The lintel of the west door is stopped with a pair of serpents' heads, and the stout crossbeams inside are ornamented.

Decoration: The paintings on the north and in the bema have been lost. What remains is an unusual series of compositions, naïve and rustic to an extreme but having a charm and character of their own. Nine scenes from the Life and Passion of Christ occupy the upper levels of the south and west walls, with the Crucifixion in the west pediment. Below are the Apostles Peter and Paul, George and the Dragon, St. Mamas and Constantine and Helen (over the west door).

Style: The unknown artist has a bold, unsubtle hand, often employing heavy outlines. Some of his figures are grotesquely distorted: see shepherd in the Nativity, for example, and the animals also. Garments are shapeless, but given an unclothed figure, anatomy is precise. His use of space is good, also his crowd scenes: the Betrayal is an example of both points. Strongest and most memorable is Christ Crucified: the contrast between the stark figure on the Cross and the foppish Venetian youth below strikes a chill. Another youth is offering the sponge impaled on a curiously convoluted reed.

205

SOUTH

AYII APOSTOLI CHURCH, *Perakhorio*
Church of the Holy Apostles, Peter and Paul

Rare, mid-12th century paintings but in poor condition.

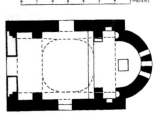

Ground plan of Ayii Apostoli, Perakhorio

Position: Off the Nicosia to Limassol road, shortly before the turn-off for Larnaca (signposted) Ayii Apostili stands on a rise beyond the village on the south-west. The key is kept at the last house but three on the right.

Dating: Built and painted between 1160 and 1180, with some repainting in the 15th century. (Dated by style.)

History: No records exist, but Ayii Apostili is known locally as 'the Monastery'. At some time, the west wall collapsed and the interior was exposed for a considerable period before being rebuilt.

Description: A small, compact building of the dome-hall type with arched recesses; the arches are rounded. It is roughly constructed of local stone with some brick incorporated. The dome is drumless and has no lantern.

Decoration: The church was fully painted in true fresco by a master, probably from Constantinople, and is the only example of his work so far discovered in Cyprus. The paintings have suffered badly from age, weathering and neglect, but were rescued as far as was possible in the 1950s. In the cup of the dome is the Pantocrator, his nimbus and book enriched with ornament. Round Him on the flattened splayed sides, a much-damaged choir of angels moves. Darkened remnants of the New Testament cycle begin with the Annunciation on the east pendentives; the Nativity and Presentation are on the south wall; in the vault of the bema, the Ascension; and the Dormition above the north door. The apse contains the Virgin orans Blachernitissa in the conch, attended by Peter and Paul in place of the customary archangels. Below is the Communion of the Apostles; and, at the lowest level, the Fathers of the Church (including Lazaros) with busts of the two greatest of Cyprus's saints. Barnabas and Epiphanios in the centre as at Asinou and Lagoudera.

Style: Shows the progress towards expressive movement and plasticity more than half a century after Asinou, (1106). The stern face of Christ is now gentler; there is more attention to ornamental detail, achieving a decorative richness that is not found at the end of the century – vide Lagoudera – when the artists rely more on line for effect. Pigments: according to Megaw and Hawkins, the basic colours used were haematite, umber, yellow ochre, purple, blue, black and white; there are also traces of gold leaf: all were used with a subtlety of combination and a wide range of tone. Backgrounds were blue and green, except in the dome where the ground is purple.

Not all is by the master. The Nativity, although contemporary, is clumsier work and possibly done by the apprentice. The Presentation belongs to the 15th century, a period when some repainting was carried out in the lower zones.

Perakhorio, Church of the Twelve Apostles

Note that:
The Fathers in the apse face front in the earlier manner as at Asinou; none wears the Polystavrion phelonian, not even John Chrysostom; instead of the Evangelists, the pendentives carry the Annunciation and a pair of seraphim.

Look especially for:
An exquisite angel in the dome
The serenely beautiful Virgin in the apse and the classical look of St Paul's raiment as he moves
The dress of the shepherds, by contrast, in the Nativity; and their lunch-bags hanging on a tree.

I am indebted to Arthur Megaw and Ernest Hawkins for much of the above. (Report in the Dumbarton Oaks Papers, number 16.)

AYIOS DIMITRIANOS, *Dhali*

Position: One mile north-east of Dhali, beside the old road.

Dating: Built probably 12th or 13th century. Restored and decorated in 1317.

Description: A small domed building with recesses cp. Ayii Apostoli but having pointed vaults and arches – legacy, no doubt, of its 14th c. restoration.

Decoration: Fragmentary, but the donor painting has survived. On the north wall, Michael the Archangel and St. George occupy the west and central recesses; notice the gothic graffiti on St. George. St. Kyriaki stands on the pier between, a female saint popular in post-Byzantine Cyprus. Over the west and south doors respectively are the Holy Tile and the Holy Handkerchief; and in the south-west recess is a soldier-saint inscribed *St. Dimitrianos* – wrongly, as A&J Stylianou point out.[1] The west vaults retain traces of three scenes from Christ's Passion: Christ with soldiers, south; the Anastasis, north; and the Crucifixion, west lunette. In the bema, south-east recess, are St. Mary of Egypt and St. Zosimos together with three others: a pair of ascetics and a Stylite.

The donor painting: Situated below the Crucifixion on the west wall over a disproportionately high entrance, which must belong to the rebuilding period and puts the painting well above eye-level. An old man and his wife are shown: his head is covered with a white coiffe over which is a black cap; and she has over her gown a heavy, full-length, lined cloak, which also covers

---

1. Dimitrianos was Bishop of Chytri (ancient Kythrea) in the 9th century. When the Arabs took a great number of his flock as captives to Baghdad, he went after them and obtained their freedom.

her head in the fashion of the day. Her hands are raised in prayer, and he is offering a large model of the church to Christ, who is giving His blessing from the top corner. The inscription on the lintel reads:

> *The most venerable church of our father among the saints,*
> *Dimitrianos Andridiotis, was renovated and painted*
> *through the donation and great desire of Michael son*
> *of Katzouroubis and of his wife and children, amen;*
> *in the year 6825, indiction . . . (1317).*[1]

Style: Good quality local post-Byzantine work, two-dimensional and traditional, with some western influence (e.g. the cusped arch of St. George and the soldiers' leggings, south west vault).

AYIOS YEORYIOS, *Dhali*

Position: Half a mile south of Dhali off the old Larnaca road.

Dating: Built probably end 12th/beginning 13th century.

Description: A cruciform church with a dome and recesses cp its neighbours, Ayios Dimitrianos and Ayii Apostoli. It stands just within the perimeter of Idalion and was largely built of material from the ancient city. A piece of blue marble with a Phoenician inscription, formerly incorporated, is now in the Cyprus Museum.

Decoration: Scraps of wall-paintings still adhere but they are in very poor condition. Part of the angelic host in the dome survives to show their former fine quality.

CHURCH OF ST. MAMAS, *Ayios Sozomenos, Potamia* *

Position: Potamia lies two miles north-east of Dhali. Turn left at junction and cross the river Yialias onto an earth road. After one-and-a-half miles come to the deserted village of Ayios Sozomenos.

Dating: Early 16th c. but in the style of 15th c. southern France.

Description: A Gothic ruin and possibly never finished, it has three short aisles separated by pillars supporting pointed arches and was probably domed. From the four central pillars spring slender colonnettes. The arched recesses with pearled mouldings in the south wall were intended for tombs; the opposite pair on the north have fallen away. The monumental west doorway is flanked by colonnettes with elongated, decorated capitals and it has a hood with elaborate moulding. Above is a stone panel containing a Latin cross, a single rose at its centre.

To the east of this abandoned church of France is a small Orthodox one, plain, barrel-vaulted and still cared for: it is dedicated to the Virgin and pre-dates St. Mamas. There are indications of an earlier, more sumptuous church here originally.

---

1. Trans: Stylianou.
*Not to be confused with St. Mamas at Dhali, which is an example of degenerate Gothic of the early 16th c.

Church of St. Mamas, Potamia

The cave of Ayios Sozomenos is located in the cliffs behind the village. It contains the saint's tomb and some wall-paintings of the late Byzantine period. Sozomenos was a reclusive holy man driven from his Syrian retreat by the Persian wars of the 5th century. An early Neophytos, he wrote copiously on Church issues.

History: The village was part of a royal estate in the 14th and 15th centuries. Beside the river Yialias, on the Potamia bank, the Lusignan king Peter II built a castle ca. 1382 and surrounded it with lovely gardens. Until 1426 – when it was burnt down by the Mamelukes – it was a favourite royal haven. Remains have been incorporated into the Turkish chiftlik, which can be seen from the bridge. Just upstream, a mound marks the site of the royal chapel of St. Catherine (later rebuilt at Pyrga).

210

LARNACA

History of Larnaca

LARNACA	The seat of the Bishop of Kition
Ancient:	Kition
Mediaeval:	Arnica (the village); Scala (the landing place): twin towns
Frankish:	Les Salines

LARNACA

History

The site of Larnaca covers the antique city of Kition, a city Lazarus would have known well as, according to tradition, he was its first bishop. By the end of the eighth century, it had been almost completely destroyed by the Arabs. In the modern town, the only place that provides a direct and continuous link with those early days is the Church of St. Lazarus, Larnaca's most treasured monument. To this spot must have come Barnabas, John Mark and most probably St. Paul; and the bishops of Kition have succeeded each other in unbroken line down to the present day. Kition seems to have dropped out of history for several hundred years following the Arab raids; all that was left being an isolated monastery church near the shore and a small village called Arnica a mile inland. Famagusta attracted all the trade. The landing place, or Scala, here was used chiefly for the export of salt from the nearby Salt Lake, and the general area was known as Salines, or Saltings.

When the Crusades began, and pilgrimages to the Holy Land, Salines became a stopping-off point, especially for pilgrims wanting to visit St. Lazarus Church; and a special mass was introduced for them there. But it was not important as a town until the loss of Famagusta to the Genoese in the 14th century forced European merchants to transfer their ships to Larnaca Bay and make a port of Salines and build residences in the adjacent village. By Venetian times, Arnica had prospered enough for a government official – a captain – to be sent to administer it. Early in the 17th century, the modern name of Larnaca was in use. Meanwhile, Salines was developing into the chief port of trade for the entire Island, and the close of the 18th century saw the two towns beginning to merge.

An extra boost had been given to this expansion by the European consuls, whose finely-appointed houses now lined the sea-front. Yet the district was not the healthiest place to live in then, surrounded as it was by marshland; and in summer death and sickness from various pestilences afflicted the population. Otherwise, it was a pleasant, leisured way of life for the European diplomats and the wealthy citizens of Larnaca. There was little to do except entertain lavishly, and an obsessive concern for social etiquette and protocol developed. The consuls almost to a man went in for money-lending and private trade.

From a half-deserted place where the dispatch of salt or the occasional landing of pilgrims must have been an event, Larnaca had grown into a lively, cosmopolitan town. Cyprus may have relapsed into an oriental backwater under an indolent Turkish regime, but through Larnaca a channel of communication was kept open to the outside world.

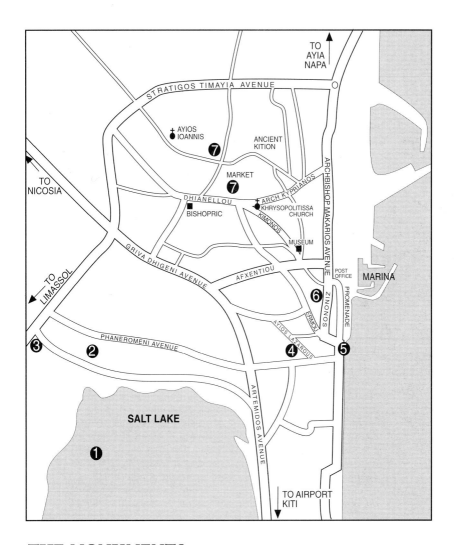

THE MONUMENTS

Note: * Indicates monuments of particular interest
         ** Indicates monuments of outstanding interest

Larnaca & Scala in 1735 (by Barsky)

THE SALT LAKE

Larnaca's Salt Lake is a very old piece of engineering, with a system of barriers, dykes and ditches.[1] Once it had a circumference of twelve miles: in the 16th century, it still enclosed nine miles; now it has shrunk to two. It is thought that the salt was already being marketed in classical times. That would account for the survival of a village and a small trading port long after Kition had disappeared, because it was a highly lucrative commodity. The process was described by travellers in the 14th and 15th centuries – previous to their reports, hardly a record exists. *At the back of the town is a place surrounded by hills which at certain times the rising sea fills with water, making a kind of lake; and when the flood retires the sea water left therein is refined into excellent salt, very white and valuable. This salt is taken for sale to many countries, and the Queen of Cyprus receives a large income from the salt merchants.*[2] It remained one of the Island's most important exports until the Second World War. The yield was prodigious, and even now summer evaporation leaves a bed of 20-50,000 tons of salt. Little is collected today and the future is uncertain.

A local explanation of this unusual lake is quite different: it was not a feat of engineering: Lazarus was responsible. Apparently in those days the Lake was a vineyard and the Saint, passing by and feeling thirsty, asked the woman who owned it for some grapes. She replied that she had none. He then said: *Because you have lied to me, let your vineyard dry up and be turned into a lake of salt!* And so it came to pass.

---

1. See Cotovicus, Ex. Cyp.
2. Felix Faber 1483, Ex. Cyp.

THE AQUEDUCT *(known as The Kamares or Arches)*

Position: Outskirts of Larnaca on the Limassol road above the Salt Lake.

Dating: Constructed between 1746 and 1750 and in use until 1941.

Description: The stone channel carried water from springs at Arpera down to Larnaca, six miles away. Three small valleys had to be spanned, involving seventy-five arches: the stretch here contains thirty-one and, towards Arpera, the other two have spans of twelve and thirty-two respectively.

The Aqueduct

History: The aqueduct is dry now and has become simply a picturesque part of the town's history and a monument to its great benefactor, Bekir Pasha. He was a man of great public spirit and, having seen the townsfolk trudging long distances to fetch water, had wells bored and this aqueduct built for them at his own expense. It cost him a lot of money, he took a personal interest in its progress and he begrudged not one piastre. It is probably the most important public work undertaken under the Turkish regime and supplied the town, almost without a break, for just about two hundred years. In 1939 the authorities considered the water to be a health-risk, open as the channels were to pollution along the way, and began the laying of pipes. Abu Bekir will go down in history as the only Turkish Governor without a blemish to his name.

MONASTERY CHURCH OF AYIOS YEORYIOS OF AGRINOU, *called Makris (the Far)*

Position: Overlooking the north-west corner of the Salt Lake. Turn off the Limassol road shortly before the Kamares aqueduct onto the road signposted 'Airport'. Very soon the church will be seen overlooking the road on the left.

Dating: Probably built mid-12th century with 14th century alterations; restored in 1706.

Description: Very small dome-hall building with arched recesses cp Ayii Apostoli at

215

Perakhorio. The fabric incorporates several massive dressed stones. Both original doorways have been blocked and later entrances made on the south and west. A stone set over the old west door is engraved with a Greek cross containing four smaller crosses in the corners. The springing for an arch on the south-east corner is all that remains of the ruined monastery buildings which have recently been demolished. They were in Franco-Byzantine style.

Decoration: Once fully decorated, the only two paintings still preserved in the immaculate interior are both of St. George and the Dragon, left and right of the screen. The northern one is behind a delicately carved, wooden arch and is a careful 1706 restoration of an earlier, superior work, the vigor of which still shines through the overpainting. The smaller St. George opposite bears the signature of the monk Anthimios: it is decorative but lacks the force of the other.

History: Ayios Yeoryios was one of two churches in the village of Agrinou, which was destroyed by the Mamelukes about 1426. Subsequently, it became the centre of a monastery and remained so until the end of the 18th century, after which it went into decline and finally ceased to function – the story of so many small, unprotected monasteries at that time.

The inscription at the foot of the larger painting records the renovation of the church and restoration of its paintings in 1706 by Manoli, its devoted priest, and his wife.

The church was called St. George the Far to distinquish it from St. George the Near or Kontos, which once stood nearer the centre of Larnaca.

ST. LAZARUS CHURCH *Larnaca's most treasured monument*

Position: In the old quarter of Scala near the Fort. Walk up Dionysou Street.

Dating: Built end 9th century, restored 17th century, arcade added 1750, campanile 1857.

Description: The building is a three-aisled basilica, the roof supported by four massive built piers in which are embedded pilasters and capitals from its Palaeo-Christian predecessor. It has lost its three domes, the side-aisles have been totally reconstructed and the windows enlarged. Faint traces of paint, discernible once, suggest that a scheme of decoration has been lost.

The gilded icon-screen was carved by a master named Taliadoros, and is considered to be one of the finest in Cyprus. Begun in 1773, it took nine years to complete. It carries some good icons, but note especially that of Lazarus on the far left, found beneath carving in 1972. Note, too, the carving of the Bishop's throne (1734) and, by the north-east pier, a Russian icon of the Virgin in an elaborate frame.

Directly under the Sanctuary is a very small, tripartite church which has been hewn out of the rock. Access is down steps beside the iconostasis. In the central aisle are two stone sarcophagi, the one on the south being revered as that of Lazarus.

Outside: Standing in the main gateway from the street, one sees, on the left of the church, the south wing of the old monastery, at the far end of which is a good small museum. The 1750 arcade runs along the south side of the church, but the view of the main building is obscured by an elaborate 19th

216

St. Lazarus Church, Larnaca

century bell-tower – which attracts the photographers but is quite alien. Under the arcade are memorial plaques in various languages, reflecting the cosmopolitan nature of Scala at the time and showing that this church was shared by all Christians. Moving west, note one of the schools set up by a committee in 1857 to educate the children of the district.

On the south-west corner of the church, observe the great, dressed stones in the wall; and on an equally large scale, pieces of columns lying in the yard: all bearing witness to an earlier, 5th or 6th century building. Do not miss the tiny English Cemetery behind its railing in the north-west corner. It commemorates members of the old Levant Company, consuls and their families, sailors and merchants between 1685 and 1850. The early deaths reflect the fevers of those days when the area was surrounded by marshland.

History: Any structure that may have existed before the end of the 9th century is subject to speculation, but it is likely that a church of some sort has been here since early Christian days. In about 890 AD, the tomb of St. Lazarus

217

was found on this spot and his relics sent to Constantinople, where they were received with much honour. The Emperor Leo VI provided funds for a church to be built over the tomb and, albeit much patched and restored, that is the building we see today. Early on, it became a monastery church and remained so for about eight hundred years, an isolated community, about a mile from the town. When the Franks came, Greek monks were replaced by Catholics. Throughout the Middle Ages, St. Lazarus was an important place of pilgrimage for visitors on their way to Jerusalem.

When the Turks arrived, the church was confiscated, but was sold back to the local community in 1589. Thenceforward, it became the main place of worship for the increasing population of Scala; and it was then that the north aisle began to be used as a Latin Chapel.

During the 18th century, a unique committee was formed in the church precincts aimed at caring for and educating the people; it continued this charitable work well into British rule. In 1970, during renovation after damage by fire, a sarcophagus was discovered under the altar with the word 'friend' inscribed on it in Greek. The few bones within are taken to belong to St. Lazarus and have not been removed. The original tomb, found in 890, was reported to have borne the inscription (in Hebrew): *Lazarus of the four days and friend of Christ.*

Tradition &
Legend:

They that were scattered abroad upon the persecution that arose about Stephen travelled as far as Phoenicia and Cyprus . . . Acts II xix.

Lazarus of Bethany, brother of Martha and Mary, after he had died and been restored to life by Christ, was a marked man. The tradition is immensely strong that he escaped to Cyprus after the stoning of Stephen in AD36. It goes on to assert that he was created first bishop of Kition by Paul and Barnabas when they were in the Island. Legends exist about the man himself. His skin, it is said, resembled parchment; moreover, he never smiled because of the sights he saw in Hades. Nevertheless, a story is told that he did smile on one occasion, when he saw a man steal a clay pot. 'The clay stealeth the clay,' he remarked (mankind being itself clay according to the Old Testament). A remarkable portrait of the saint exists in Lagoudera Church: painted in 1192, it is faithful to the reports of his looks. Lazarus is thought finally to have died in about 77AD, having been bishop of Kition for thirty years.

THE FORT

Position: At the southern end of the promenade.

Dating: Late 14th century, rebuilt 1625.

Description: The fort stands on the sea-shore. The courtyard is surrounded by a thick wall which has a number of rooms built into it, and the entrance is through a cool and cobble-stoned gatehouse. For the best view, walk down to the beach first – and notice too the blocked gunports. The fort is squat and strongly built, its massive walls splaying markedly outwards towards their base: it probably incorporates an earlier Byzantine structure, and it has been adapted to take artillery. The rooms to the west of the gatehouse contain the mediaeval museum for the district of Larnaca.

History: In the late 14th century, a chain of forts and blockhouses stretched from Larnaca to Kantara Castle in the north, and this was one of the chain. They were put up by James I as protection from the incursions of the Genoese,

who were then occupying Famagusta. After the Genoese were driven out, they were no longer needed, and only this fort was retained for defence. It was strengthened by the Venetians and rebuilt by the Turks. In the 1760's, the Abbé Maritis reported that it was by then *a wretched building and almost in ruins on the sea side.*[1] Its chief use then was to exchange salutes with visiting ships in an elaborate ceremony of exchange cannon shots. During the early days of British rule, the fort was used as a prison.

Adjacent is the Great Mosque which was erected in the late 16th century on the site of the Latin church of the Holy Cross: some Gothic features can still be observed.

THE PIERIDES COLLECTION at 4 Zenon Kitios Street, Larnaca (also the Swedish Consulate)

From the Tourist Office, turn left at the traffic lights. The house is a short way along on the right. Admission: Mon-Sat. 9.00 to 13.00.

It is the private residence of the Pierides family, leading citizens in Larnaca for generations. The collection was begun more than 150 years ago to prevent antiquities from being pillaged. Look for mediaeval and Byzantine exhibits in the entrance hall and right-hand rooms.

Examples of Byzantine pottery in the wall-cases:
Slip-painted, early 13th century: jug and bowl with spirals and bands
Plain sgraffito, early 13th century: bowl inscribed Theodoros
Monochrome sgraffito, 13th century: bowl – falconer with hawks (note the jesses)
Brown and green sgraffito, 14th century: marriage bowls – coiled snake – centaur – large bird
Sgraffito ware, late 14th century: chalice with heraldic Lusignan lion
Sgraffito ware, end 14th century: goblet (pride of the display)
Sgraffito ware, 15th century: schematised designs using fewest possible incisions
Venetian period, 16th century: small output, designs sketchy, abstract and poor quality.

---

1. Travels in the Island of Cyprus ch. 2.

Larnaca Central

All the previous monuments have been in the Scala area of this double town. Larnaca proper is divided into three quarters: **Khrysosotiros, Khrysopolitissa** and **Ayios Ioannis,** all built directly over ancient Kition and each with its own church. At the top of Archbishop Kyprianos Avenue is Panayia Khrysopolitissa, built 1815, of odd proportions and little intrinsic interest. Continue west to reach the cathedral and palace of the Bishop of Kition, set in the precincts of the monastery of **Khrysosotiros.** This church is altogether simpler and more dignified and has attractive 18th century furnishings; it was largely rebuilt in 1853.

A north turn leads to the third quarter and the Church of **Ayios Ioannis Theologos.** A 17th century building, it was extensively repaired in 1850. Of interest are the outdoor pulpit on the narthex wall, dating from 1849 and used at Easter for readings from the Gospel in four languages. An adjacent Venetian door made of black and white marble was formerly the west entrance to the church.

220

LARNACA DISTRICT

THE MONUMENTS

Note: * Indicates monuments of particular interest
        ** Indicates monuments of outstanding interest

SOUTH

THE TEKKE OF UMM HARAM, *(Hala Sultan): Shrine of Mohammed's foster-mother*

Third most holy place in Islam.

Position: Three miles south-west of Larnaca. Take first turning right after airport.

Tekke of Umm Haram

Description: The mosque and Tekke stand in solitude in an Eastern garden of palms, citrus trees and flowering shrubs overlooking the Salt Lake. It is first seen at a distance, and, with water in the Lake and a reflection, is a lovely sight. The approach is through a gateway set with elegant inscriptions in Arabic. The mosque itself is considered to be the best sort of Ottoman architecture in Cyprus. As customary, one enters it without shoes.

Note the mihrab, orientated towards Mecca, the latticed women's gallery, the stand for the Koran, the water-cistern and the arabic clock. The shrine is reached through a doorway left of the mihrab. It admits to a vestibule beyond which is the chamber containing the tomb of Umm Haram. Before entering that, examine the second doorway: it is mediaeval with dog-tooth moulding and the threshold has a marble frieze, apparently Roman. Within stands a trilithon swathed in cloth. Although the two massive uprights are now partly constructed of masonry and wood, the horizontal stone is a single gigantic meteorite, weighing fifteen tons.

Inland lies a Bronze-age city and this could be a cromlech relating to it. The lower parts of the uprights are decorated with tree-of-life, star of David and rosette motifs in low relief. The tomb itself is smothered in fine embroidered

222

cloths and is protected by bronze gates. In the cloister, another tomb commemorates the 20th century wife of King Hussein of the Hedjaz. Until the first World War, every Turkish ship dipped its flag as it passed, the Tekke being visible out at sea.

History: In the year 649, the Prophet Mohammed's foster-mother, Umm Haram, arrived in Salamis with her husband, the Governor of Palestine and second-in-command of the first Arab raid in a Holy War against Christian Cyprus. Whilst riding on the shore of the Salt Lake, she was thrown from her mule and, in the words of a Turkish historian, writing ca 1800, *Broke her pellucid neck and yielded up her victorious soul and in that fragrant spot was at once buried.*[1]

The Byzantine centuries passed, the Latins came and went: and some time in the 17th century a Turkish dervish found this ancient Moslem tomb, practically buried under a dolmen and obviously that of a person of great rank. By 1761, the shrine was walled and had acquired its bronze gates and pilgrims were arriving. The Sultan in Istanbul conferred his special protection on the Tekke and appointed a sheikh to guard it. A mosque, a fountain and accommodation were provided and large numbers of Moslems came to pray at the shrine of Umm Haram. The present mosque was built in 1816.

Legends: According to popular belief, the meteorite was miraculously transported from Mecca when Umm Haram died and hovered, unsupported, over her tomb. Another claim was that all three stones were on Mount Sinai, being transferred here by angels.

PANAYIA ANGELOKTISTOS CHURCH, *Kiti*
(built by the angels)
Contains a unique wall-mosaic of the 6th/7th century.

Position: In Kiti village (signposted). Seven miles south-west of Larnaca on the airport road.

Dating: Built ca. 1000 AD on 5th century ruins. Rebuilt 12th c; Latin chapel attached 13th; restoration 16th.

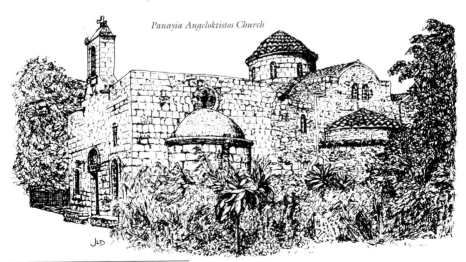

Panayia Angeloktistos Church

---

1. Excerpta Cypria, trans. Cobham.

Description: **The Byzantine Church** is a lofty 12th century cruciform building with a
lantern dome. Entrance is through the Latin Chapel on the south side, now
used as a vestibule. Few traces of the original decoration remain, but a good
painting of John the Baptist can be seen on the north-east pillar (probably
13th century). The icon screen is part templon, with painted panels and
posts, and part iconostasis. On the right hangs a large icon of the Archangel
Michael (14th century): although overpainted several times, the calm oval
face is still strikingly lovely.

The Mosaic

Embedded in the conch of the apse, it is the only known example of its kind
in monumental art to have survived from before iconoclasm. In the centre
stands the Virgin with Christ on her left arm; she is presenting Him to us
with a gesture and He is making the sign of blessing.[1] She is standing on a
footstool, yet appears to be floating in space – an effect achieved by placing
her stool over the frieze. The background of gilded glass tesserae, reflecting
light above a strip of blue floor, enhances the three-dimensional effect. The
Archangels Michael and Gabriel, each holding a wand of office, bow towards
the Holy Pair and offer the Christchild the orbs of supreme spiritual
authority. Their wings are feathered with peacock-eyes, which are symbols of
eternal life. Gabriel's classical, moulded robes, the elegance and grace of all
the figures, betray a strong Hellenistic influence. The patterned border
includes symbolic motifs of fountains, stags, parrots and ducks.

The dating of this work was controversial until the border was uncovered in
1952 and seen to have similarities with decoration elsewhere known to have
a 6th century date: the Dome of the Rock, for example. The inscription
HAGIA MAPIA, Holy Mary, above the Virgin's head is a curious
anachronism, *THEOTOKOS*, Mother of God, having long superseded it
(vide Council of Ephesus 431AD).

The Mortuary Chapel on the north east is a 12th century construction and
is dedicated to the medical saints Cosmas and Damian. It contains several
well-executed wall-paintings of the 15th century, including a mounted St.
George.

The Latin Chapel was attached in the late 13th century. It is a Gothic
building divided into four rib-vaulted bays, the ribs springing from internal
buttresses which form arched recesses between each pair. Above the apse is a
small round window with quatrefoil tracery. At the west end is the
tombstone of Simone Guers dd. 1302. On the east are displayed a number of
icons in poor condition; but note the St. John, which was probably painted
for the chapel, forming part of a Crucifixion scene; it shows marked Italian
influence. Built into the wall outside are three coats-of-arms, including one
of three lions heads – almost certainly that of the Gibelet family. Note the
stone water-spout in the form of a sheep, west of the chapel.

History: The 5th century basilica would certainly have been wrecked by the Arabs; yet
the apse containing the 6th century mosaic somehow miraculously survived
to be incorporated into the rebuilding of 1000 AD – also a basilica. Under
the Comnenians it was rebuilt again and became cruciform. The Latin
Chapel was added by the powerful Gibelet family, who were lords of the
fiefdom here in the 13th century.

---

1. A disposition known as Hodegetria, describing the Virgin as a conductress of prayer.

KITI VILLAGE

It is on the old Roman coast road and is thought to have been founded in the 4th century by settlers from Kittim (Kition). Later the settlement was walled. Under the Latins it was known as Le Quid. Kiti became a royal dhomaine in 1367 when King Peter established a palace on the west bank of the river Tremithios, not far from the church. The king was fresh from his capture of Alexandria. The palace stood for barely sixty years, being destroyed by the Mameluke army in 1426: the few remaining stones may be viewed from the bridge.

THE WATCH TOWERS

At Cape Kiti, not far from the lighthouse, stands a sturdy **Venetian watch-tower,** which could not have been built, according to Enlart, before the very end of the 15th century. Its first-floor entrance leads into a room vaulted and with broad squared ribs. In the west wall is a staircase leading to the roof, which has impressive machicolations round its parapet. The blind ground floor gives internal access to a cistern. Three coats-of-arms are carved on the lintel of the doorway: in the centre is the lion of St. Mark and on each side is a shield bearing arms so far unidentified. The tower was repaired in 1977/78.

Venetian Watch-Tower, Kiti

About eight miles west, at Alaminos, is another watch-tower, constructed in the 15th century – ruinous now but poorly built anyhow. It had three floors, the entrance being on the middle level with a long narrow recess over it to house the raised drawbridge.

225

AYIOS YEORYIOS, *Arpera*

Moving testimony to life in the 18th century. (See also *House of the Dragoman*, Nicosia.)

Position: Go through Tersephanou village, then take the lower road (right) for 1½ miles to the dam. (Source of the springs that once fed Larnaca's aqueduct.) If church locked, apply for key at the farm across the field.

Dating: Built 1745, decorated 1747, renovated 1785.

Description: The village has gone and only the church remains, standing on the rubble of its predecessor. Built and buttressed in Franco-Byzantine style, it is single-aisled with a vaulted roof. A door on the north-west leads to a latticed women's gallery, recently restored.

Decoration: Never fully painted. All the wall-paintings and accompanying inscriptions belong to the first period, 1745-7; also the iconostasis and lowest row of icons.

Donor painting (above north door): Christofakis Constantinou is shown with his family offering his church to his chosen patron, St. George. These are portraits and have been rendered with great care. All are wearing clothes such as befit a leading Cypriot family whose head is Chief Dragoman to the Serai. The rich robes are trimmed with ermine, the ladies wear exotic hats, and the wide, black fur head-gear of Christofakis and the two boys are official dragoman calpacs. There is considerable Turkish influence. The two inscriptions are prayers to St. George.

Other paintings include Symeon Stylites on his pillar, and an outsize George and the Dragon signed and dated *Hand of Philaretos 1747*. (Cp the St. George in Ayios Minas by same hand ten years later.) The left compartment of the sanctuary, or bema, is partly decorated; and here yet another inscription records the names of all the children of the family, living and dead, whom the priest should pray for.

The Iconostasis: contemporary with the building. Note the unusual double icon of St. George and a dog-headed St. Christopher painted by a monk called Ioannikos. (See legend.) The icons on the upper rows were painted in 1785 together with the inscription explaining the reason for the forty-year delay.

History: To be the Grand Dragoman, or Interpreter in the Governor's Palace, called for the utmost diplomacy and skill. In 1745, Christofakis knew his life was in danger. After a threat of exile, he had this church built and decorated at his own expense in thanksgiving to St. George for continuing to safeguard himself and his family (see dedicatory inscription).

Three years later he was murdered as he made his way to church in Nicosia on Easter Day. The instigator was Haji Baki Ali who was the most detested Turkish official of the century: later he was to become Governor of Cyprus. Nothing happened to Arpera for thirty-five years; but, as soon as public outcry overthrew the tyrant, Meletios the Bishop of Kitium renovated Christofakis' church, put the remaining icons on the screen and added there some lines of verse recording all this.

Legend: An eastern story tells of St. Christopher's great beauty, which made him very attractive to women. As he wanted to devote his life to God in prayer and

226

meditation, he prayed to the Virgin for help; so she gave him the head of a dog. Afterwards, no woman would look at him again and he was left in peace. (A connection with Anubis, the jackal-headed god of Egypt suggests itself.)

NORTH WEST

STAVROVOUNI MONASTERY: *Mountain of the Holy Cross; mediaeval Santa Croce*

One of the oldest foundations in Cyprus.

Warning: Since the death of the previous abbot in 1982, the monastery has been run on Mount Athos lines. It is therefore inaccessible to tourists. Only if you are male and devout will you be admitted.

Stavrovouni Monastery

Position: Twenty-three miles west of Larnaca on an isolated peak 2,260' high and clearly visible from the airport. From the old Nicosia/Limassol road, just over a mile south of the Kornos/Pyrga crossroads, look for the turn-off for Stavrovouni on the east (signpost). Passing a military camp and the small dependent monastery, Ayia Varvara, the road climbs and twists steeply to the car park on the shoulder: easy steps lead up to the summit.

Description: The tremendous views and the pure, clear air are quite stupifying but the monastery is rather disappointing. The visible buildings are relatively modern although on pre-existing foundations, and the crypt could well be original. The church is tripartite – a very early plan – and has two central domes. To the east are the scant remains of the Roman temple of Aphrodite; and on the west three massive flying buttresses support the outer wall of the monastery – legacy of the Latin monks and added in the 14th/15th century.

The monks live very plainly, keep strictly to their vows and are some of the most devout in the land; and the monastery itself, which used to be embellished with many treasures, is now austere. There is a large wooden cross dated 1476 and minutely carved with scenes from the life of Christ, encased in silver in 1702 and containing a splinter of the True Cross in a gold cover. In the north corridor is a plaque engraved with a prayer from an 11th century monk. Until very recently, the only water supply was from four rain-water tanks.

History &
Tradition:
The mountain was called Olympus in classical times and was crowned with a temple to Aphrodite, which became a place of pilgrimage. In about AD 327, Helena, mother of Constantine, built a church over the temple ruins and placed within it the cross of the Good Thief which she had brought from Jerusalem. Again pilgrims started coming to the Holy mountain, and the place has been honoured ever since. St. Helena is also credited with sending the first monks here, from Palestine – and the first monastic cats.

Records of the early part of Stavrovouni's history have not survived its later pillaging and destruction; but mediaeval visitors mention the miraculous Cross which hung unsupported in the air beside the altar. In 1197, the Lusignans established Benedictine monks in the monastery. They remained until the Mamelukes sacked and destroyed it in 1426 and carried off the Cross, by then encased in gold. In that year all Benedictines left Cyprus for good. It is uncertain who succeeded them, but the buildings were repaired only to be burnt down again by the Turks in 1570. After that, they remained unoccupied until some time in the 17th century, when at long last the Orthodox monks came back. During the Greek uprising of 1821, Stavrovouni was searched, the monks discovered hiding in the secret crypt, and all were massacred. Now it is very peaceful. The monks produce the best honey and halloumi cheese and both are sold to visitors at Ayia Varvara.

Legend:
St. Helena was returning to Constantinople from Jerusalem with the Cross of Jesus and that of the Good Thief when her ship was driven by storms to the south coast of Cyprus and she came ashore at a place still called Vasilikos, 'Queen', in memory. She fell asleep, *being wearied of the sea,* and dreamed that a young man commanded her to build many churches here, just as she had done in Jerusalem. On waking, she discovered that the cross of the Good Thief had been miraculously transported to the top of the mountain. So the first church she built was Stavrovouni.[1]

AYIA THEKLA MONASTERY, *Mosphiloti*

It stands back from the old Nicosia/Limassol road, east side, hidden by trees. Take the track immediately south of the Mosphiloti turning. The monastery dates from 1471 and is unremarkable in itself. There are associations, though, with St. Helena, who by tradition established the first monastery on this spot in the 4th century. A large cave containing a holy well lies under the apse of the church. Nuns have recently come to Ayia Thekla.

---

1. Chronicle of Makhairas.

AYIA EKATERINA CHAPEL, *Pyrga*

Position: One mile east of the old Nicosia/Limassol road, first turning north of Stavrovouni. The chapel is on the right before entering the village, overlooking a stream. It represents a bit of late Lusignan history and contains portraits of King Janus and Charlotte, his Queen.

Dating: A Franco-Byzantine building of 1421; decorated same year; further work done in 1432.

*Ayia Ekaterina
Chapel, Pyrga*

Description: Small, single-aisled and barrel-vaulted; strengthened in Gothic style with transverse ribs; it has no apse. Traces remain of other buildings which once surrounded the chapel. A wooden portico formerly enclosed it on three sides, leaving the east free. Despite its small size, it is well lighted and airy, having six windows and three doors. On the south, a tiny belfry carries stone fitments for banners; and on the lintel of the door below it the enigmatic word *Bazoges* is cut. The legend is incomplete but, as the word derives from *basilica,*[1] it might indicate the royal entrance.

Interior: A lost inscription in French under the west window recorded the dedication of the chapel in 1421 *in honour of God and of the Passion of our Lord.* The walls and vault were originally completely painted. From what remains, it can be seen that the Crucifixion and scenes from the Life of Christ covered the eastern part and the Annunciation and scenes from the Life of the Virgin the western. A simple plan, but not Byzantine – although the style and iconography are, basically. The Crucifixion above the altar is the most interesting painting: Janus and Charlotte, wearing crowns, can be seen kneeling at the foot of the cross. Below is the Entombment. See on the right a figure wearing a mitre: he could be Hugh de Lusignan, brother of Janus and Archbishop of Cyprus, who acted as Regent during the year of Janus' captivity in Egypt. Opposite, on the west wall right of the lunette is the Virgin (part of an Annunciation): note the black bird looking towards the – missing – Archangel.[2]

---

1. Enlart
2. A&J Stylianou

229

To help identification of the rest of the scenes, here is a summary:

East wall: Crucifixion, Deposition, Entombment, Empty Tomb (twice). *North vault:* Raising of Lazarus, The Last Supper (best preserved), Washing of the Feet. *West wall:* Annunciation. *South vault:* Birth of Virgin, Blessing, Presentation.

Lower register

Individual saints in relief, but covered in salt deposits.

West door: rt. BVM with Christchild above three female saints.

South wall east: four saints – two of them wearing Catholic bishops' mitres.

So far, the painter has revealed himself as trained in the Byzantine tradition, but adapting where necessary to the demands of the Franks. He seems to have picked up his French by ear because one or two inscriptions read strangely – La Pente Couste, for example! A complete departure can be seen on the ribs of the vaulting, which are ornamented with Royal Lusignan coats of arms and bring an echo of mediaeval western pageantry into the chapel.

History: A chapel to Ayia Ekaterina once stood on the royal estate of Potamia a day's march north of Pyrga. In 1426, it was reduced to rubble by the Mamelukes and never rebuilt. The small church at Pyrga had been dedicated to The Passion, originally, and the foundations surrounding it indicate the presence of old monastic buildings. It is quite likely that the title of Chapel Royal and the dedication to St. Catherine were subsequently transferred here and the paintings reproduced.

WEST

STAVROS CHURCH, *Tokhni*

Venerated place of pilgrimage associated with St. Helena.

Position: Turn off the Nicosia/Limassol road four miles south of the junction for Khirokitia and continue north to the village along an access road.

Dating: Founded 325 or 327 AD; rebuilt on new site, date unknown; Latin Chapel attached 14th century; burnt down 1426; rebuilt on original site in the 19th century.

Description: At the top of a picturesque village a sturdy bridge spans the dry river-bed. It carries on its back a not unattractive modern church which stands on the site of one of the very early churches of Cyprus – that erected by St. Helena in the 4th century. It used to contain a piece of the True Cross; and a cave exists under the south portico in which that and other treasures were hidden during times of trouble. The church was rebuilt in the mid-Byzantine period on the hillside opposite, using the old stones.

When the Mamelukes passed through in 1426, they destroyed the new church and now only the ruins of the 14th century Latin chapel attached to it remain, on which traces of intense heat can be seen. Preserved within the modern church is a slab of rock formerly part of the cliff-face upstream: it was incised at a remote period with a floriate cross and some lettering in Greek coloured in red – which has been renewed so often that it has become unreadable. (Locally it is said that the inscription marked the point where St. Helena crossed the river and had her vision.)

Tradition &
History:
St. Helena, after founding Stavrovouni, wished also to leave a piece of the True Cross with the Christian community in this area. As the royal party was crossing the river-bed to return to their ship, a sign from Heaven in the shape of a pillar of fire directed the Queen to Tokhni, and she built her second church there accordingly. The wood from the True Cross was preserved within for almost a thousand years. Then, according to two Venetian texts, in 1318 a Latin priest stole it and it was lost for twenty-two years, when a shepherd-boy discovered it hidden in a carob tree.

It then became the centre of a fierce argument between the Latin and the Orthodox Churches, the former declaring it to be not genuine. As the True Cross could not be destroyed by fire, to resolve matters the piece was tested over a brazier in the presence of King Hugh IV and Queen Alice; and although it became red hot it stayed entire. Then a miracle occurred, for the Queen had been dumb for three years[1] and, when she saw the Cross unburnt after an hour, suddenly cried out, *I believe that this cross is of the wood of the Cross upon which Christ the Son of God was crucified.* And all present realised the miracle.

The piece of the True Cross, incidentally, was never returned to the church of Tokhni but taken by the Queen's mother to Nicosia to a church specially built for it. It was last heard of in the Phaneromeni Monastery in Nicosia.

---

1. See Makheras Monastery

231

Legend: In times gone by, before the church was built, Tokhni was infested by forty devils. To get rid of them, the inhabitants dug a pit at the far end of the bridge and a priest managed to entice the devils into it. *Hardly were they inside than masons who had been standing ready, clapped a cover over the hole, and at once built a church; and so long as the church stands the devils must remain bottled up.*[1]

SITE OF THE BATTLE OF KHIROKITIA (7th July 1426)

It is also the site of an earlier encounter, for it was here that Richard Coeur de Lion caught up with Isaac Comnenus in 1191.

Position: Go past the Neolithic site towards the village and take first turning left.

Description: The sparse ruins are known locally as 'the old Serai,' but are in reality the remains of a Commanderie of the Knights of St. John. Part of a large vaulted hall can be seen, built of the same fine, ashlar stone and in the same style as Kolossi Castle (which puts its date well after the battle). The contemporary building, constructed by the Templars around 1300, was destroyed in the battle and all that remains is the well.

Close by stands the small church of **PANAYIA TOU KAMPOU** (Our Lady of the Field), which probably served as the Knights' chapel and is of late 13th/early 14th century origin. The fragmentary paintings date from 1509. Notice the French-derived finial, a face amid leaves, over the west door. At the village there is a mediaeval bridge with pointed arches.

History: Ever since Peter I sacked Alexandria in 1365, the Egyptians had felt bitter towards Cyprus; and Cypriot sailors had helped further the antagonism by constantly raiding their shores. Now, under a strong Sultan, they followed the example of the Genoese and began to retaliate. Twice already a Saracen force had landed to harass and plunder Limassol and the countryside round; but this time it was a much larger contingent.

On July 4th 1426, with an army hastily raised at Potamia, King Janus and his knights marched south to Pyrga. Next day they moved to the

Panayia tou Kambou, Khirokitia

Commanderie at Khirokitia, and on the third day following battle was joined. Gross inefficiency, poor discipline and the rawness of the troops ensured that what ought to have been an easy victory turned into a lost battle after the first clash. The ranks broke and fled, leaving the King and his cavalry to their fate. Janus was taken alive only because he shouted *"Melek"* – King! – before

---

1. Gunnis, Historic Cyprus.

a lance struck. That night his brother Hugh, Archbishop, brought the royal family and treasure out of Nicosia to refuge in Kyrenia Castle.[1]

Four days later, wrecking all the way, the Mamelukes reached the capital and sacked it and Alexandria was avenged. King Janus was forced to ride in a victory procession in Cairo and was publicly humiliated. Next year he was ransomed for an immense sum and returned to end his days a broken, sick man. It was left to the Archbishop to restore order, acting as his brother's regent: he seems altogether to have been the abler man.

THE MONASTERY OF AYIOS MINAS, *near Lefkara*
(Now occupied by nuns)

Position: South of Lefkara, between Kato Dhrys and Vavla in the valley.

Dating: 15th century, restored in 1754 by Parthenios, Bishop of Kition.

Description: Probably began as a Dominican establishment. The church is the common Cyprus mix of Byzantine and Gothic: pointed vault with transverse ribs and side porticos. It is surrounded by 18th century monastic buildings with a cloister on the west. The paintings of St. George and St. Minas on the north and south walls were done by Philaretos in 1757 – the same who painted the large St. George in Arpera Church ten years earlier. The nuns paint icons and produce excellent honey.

CHURCH OF ARKHANGELOS MIKHAIL, *Kato Lefkara*

Position: Isolated in a field west of the village along a chalk track.

Kato Lefkara

---

1. The eyewitness account of the battle in the Chronicle of Makhairas is worth reading (see Gunnis page 263).

Dating: End 12th century; modern extension, west end.

Description: A single-aisled building, domed and vaulted, with arched recesses cp. Laghoudera.

Decoration: End of 12th century paintings in the apse, the drum of the dome and south central recess. Best preserved are the Communion of the Apostles and the Fathers of the Church in the apse, the Baptism in the recess and the Mandylion above the south door. Notice the Christchild in the paten on the painted altar. The celebrating Fathers are converging towards the altar in a semi-frontal position, and all but one (name lost) are wearing the polystavrion phelonian. It is this last feature that reveals the late 12th century date of the paintings as before that few bishops other than St. John Chrysostom had the right to wear such a garment. See also Ayia Solomoni in Paphos, decorated in the same period and in similar style and where the Fathers are mainly dressed in the polystavrion.

The Anastasis, west vault, is 15th century, and the paintings on the north walls are very late in date.

History: Kato Lefkara is the smaller of the two lace-making villages. It is where the Orthodox Bishop of Limassol had his seat when the Latins expelled the Greek prelates from the main towns in 1222. Rupert Gunnis writes: *While repairs were being carried out to the church about 1865 a bishop's crown and other relics were found under the floor. These were sold to one of the foreign consuls at Larnaca, probably General Cesnola.*

St. Neophytos was born in the neighbouring village of Kato Dhrys and is said to have attended this church as a boy, but it must have been in an earlier building.

NORTH EAST

AYIOS ANTONIOS CHURCH, *Kellia*

('Kellia' means cells and indicates a monastery).

Rare painting of the Crucifixion, 9th century.

Position: About 5½ miles north-east of Larnaca. One mile along the Famagusta road, look for sign for Livadhia; then, after passing through that village, turn left at the fork. Coming from Nicosia, take the Aradhippou by-pass for four miles to the Kellia turn-off.

Dating: Built 9th century on earlier foundations; reconstructed early 11th century; further rebuilding 15th century; narthex and external arcading possibly 18th century.

Description: On a mound of stones and rubble, site of an Early Christian church, St. Anthony has been considerably altered over the centuries. It probably began as a three-aisled basilica similar to St. Lazaros – and likewise with three domes; but in the late 10th/early 11th century it was reconstructed to become a cross-in-square church. The present apse and high transept vault are 15th century work, made necessary, perhaps, after the destruction of the village by Mamelukes in 1425. Later, internal buttresses were built between the pillars. (They have now been removed.) Built into the fabric and lying about are fragments of various periods.

Ayios Antonios Church, Kellia

Look especially for:

i) the arms of the Gourri family above the south west door – a sun displayed

ii) part of a sarcophagus lid, 4th century BC, acting as lintel over west door into narthex

iii) a pair of heraldic rodents in stone relief above north door

iv) palaeo-Christian consecration crosses with red infill on two of the pillars

The roof was a look-out post in the second world war, and local people say that it commands a view as far as Syria on a clear evening.

Decoration: Chiefly of the mid-Byzantine period. Until very recently, all was hidden under whitewash which, when removed, revealed in some places as many as three superimposed layers of plastering. The wall-paintings date from the

Plan of church (showing construction dates and distribution of wall-paintings)

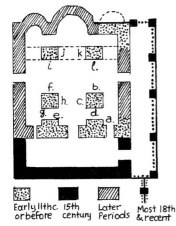

Ground plan of Ayios Antonios, Kellia

a. Sacrifice of Isaac (twice): early 11th & 12th c.

b. Sts. Andronicos & Athanasia: early 11th c.

c. Virgin & Child enthroned: early 12th c.

d. Virgin & Child: early 12th c. – by a master and very fine

e. Sts. Cosmas & Damian possibly: early 11th c.

f. St. George mounted; two female saints: early 12th c.

g. Early Byzantine anchor-type crosses on marble.

h. St. George mounted: possibly 13th c. Below: early dedication cross with inscription.

i, j, k. Prelates and saints.

l. Crucifixion, 9th c. and fragment of Betrayal above (11th c.)

235

early 11th to the 13th century; also an eastern-style Crucifixion of the 9th century with archaic iconography. A few paintings are at present in the Cyprus Museum: they were removed to expose earlier work and will be returned to other positions. The paintings are distributed in a seemingly arbitrary manner, the customary plan, which would have included a Christological cycle in the vaults, having been lost.

(For dates and assessment concerning both fabric and frescoes, I am for the most part indebted to The Painted Churches of Cyprus, A&J Stylianou.)

AYIOS YEORYIOS CHURCH, *Xylophagou*

Position: On the Larnaca – Ayia Napa road, about seven miles east of Dhekelia, behind the main square and dwarfed by the modern church alongside. Key kept at the priest's house.

Dating: Built and decorated late 15th century; renovated 1770; some later painting.

Description: Built as a single-aisled domed church with three bays and extended later at the west end and a gallery added. Above the south door is an emplacement for a banner: the quoin in the right-hand angle of the frame is carved with a coat-of-arms showing two heraldic beasts with foliage. Inside is further evidence of heraldry: above the apse another coat-of-arms displays the Byzantine double-headed eagle. A&J Stylianou consider it possible that the lord of the fiefdom here in Venetian times was not a Latin but a Greek of the old Palaeologue nobility.

In 1770, structural alterations and a general renovation were carried out, including a new iconostasis, the funds being provided by two benefactors. After that, the church was apparently monastic. Then, at some point, Christ Pantocrator replaced the Virgin in the conch of the apse, indicating a change of function for the church, it becoming a cemetery chapel.

Decoration: The paintings were badly blacked in a fire many years ago. The Annunciation (east lunette) and the Nativity (bema, south wall) have been cleaned and proved to belong to the first period of decoration, end 15th century. The Festival Cycle continues round the vaults as far as the north-west bay; then comes a Tree of Jesse followed by a short Life of the Virgin in the south-east bay. All appear to belong to the first period except for the south-west vault: in this case, the whole bay has been cleaned, revealing a Crucifixion and related scenes to be naive work done in 1805 (commissioned, no doubt, to replace those lost when the old west wall was destroyed). St. George and the Dragon, right of the icon screen, belongs to the period of renovation and is dated 1772. The lower walls are lined with saints, some overpainted.

Ayios Yeoryios Chapel

Associated with Xylophagou church is the simple chapel of **Ayios Yeoryios** at the mouth of Potamos tou Liopetriou. It stands near a picturesque creek which is lined with small gaily-painted craft, and is the fishermen's church. To reach it, drive two-and-a-half miles out of Xylophagou on the Ayia Napa road; at the crossroad, turn left onto a poor surface (signposted 'Potamos') and continue to its terminus.

Watch Tower

Two miles south of Xylophagou stands a third watch tower cp. those at Kiti and Alaminos: it is Venetian, 16th century and ruinous.

FAMAGUSTA

*The Free Parts of the District
around the Ayia Napa – Protaras Area and Kokkinohoria.*

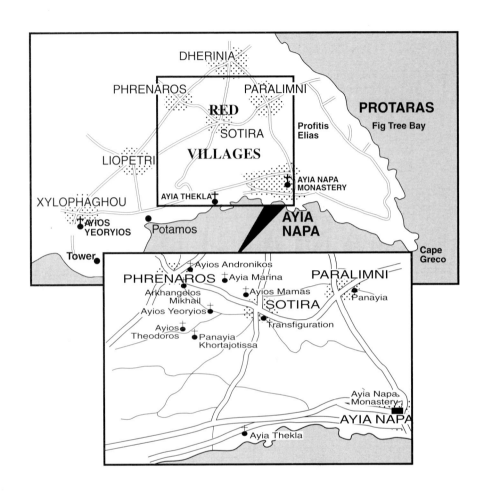

Note: *   Indicates monuments of particular interest
           ** Indicates monuments of outstanding interest

AYIA THEKLA

Small church of a former monastery, Ayia Thekla can be found on the rocky coast midway between Xylophagou and Ayia Napa. It is reputed to stand on an early Byzantine site, and the considerable debris of tile and broken stone to the south and east seems to bear this out. The chief interest here is the saint's shrine cut out of the solid rock, which is located on the shore a short distance to the south-west. It has a long, narrow aisle, an apse and deep west, central and east recesses like a miniature church, and an oil-lamp burns continuously. It does not have the appearance of a converted Roman or Hellenistic tomb. The shrine is held in high regard by the people of the district.

Plan of Ayia Thekla's shrine (not to scale)

AYIA NAPA MONASTERY: *Our Lady of the Forest*

One of the last monuments built by the Venetians.

Position: In the central square of the village.

Dating: Founded 16th century, completed 1570, restored 1813 and again in 1950.

Description: The monastery is entered through an imposing gateway which leads into a large open courtyard surrounded on three sides by cloisters. To the right is a solid two-storey gatehouse. Notice the boar's head fountain at its base, thought to be Roman. In the centre stands a marble basin in a domed fountain-house. Beyond the basin, built against the cliff, is an unusual-looking church. Beyond the cloister on the far side, facing the sea, stands a large open cistern in which huge goldfish swim. Here two magnificent sacred trees cast their shadows: they are the sycamore-figs of the Bible and are reputed to be six hundred years old.

The Church: far older than the monastery, possibly 8th or 9th century, it has been built round an underground rock-cut chamber in which, it is

Ayia Napa Monastery

239

claimed, a holy icon of the Virgin was found – hence the name 'Ayia Napa'. A well inside still contains water. The built portions of the church are unremarkable, and they incorporate a Latin Chapel, not unexpectedly. The front, however, has attractive architectural features including a small rose window. According to an inscription in Latin noted by Drummond in 1754, the date of this facade – and also of the central fountain – is 1530.

The Fountain-house: contains a fine octagonal marble basin, decorated Roman-style with heavy swags of garlands interspersed with sculpted figures and coats-of-arms, somewhat defaced. Between the four broad arches below the canopy are cool and welcome seats.

The Venetian Gatehouse: a perplexing structure seemingly at variance with the rest. From without, it is easily defended, having a small gateway and impregnable ground-floor store-rooms. Viewed from the courtyard, it has the look of a Lusignan watch tower, complete with an external flight of stone steps leading to a first-floor entry. The living quarters are all on that level and have richly ornamented window jambs and arches, and a loggia overlooking the gate. The gateway itself carries stone sockets for flags or an awning. Altogether, the house accords well with the tradition that a noble Venetian lady came to live in the monastery.

History &   *Cape Graecia was probably Cape Throni of the ancients, where there was a city*
Tradition: *of the same name.* Pococke, Exp. Cyp.

Remains of massive walls and a Roman aqueduct bringing water over four miles to the monastery site indicate that this was a Roman settlement which subsequently reverted to forest. Some reference is made to a convent being here in the 14th century; but any records that might have survived were burnt, according to one historian,[1] by a monk towards the end of last century because he could see no use for them! Of the Venetian monastery – a nunnery – the story is told that the daughter of a rich and aristocratic family was refused permission to marry the man she loved; so she retreated from the world to live the religious life. The story tells further that the faces on the fountain are those of the girl's father and mother.

There was still a convent here well into the 17th century; then, for about a hundred years, Orthodox monks were in possession. The monastery fell into disuse in 1790. Now it houses the Ayia Napa Conference Centre, serving various churches of the Middle East.

AMONG THE RED VILLAGES – THE KOKKINOHORIA

The Paralimni Lake area possesses a number of churches, none of which has any outstanding interest, but which collectively are worth visiting.

At Paralimni: The Church of the Panayia

This was originally a single-aisled building with a dome and barrel-vault – possibly 16th century; the south aisle was added later. An unusual feature is the vaulting, which is decorated with porcelain plates mostly of the early 18th century. The church has some late 18th century wall-painting and a good iconostasis of the 17th century.

---

1. Kyrris: Cyprus Studies, 1968

Vicinity Sotira/Phrenaros

The feudal estate of Frinaria flourished here in mediaeval times, its centre a mile south of the relatively new village of Phrenaros. The domestic buildings have disappeared, leaving only the churches. The Greek word 'freminors', it is sometimes suggested, gave rise to the name, a corruption of 'freres mineurs'.

The **Monastery of Panayia Khortajotissa** – or Kourdali – was still here in the late 18th century: its early 16th century church has recently been restored. The nearby remains of **Ayios Theodoros Church** consist solely of the dome of its narthex; but to the north-east is the splendid church of **Ayios Georgios of Khortakia** (the name of the locality). It is an early 12th century cross-in-square type, lofty and well-built, with a later elongated narthex of rougher construction. The original west doorway has five crosses cut into the lintel. This church retained a considerable amount of its wall-paintings well into the present century; now very few are left.

Of the group of churches in the north, recommended are:

Ayia Marina: 15th century, barrel-vaulted with wall-paintings.

Arkhangelos Mikhail: dwarfed by the new church in Phrenaros village, restored 1883 and paintings lost, but an attractive building.

Ayios Andronikos: a small chapel.

At Sotira: **St. Mamas:** possibly 12th century, extensively rebuilt 15th or 16th c. Partly ruined but still containing late 16th c. wall paintings.

Church of the Transfiguration: close by with fine bell-tower. History unknown, but rebuilt 1553; lost its side-aisles.

Ayios Andronikos, Phrenaros

241

MONUMENTS IN OCCUPIED TERRITORY

Important Byzantine and Mediaeval Monuments in the Turkish-occupied part of Cyprus.

A. NICOSIA DISTRICT

Nicosia

1. **Kyrenia Gate** (see under Venetian Walls & Gates, p.180).

2. **Monastery of the Whirling Dervishes:** founded 13th c.; multidomed building dates from early 17th c.; Museum of Turkish Art since 1963.

3. **Venetian Column:** in Ataturk Square. Roman. Coats of arms round base and originally surmounted with the Lion of St. Mark.

4. **Buyuk Hamam** formerly St. George of the Latins: 14th c. and a public bath since 1570; now about six feet below street level.

5. **Buyuk Khan** (the Great Inn): built 1572 from stone from earlier buildings; small hexagonal mosque in centre.

*6. **The Bedestan** (covered market just south of Ayia Sophia): a hall contrived from the remains of two abutting churches: north, the Latin St. George of the English – 16th c.; south, the Greek Orthodox Cathedral – 14th c. Site of 6th century early Christian basilica.

*7. **Selimiye Mosque** formerly the Latin Cathedral of Ayia Sophia: founded 1209 and, despite damage and alterations over the years, a superb example of French Gothic.

*8. **Haidar Pasha Mosque** formerly the Latin church of St. Catherine, late 14th c. and perfect example of the architecture of Southern France. (Lies north-east of Ayia Sophia.)

*9. **The Armenian Church,** former church of the Benedictine nunnery of Our Lady of Tyre, 13th century Gothic. (Near the Roccas bastion on the south-west edge of Green Line.)

Morphou

Monastery church of **Ayios Mamas:** Byzantine, rebuilt ca. 1500 & 1725. Interesting iconostasis.

B. FAMAGUSTA DISTRICT

Famagusta Walled city

1. **The Walls:** constructed by Venetians on Lusignan foundations; note particularly the Martinengro bastion and the Citadel (Othello's Tower).

2. **The Latin church** of St. Peter and St. Paul, mid 14th c: has remained in use – latterly as mosque, library and now theatre.

3. **The Royal Palace** or **Palazzo del Proveditore** (west of the cathedral): now only the Venetian facade remains.

*4. **The Latin Cathedral** of St. Nicholas, early 14th c.; now Lala Mustafa Pasha mosque, previously "Aysofya"; dominates the city. Still the loveliest of all.

5. **St. George of the Latins:** late 13th c. and ruinous (near the Citadel).

6. **St. George of the Greeks & Ayios Symeon** – the original Byzantine Cathedral (south)

Salamis

Monastery of Apostolos Varnavas: 18th c. buildings; the Apostle's tomb. (Monastery now an archaeological museum.)

Basilicas of Ayios Epiphanios and the **Kampanopetra.**

Northern and Karpas

Trikomo: chapel of **Ayios Iakovos,** 15th c.(?); **Panayia Theotokos,** early 12th c. containing important wall paintings.

Lythrankomi: **Panayia Kanakaria:** early Christian basilica remodelled ca. 1160. Contained priceless 6th c. mosaics until stolen (now safely in the Byzantine Museum, Archbishopric, Nicosia).

***Kantara Castle:** Byzantine foundation with Lusignan fortifications; dismantled by the Venetians. Splendid panoramic views.

C. KYRENIA DISTRICT

*1. **Kyrenia Castle:** Byzantine, reconstructed in Lusignan and Venetian periods; has a stormy history.

*2. **Bellapais Abbey:** founded ca. 1200 on magnificent site.

3. **Lambousa:** important city and port in Roman and early Christian periods; by Lapithos.

*4. **St. Hilarion Castle:** early 13th c. on Byzantine foundations; dismantled by the Venetians; a romantic, fairy-tale place.

5. **Buffavento Castle:** bleak mid-Byzantine fastness, dismantled by the Venetians.

*6. **Monastery of Ayios Khrysostomos,** Koutsovendis: 11th century foundation with several churches and chapels; important early 12th c. wall paintings.

7. **Church of Christ Antiphonitis,** near Kalogrea: built ca. 1200 with later additions. (The magnificent wall paintings have now been destroyed.)

TOURS

A Suggested Week's Tour of the best of the Painted Churches and Historic Sites.

DAY ONE
Larnaca & Nicosia

a.m.   Angeloktistos, Kiti .... 10th/11th c.
early apse with 6th c. mosaic
St. Lazarus, Larnaca.. late 9th c.
general interest, no wall paintings
Ayios Antonios, Kellia .... probably 9th c.
9th, 10th & 11th c. paintings
Ayii Apostoli, Perakhorio .... 12th c.
1160-80 paintings. Rare period.
p.m.   St. John's Cathedral, Nicosia............................. 1665
completely decorated in mid 18th c.
Byzantine Museum ....
First rate collection of icons
Night in Nicosia.

DAY TWO
Troodos Mountains (east side)

a.m.   The Cyprus Museum
Metamorphosis tou Soteros, Palekhori .... early 16th c.
Local post-Byzantine, ca. 1510-20
p.m.   Stavros tou Ayiasmati, Platanistasa....................... late 15th c.
painted 1494 by Philip tou Goul
Panayia tou Arakos, Lagoudera .... mid 12th c.
painted 1192 by Constantinople master
Night in Kakopetria

DAY THREE
Around Kakopetria

a.m.   Panayia Theotokos Chapel 1520
local post-Byzantine
Dormition, Kourdali .... early 16th c.
Italo-Byzantine frescoes and icons
Ayios Nikolaos tis Steyis, Kakopetria........................ early 11th c.
rare Macedonian paintings; also post Byzantine
p.m.   Panayia Podithou, Galata 1502
Italo-Byzantine
Arkhangelos chapel .... early 16th c.
painted 1514 by Symeon Axenti
Ayios Sozomenos... early 16th c.
painted 1513 by Symeon Axenti
Night in Kakopetria

DAY FOUR
Troodos, the northern valleys

a.m.   Panayia Phorbiotissa, Asinou................................. 1105/6
two-thirds of original painting kept
Lampadistis Monastery, Kalopanayiotis
a) Ayios Herakleidios.. 11th c.
13th & 15th c. paintings, local post-Byzantine
b) The Latin Chapel... end 15th c.
Italo-Byzantine

244

p.m.	Panayia tou Moutoulla	1280
	Cappadocian style, 13th c. rendering	
	Arkhangelos Mikhail, Pedhoulas	1474
	local post Byzantine	

Night in Limassol

DAY FIVE
The South Coast

a.m.	Limassol Castle	13th c.
	mediaeval museum	
	Kolossi Castle and church	1454
	well-preserved keep, 12th c. church	
p.m.	Kourion	
	Roman and early Christian mosaics	
	Yeroskipos	9th c.
	late 15th c. paintings	

Night in Paphos

DAY SIX
Paphos

a.m.	Nea Paphos: Ayia Solomoni, Basilica, Saranda Kolones, Roman Mosaics	
	within the Roman city	
p.m.	Peyia Basilica, Cape Drepanum	6th c.
	mosaic floors	
	Panayia Khryseleousa, Emba	12th c.
	paintings end 15th c.	

Night in Paphos

DAY SEVEN
Paphos

a.m.	Byzantine Museum, Bishopric	
	Ayios Neophytos Monastery	
	a) The Katholikon	c. 1500
	fine early 16th c. frescoes, later icons	
	b) The Enkleistra	12th c.
	painted 1183 and 1196 in two distinct styles	
p.m.	Khrysorroyiatissa Monastery	founded 1152
	famous for its position and its wine	
	Ayia Moni	founded ca. 300
	on site of Temple of Hera, 4th c. BC	

TOURS
Suggested one-day excursions in each area

1. PAPHOS first day:
a.m.   Nea Paphos: Ayia Solomoni, Basilica, Saranda Kolones and Roman Mosaics.
p.m.   Byzantine Museum, Ktima; Ayios Neophytos Monastery.

2. PAPHOS second day:
a.m.   Ayia Paraskevi Church and Folk Museum, Yeroskipos;
        Lusignan Manor House, Sugar Factory* and Katholiki Church, Kouklia.
p.m.   Khrysorroyiatissa Monastery and Ayia Moni.

3. LIMASSOL:
a.m.   Limassol Castle and Kolossi Castle; Kourion Museum, Episkopi.
p.m.   House of Eustolios, Basilica and Baptistery, Kourion.

4. TROODOS first day (based on Agros):
a.m.   Panayia tou Arakos, Laghoudera and Stavros tou Ayiasmati Church, Platanistasa.
p.m.   tou Soteras Church, Palekhori & Ayios Ioannis Vaptistis Church, Askas.

5. TROODOS second day (based on Kakopetria):
a.m.   Ayios Nikolaos tis Steyis and *either* the three Galata churches *or* the Church of the Dormition, Kourdali.
p.m.   Ayios Ioannis Lampadistis Monastery & Panayia tou Moutoulla, Moutoullas.

6. NICOSIA first day:
a.m.   St. John's Cathedral and Byzantine Museum; House of the Grand Dragoman.
p.m.   Panayia Phorbiotissa, Asinou; Ayii Varnavas and Ilarion Church, Peristerona.

7. NICOSIA second day:
a.m.   The Cyprus Museum; Monastery of Ayios Herakleidios.
p.m.   Makheras Monastery; Khrysospiliotissa Church.

8. LARNACA:
a.m.   The Fort, Ayios Lazaros Church and Pierides Collection;
        Angeloktistos Church, Kiti, Tekke and Salt Lake (refreshments).
p.m.   Ayios Antonios, Kellia; Ayia Ekaterina Chapel, Pyrga; and Stavrovouni Monastery*

Not always possible to visit.

SUPPLEMENT

MEDIAEVAL BRIDGES

Old bridges abound. Many are still in use, others can be spotted spanning channels on disused stretches of road, some simply arch over nothing or lead nowhere. A lot cross very small streams or dried-up courses – an indication that the flow of water was much greater when they were built. The oldest identifiable are more than five hundred years old, being **Lusignan.** Examples: **i. the ruined bridge at Kiti; ii. the bridge just west of Malounda** on the Nicosia-Mitsero road, still in use and bearing a small, defaced coat-of-arms; **iii. Skarphos bridge** standing on the old Lusignan road from Polis to Paphos (which vanishes at that point) below a newly-made highway, 1½ miles upstream from Evretou; the shrunken water-course has moved away from the bridge altogether. **Venetian** bridges are more numerous and some romantically-sited are old pack-bridges built for the passage of camel-trains which brought ore down to Paphos from Troodos. Three of these last stand on the southern edge of the Paphos Forest on roughish earth roads: **i. Elea bridge,** south of Kaminaria and west of Phini, in a wooded dell; **ii. Kelaphos bridge,** where the water flows year-round; **iii. Roudhias bridge,** which crosses the dry upper reaches of the Xeros Potamios river, east of Vrecha village and just south of the present track. See also the **Ana Bridge** at Peristerona, Nicosia district; and the small example beyond the bend on the road to **Kalopanayotis,** above the dam.

Roudhias Bridge

MEDIAEVAL POTTERY

An essential commodity, excavations have revealed a steady output of assorted pottery from late Antiquity onwards throughout the Middle East. Almost all was made on a wheel and fired in a kiln. The products were used for transporting goods, for storage, for cooking and for table use. Up to the 13th century, they were chiefly either pithoi for storage – the pot usually embedded in the ground – or amphorae for both transport and storage, or a variety of smaller vessels for domestic use. (The production of very large, round-bellied pithoi, unique to Cyprus, was discontinued only in 1972; and coarse red-clay ware is still being made at Kornos at a very ancient pottery indeed.) Throughout the Empire, as early as the 7th century AD, vitreous glazing had begun to replace the old red slip on fine ware. The main source for it appears to have been the area around Constantinople. Monochrome at first, from the 9th century onwards the art of glazing in various colours was perfected. In the 10th and 11th centuries, fine Byzantine glazed ware was being distributed from central production sites and was also being copied locally. A hundred years later, in more beleagured times, export dwindled and the local potters were on their own. In design and technique, the industry was considerably influenced by Islamic culture, particularly sgraffito, splash and incised work, decoration in the form of imitation Arabic writing (called pseudo-Kufik), and simple geometric patterns. Floral, bird and hunting motifs were used also, possibly re-introduced to Byzantium by way of Islamic textile designs, but originating from a common source in antiquity. Deriving directly from the Classical world were repetitive rinceaux and running spirals and the occasional use of human figures.

Cypriot potters were skilled craftsmen, and when the Lusignans came to rule over the Island in the late 12th century, cut off from further Byzantine influence, they developed their own local styles. So it was that glazed pottery entirely native to Cyprus appeared early in the 13th century. It continued to be made in the Byzantine fashion, but gradually emblems reflecting the culture of the Crusaders and the Franks came into the decoration. Representations of knights and ladies were in demand, either in pairs on marriage bowls or pursuing a pastime severally or singly. Some dishes bore vague heraldic symbols, suggesting perhaps the owner's noble connections – the Lusignan lion was popular. These all provide interesting

Raised base

Flanged edge

248

glimpses into the courtly life and dress of the period, seen through the eyes of the maker of pots. And what else emerges time and again is the potter's gleeful sense of humour.

Three different potteries turning out glazed work can be discerned. Between them, they functioned from the 13th to the 15th centuries. Lemba workshop, near Paphos, produced coarse-grained, hard grey clay ware with a characteristic upturned ring round the foot. Lapethos, near Kyrenia, was the only pottery with a continuous history, preserving the traditional glazed pot which had both ring-base and neck (raised base). The third workshop was at Engomi, near Salamis, working with a grey, light-coloured clay, their bowls having a characteristic white flanged edge.

Methods of decorating in Cyprus

1. **By painting.** A slip of watered pink or white clay was used, chiefly in the 13th century, to paint lines and spirals on the pot's own dark ground.

2. **By sgraffito.** This was the more popular. The vase was dried to a degree of hardness and covered with the slip. Then a sharpened instrument – usually cane – was used to cut into the slip and expose the dark surface of the pot. Incised lines could be wide or narrow. After engraving, a transparent glaze was applied and the pot was fired a second time. The first local sgraffito vases usually had wide incisions and were in monochrome – either yellow-brown or green from the iron or copper oxide which had been mixed with the glaze. By the 14th century, incisions were narrow, the patterns had proliferated and both oxides were being applied to the same surface to give a two-toned effect. As the potters moved into the 15th century, vases became chalice-like, possibly copying their metal counterparts, and the subjects on the bowls were eventually so simplified as to be virtually schematic, displaying an extreme economy of line; arms and legs were omitted, for example, and a few squiggles suggested a bird: yet the creations have force.

Under the Venetians there was a steady decline in output and a deterioration in quality, variety and decoration. It seems that demand for local ware had almost stopped and everyone wanted to buy the Italian goods which were then being imported on a large scale.

Indebted for much of this to
Demetra Papanikola - Bakirtzis, Kavala

COINAGE

Important collections in the Cyprus Museum, the Central Bank and the Cultural Foundation of the Bank of Cyprus.

In the past, as well as copper, Cyprus has mined silver in quantity. The first silver coins were issued at Salamis in 538 BC and the mints of Cyprus continued in production until Roman times.

Under the Romans from the reign of Augustus a series of bronze coins were struck, and under Claudius (41-54 AD) the words Koinon Kyprion, the Union of Cypriots, appear for the first time, together with the name of the pro-consul. Thenceforward, the Union was responsible for the issue of all bronze coinage. The silver coins were produced in Antioch until 76/77 AD when the mint was transferred to Cyprus – a move possibly connected with Vespasian's measures to help the Island, recently devastated by earthquake.

Early Byzantine coinage was still that of the Late Roman Empire. When the Empire was divided in 395, Cyprus coinage was synonymous with that of Constantinople. In 498, the creation of the heavy copper Follis determined much of the pattern for minting throughout the Byzantine Empire. Together with a silver piece called a Miliaresia, it continued in circulation until the late 11th century. Then both coins were replaced by alloys of silver/copper and gold/silver respectively.

From the outset, however, the images on the coinage had been changed, anything pagan being omitted. Representations of the Emperor, which on Roman coins had been true portraits in high relief, had now become formal symbols in low relief, majesty being shown by dress and insignia. From the mid-5th century came the Cross on the reverse; but Christ, the Virgin and saints were regular features only after iconoclasm (from 843).

Lusignan Coinage was introduced by Guy de Lusignan in 1192 and was based on the numismatic system of the Holy Land. It consisted of the copper Denier, the white/gold Bezant and the Imperial Bezant. These remained the currency for about one hundred years. Henry II stopped the white Bezant and struck the silver Gros and half Gros to bring Cyprus in line with the system in the Latin East. The Gros remained the official coin of the Island until the end of the Frankish period.

By 1310 there were two main mints, the economy flourished, and during the 14th c. output was at its maximum. But the loss of Famagusta in 1372 and the constant harassment by the Genoese led to a decline. Many hoards have been discovered, hidden during this uncertain period. The disastrous reign of Janus (1398-1432), culminating in ransom money and yearly heavy tribute to Egypt, was the final blow, and the economy never recovered. Yet some of the most attractive coins were struck towards the end of the Lusignan dynasty: the silver gros of James II, for example.

Venetian coins began to circulate alongside a variety of others after 1489, creating confusion. Therefore, early in the 16th century, all gold and silver coins were counterstamped and small coins called Carzia were struck. From mid-century until 1570, the Carzia came from Venice and showed the head of the Doge on the obverse.

The Turkish Occupation: For the next three hundred years, there was no Cyprus coinage, only that of the Ottoman Empire.

Bronze coin of Trajan c. 112-117 AD with inscription KOINON KΥΠΡΙΩΝ.

Bronze follis of Heraklion (608-610AD)

Silver gros of Henry II (1285-1324)

Silver gross of James II (1460-1473)

BARSKY 1701-1747

Basil Gregorovitch Barsky was a Russian Orthodox monk from Kiev who spent half his life wandering in the Near East, taking notes of what he saw. He made three visits to Cyprus: in 1726, 1727 and from 1734 to 1736. He kept a journal and stayed in whichever monasteries offered him hospitality. He would sketch each one and write an account of its history, its treasures and its circumstances at the time.

Barsky's acute observations provide us with a reliable and valuable insight into Cyprus as it was after one hundred and sixty years of Turkish rule – a period that is otherwise obscure. He recorded each visit in a cartouche in the monastery church. (See: Ayios Nikolaos tis Steyis, Ayios Joannis Lampadistis and Panayia tou Arakos.)

There are more than sixty monasteries where you can still find monks. The smallest have only five or six while the big ones have as many as fifty or even one hundred.

Barsky in 1735

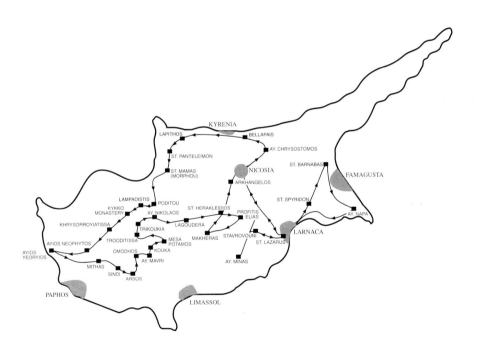

(A) IN CONSTANTINOPLE

324-37	Constantine the Great	
313	Edict of Milan	Acknowledged Christianity.
325	First Church Council	In Nicaea – called by Constantine. (Cyprus sends three bishops)
330	Constantinople founded	A new Rome but Christian

381	Second Church Council	In Constantinople. The great Theologians.
379-95	Theodosios I	Christianity the official religion of the Roman Empire.
396	Division of the Roman Empire	
431	Third Church Council	At Ephesus. (Cyprus sends five bishops).

527-565	Reign of Justinian	Ayia Sophia built. His new Codex of Roman Law was in Latin, but the tongue of Constantinople was Greek.

mid 7th-mid 10th c:
Arab invasions

726-843	The Iconoclast dispute	All images possible removed and smashed.

867-1056 THE MACEDONIAN DYNASTY

867-886	Basil I	Now cruciform domed churches give scope for new scheme of decoration.
963-969	Nicephoros Phocus	
976-1025	Basil II	Brilliant commander. Russia adopts Orthodoxy.
1042-55	Constantine Monomachos	Time of wealth and splendour centred in the Imperial Court.
1054	The Great Schism	Split between the Latin and Orthodox Churches.

1057–1204 THE COMNENIAN DYNASTY

1081-1118	Alexios I Comnenos	Rise of the Seljuk Turks.
1096	Start of the Crusades	Empire shrunk and wealth reduced.

1143-80	Manuel Comnenos	
1191	The Third Crusade	

1204	The Fourth Crusade	Sack of Constantinople by the Venetians. Now only pockets of Empire left.
1204-61	Imperial Court at Nicaea	Art continues to develop.

1256-1453 THE PALAEOLOGUE DYNASTY

1261	Back in Constantinople	Impoverished Court finds decayed city; but arts reach new peak, vide Church of the Saviour in Khora c. 1310.

1291	Fall of Acre.	

1453	Fall of Constantinople to the Turks.	

HRONOLOGY
(B) IN CYPRUS

EARLY BYZANTINE
327	St. Helena, mother of Constantine the Great, in Cyprus.
mid 4th	Earthquakes raze Salamis, Kourion and Paphos.
368	Salamis rebuilt as Constantia and becomes new capital city.
368-403	Archbishop Epiphanios re-unites the Church of Cyprus.
395	Emperor Theodosios bans the rites of Aphrodite.
396	Governors now appointed from Constantinople.
400	Now fifteen bishops, mass baptism and much rebuilding.
488	Discovery of St. Barnabas's tomb at Salamis.
	Recognition of Apostolic foundation of the Church of Cyprus and its right to be independent.
mid 6th	Establishment of the silk industry in Cyprus.
649	First Arab raid.
653	Sack of Nea Paphos; Islamic garrison based there.

MID-BYZANTINE
965	Cyprus securely part of the Byzantine Empire once more.
et seq.	Period of intense building and creative activity.
	Emergence of Nicosia, Famagusta, Limassol and Kyrenia in place of the ruined antique cities.
	Under Alexios, the island becomes a military base.
1185-91	Nephew Isaac Comnenos self-styled emperor of Cyprus.
1191	Richard Coeur de Lion takes Cyprus on his way to Syria, ending seven hundred years of Byzantine rule.

1192 – 1489 THE LUSIGNAN DYNASTY
1192	Coeur de Lion leases the island to Guy de Lusignan.
13th c.	Establishment of the Latin Church in the cities.
	Orthodox priests and bishops banished to rural areas.
1260	The Bulla Cypria – a Papal edict making the Church of Cyprus subordinate to the Latin.
1291	Crusader knights and entourages pour into Cyprus.
1373	Loss of Famagusta to the Genoese.
1426	The Mameluke invasion causes immense damage.
	King Janus made captive.
1442	Lusignan/Palaeologue marriage improves standing of the Orthodox Church in Cyprus.
1453	Influx of refugees brings fresh impulse to Byzantine culture on the island.
1464	Genoese expelled from Famagusta by James II.
1470	Plague kills half the population.
1474	Katerina Kornaro, Venetian, becomes Queen of Cyprus.
1489	Katerina is persuaded to retire and the island is ceded to Venice.

1489 – 1571 VENETIAN RULE
1567	Present fortification of Nicosia began.
1570	The Turkish invasion: they take Nicosia and sack Limassol.
1571	Fall of Famagusta.

1571 – 1878 TURKISH RULE
1572	Latin churches now mosques, store-houses etc. and Orthodox Church restored.
	Period one of general decline marked by a succession of corrupt governors.

FOUNDATIONS (not comprehensive)

EARLY BYZANTINE

300	Ayia Moni Monastery.
325	Ayios Nikolaos of the Cats.
327	Stavrovouni Monastery; also possibly Omodhos.

late 4th   Church basilicas built at Constantia and Paphos;
           Annex of Eustolios at Kourion.

early 5th Church basilica at Kourion.
5th c.   Angeloktistos Church, Kiti (6th c. mosaic).
           Ayios Herakleidios Church, Politiko.

6th c.   Church basilica built at Drepanum (Peyia).

MID-BYZANTINE

9th c.
or earlier Ayia Paraskevi five-domed church, Yeroskipos.
9th c.   Ayios Antonios, Kellia.
end 9th c. Ayios Lazaros, Larnaca.
early 10th Ayii Varnavas and Ilarion 5-domed church, Peristerona.
early 11th Ayios Herakleidios Church, Lampadistis Monastery.
end 11th   Kykko Monastery. Castles built on northern range.
1105/6   Panayia Phorbiotissa, Asinou.
12th c.   Panayia Khryseleousa, Emba.
mid 12th   Makheras Monastery.
1152   Khrysorroyiatissa Monastery.
1160   Ayios Neophytos Enkleistra – cell and sanctuary (ptd 1183).
1160/80   Ayii Apostoli, Perakhorio.
1183   Nave of Enkleistra completed (painted 1196).
1192   Panayia tou Arakos, Lagoudhera.

POST-BYZANTINE
Lusignan Period

1200   Paphos Castle built (Saranda Kolones).
1209   Latin Cathedral of Ayia Sophia begun.
mid 13th   Limassol Castle built.
1250   Troodhitissa Monastery.
1280   Moutoullas Chapel.
First half
14th c.   St. Mary of the Augustinians (Omeriyeh Mosque)
1421   Royal Chapel at Pyrga.
1454   Kolossi Castle.
1474   Arkhangelos Mikhail Church, Pedhoulas.

Venetian Period

1494   Stavros tou Ayiasmati Church, Platanistasa.
1495   Ayias Mamas Church, Louveras.
ca. 1500 Katholikon, Ayios Neophytos Monastery.
          Khrysopolitissa, Paphos.
          Arkhangelos Monastery, Kato Lakatamia.
          Latin Chapel, Lampadistis Monastery. Italo-Byzantine.
1502   Panayia Podithou, Galata. Italo-Byzantine.
1513   Ayios Sozomenos Church, Galata.
1514   Theotokos Chapel, Galata (Arkhangelos).
early 16th Metamorphosis tou Soteros Church, Palekhori.
          Church of the Dormition, Kourdali. Italo-Byzantine.
mid 16th Ayia Napa Monastery.
1560   Ayios Ioannis tou Prodhromo, Askas.

Turkish Period

1665   Orthodox Cathedral of Ayios Ioannis, Nicosia.
1745   Ayios Yeoryios Church, Arpera.

ICONS AND THE ICONOSTASIS

An icon is simply an image, whether displayed on a portable wooden panel or monumentally on a wall. It can be in any medium: ivory, silk, mosaic, stone, paint. In the narrow sense, it is the portable sort that is referred to – usually hanging on the iconostasis – and that is the sense in which it is used here.

The icon itself is not an object of worship but a vehicle of prayer through which the real saint can be reached. That is why the icon is venerated. In order to bond with its prototype in Heaven, the icon must convey as far as possible the attributes and essence of that particular saint: an image of St. Peter, for example, grizzled and burly, is immediately recognisable as of Peter whether the likeness was made in the 7th century or the 14th. And the same applies to all Orthodox religious icons of sacred personages and Biblical or Apocryphal scenes both monumental and on panels.

(For more on icons see Introduction pages 14, 19 & 26; also Byzantine Museum 183)

THE ICONOSTASIS

It grew out of the Templon, which is a low screen dividing the sanctuary from the nave, and which is still met with in some churches. In early times, the templon was made of stone, but by the 12th century wood had replaced stone and the screen had increased in height. It often had slender columns supporting an architrave or epistyle. In the 13th and 14th centuries, the spaces between the columns were closed, icons were transferred from the church walls and the iconostasis was born.

The screen most often met with now is beautifully carved and gilded and carries two tiers of icons: on the lower, large boards of Christ, the Virgin, John the Baptist and chosen saints for devotions; above, on the epistyle, twelve miniature scenes of the great feasts of the Church.[1] Central is the Holy Door, which usually has the Annunciation painted on it with selected Fathers of the Church below; but the subject can vary. Where there are side chapels, parabema, they also are screened and have doors. In the bigger churches, the iconostasis may be in three tiers and carry a large number of icons, the additional, upper row comprising a Great Deesis, namely: Christ between the Virgin and the Baptist with St Peter and St Paul, the Apostles, on either side and the Archangels Michael and Gabriel at each end. Moreover, above that stands an icon of Christ on the Cross, the Virgin and St John on smaller frames at the foot.

---

1. Known as the Dodekaorton, the Twelve Feasts of the Orthodox Church are: Annunciation, Nativity, Presentation in the Temple, Baptism, Transfiguration, Raising of Lazarus, Entry into Jerusalem, Crucifixion, Resurrection, Ascension, Pentecost, Dormition of the Virgin.

Iconostases are a highly developed form of wood-carving and some fine examples can be found in Cyprus. For examples, see:

Early 16th c.	Church of the Dormition, Kourdali
Mid-16th c.	Ayios Neophytos Katholiki, Paphos*
16th c.	Panayia Khryseleousa, Emba
Early 17th c.	Ayios Herakleidios Monastery church (south screen)
1774	Ayios Herakleidios Monastery church (north screen)
17th c.	Joachim & Anna Church, Kaliana
Mid-18th c.	Ayios Ioannis Cathedral, Nicosia
1773:	Ayios Lazaros Church, Larnaca*

Outstanding.

Plan of iconostasis showing distribution of icons

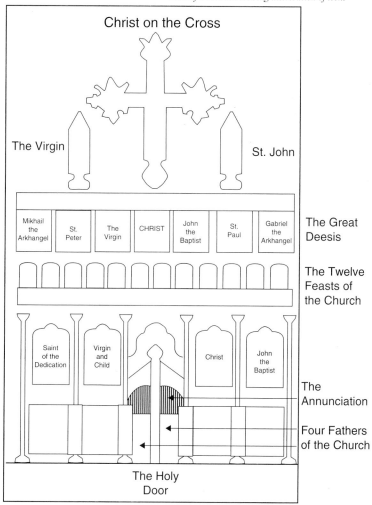

Christ on the Cross

The Virgin

St. John

Mikhail the Arkhangel	St. Peter	The Virgin	CHRIST	John the Baptist	St. Paul	Gabriel the Arkhangel

The Great Deesis

The Twelve Feasts of the Church

Saint of the Dedication

Virgin and Child

Christ

John the Baptist

The Annunciation

Four Fathers of the Church

The Holy Door

Paphos Basilica – late 4th c.

Mosaic from the House of Eustolios, Kourion – early 5th c.

259

Above: Mosaic, Angeloktistis Church, Kiti

*Left: Kanakaria mosaic of Christ Child
Both early 6th c.*

260

The Transfiguration and the Raising of Lazarus, Ayios Nikolaos, Kakopetria – ca. 1000 AD wall painting

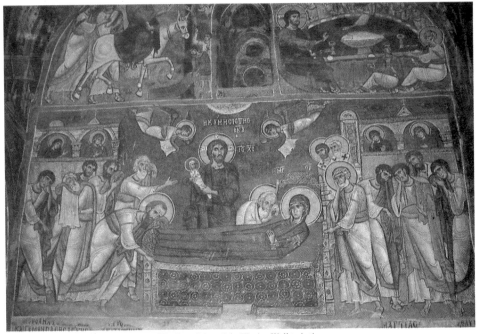

The Dormition of the Virgin. Wall painting

The Communion of the Apostles, Panayia Phorbiotissa, Asinou – 1105/6 AD. Wall painting

Ayios Neophytos Enkleistra – 1183. Wall paintings
Top: *Virgin, Fathers of the Church and Ascension*
(sanctuary)
Right: *Crucifixion (cell)*
Below: *St. Neophytos between archangels (sanctuary)*

Mid-Byzantine

Panayia tou Arakos, Lagoudera, 1192.
Wall paintings

Archangel Gabriel
(part of The Annunciation)

Panayia Arakiotissa

Ayios Lazaros

Entry into Jerusalem, Ayios Herakleidios, Lampadistis Monastery – end 13th c. Wall painting

Crucifixion, Ay. Nikolaos – mid 14th c.) Wall painting

Washing of the Feet, Ay. Herakleidios, Lampadistis Monastery – 1400 AD. Wall painting

The Nativity, Stavros tou Ayiasmati – 1494 AD. Wall painting

Ayios Mamas, Metamorphosis tou Soteros, Palekhori – early 16th c. Wall painting

268

Top: The Crucifixion
Below: Virgin Enthroned with Christchild & Archangels
Panayia tis Podithou, Galata – 1502 AD. Wall paintings

269

Top: The Betrayal & Christ before Pilate
Below: Rare depiction of St. Paul dictating (in the squinch)
Ayia Paraskevi, Yeroskipos – late 15th c. Wall painting

270

Ayios Neophytos Monastery Church – Wallpaintings ca. 1500.

Above: *The three Kings in continuous strip. (Part of the Akathistos Hymn in the north vault).*

Left: *Joachim's Dream (south vault).*

Panayia Kaminaria
First quarter 16th c.

The Dragoman & Family, Ayios Yeoryios, Arpera – mid 18th c.

272

Icon Screen: Ayios Neophytos Katholikon south – showing part of the Great Deesis above Festivals of the Church

Interior of St. Lazarus Church looking east showing central part of the Iconostasis – late 18th c.

REFERENCE SECTION

Examples of different forms of Byzantine Churches in Cyprus.

Cross-section of an Orthodox church

The Byzantine Emperors and the Lusignan Kings

Some outstanding Cypriot saints and other popular saints

The Seven Councils of the Church

Some basic Christian symbols

Dictionary of terms

Sources

In 1986, UNESCO included the following painted churches in their World Heritage list:

Panayia Phorbiotissa, Asinou
Ayios Nikolaos tis Steyis, Kakopetria
Panayia tis Podithou, Galata
Ayios Herakleidios Church and the Latin Chapel, Lampadistis Monastery
Panayia tou Moutoulla, Moutoullas
Arkhangelos Chapel, Pedhoulas
Ayios Stavros, Pelendria
Panayia tou Arakos, Lagoudhera
Stavros tou Ayiasmati, Platanistasa

N.B.   Photography is not allowed in the interiors of the above churches without written permission. To obtain a permit, apply to the Director, Department of Antiquities, The Cyprus Museum, 1, Museum Avenue, Nicosia.

EXAMPLES OF DIFFERENT FORMS OF BYZANTINE CHURCHES IN CYPRUS

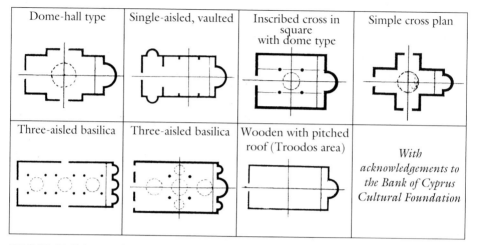

Dome-hall type	Single-aisled, vaulted	Inscribed cross in square with dome type	Simple cross plan
Three-aisled basilica	Three-aisled basilica	Wooden with pitched roof (Troodos area)	*With acknowledgements to the Bank of Cyprus Cultural Foundation*

CROSS-SECTION OF DOMED CHURCH LOOKING EAST, SHOWING POSITION OF WALL-PAINTINGS

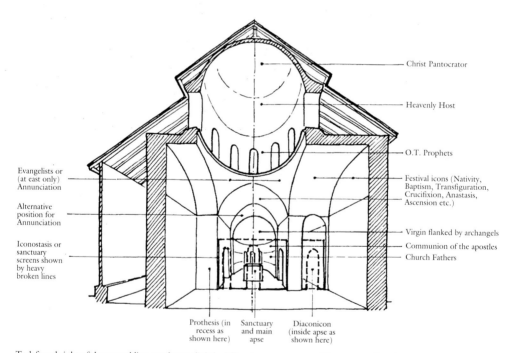

Christ Pantocrator

Heavenly Host

O.T. Prophets

Evangelists or (at east only) Annunciation

Festival icons (Nativity, Baptism, Transfiguration, Crucifixion, Anastasis, Ascension etc.)

Alternative position for Annunciation

Virgin flanked by archangels

Iconostasis or sanctuary screens shown by heavy broken lines

Communion of the apostles

Church Fathers

Prothesis (in recess as shown here) Sanctuary and main apse Diaconicon (inside apse as shown here)

To left and right of the central line are shown slightly different arrangements, with narrow or broader cross arms flanking the dome, the first without and the second with secondary apses flanking the main central apse for prothesis and diaconicon.

Acknowledgements to Dr R. J. Mainstone for kindly making the plan shown above.

THE BYZANTINE EMPERORS

As it has been reckoned that, between 324 and 1453, there were eighty-eight of them, only the most relevant are listed below.

324-337	CONSTANTINE THE GREAT	886-912	Leo VI
361-363	Julian	963-969	Nicephoros Phocas
364-378	Valens	976-1025	BASIL II
379-395	THEODOSIOS I	1042-1055	Constantine Monomachos
395-408	Arcadios		
408-450	Theodosios II		**The Comnenian Dynasty**
457-474	Leo I	1057-1059	Isaac Comnenos
474-491	Zeno	1059-1067	Constantine Ducas
491-518	Anastasios I	1081-1118	ALEXIOS I COMNENOS
518-527	Justin I	1118-1143	John II Comnenos
527-565	JUSTINIAN I	1143-1180	Manuel I Comnenos
565-578	Justin II	1180-1183	Alexios II Comnenos
610-641	HERACLIUS	1183-1185	Andronicos I Comnenos
797-802	Irene	1185-1195	Isaac II Angelos
802-811	Nicephoros	1195-1203	Alexios III Angelos
829-842	Theophilos		

The Palaeologue Dynasty 1258-1453

The Macedonian Dynasty
867-886   BASIL I

THE LUSIGNAN KINGS OF CYPRUS

1. Guy de Lusignan	1192-1194	12. James I (uncle)	1382-1398
2. Aimery (brother)	1194-1205	13. Janus (son)	1398-1432
3. Hugh I (son)	1205-1218	14. John II (son)	1432-1458
4. Henry I (son)	1218-1253	15. Charlotte (daughter)	1458-1459
5. Hugh II (son)	1253-1267	16. Louis of Savoy (husband)	1459-1460
6. Hugh III (cousin)	1267-1284	17. James II (bastard son	
7. John I (son)	1284-1285	of John II)	1460-1473
8. Henry II (brother)	1285-1324	18. James III (son)	1473-1474
9. Hugh IV (nephew)	1324-1359	19. Catherine Cornaro	
10. Peter I (son)	1359-1369	(mother)	1474-1489
11. Peter II (son)	1369-1382		

SOME OUTSTANDING CYPRIOT SAINTS

BARNABAS, 1st century: Apostle and founder of the Church of Cyprus; martyred.

EPIPHANIOS, 315 to 403: Archbishop of Constantia from 368; known as 'the Great'.

HERAKLEIDIOS, mid-1st c: baptised by Barnabas and Paul, first bishop of Tamassos.

JOHN THE ALMONER, ca. 560 to 619: Patriarch of Alexandria, native of Amathus. Wrote the life of St. Tykhon.

LAZAROS, 1st century: brother of Mary and Martha of Bethany, resurrected by Christ; first bishop of Kition.

LEONTIOS OF NEAPOLIS, 7th c. Bishop of Limassol and hagiographer (including lives of John the Almoner and Spyridon).

MNASON, 1st century: second bishop of Tamassos, known to Paul and Barnabas (Acts 21).

NEOPHYTOS, 1134 TO 1219: famous Paphos recluse and founder of St. Neophytos Monastery.

SOZOMENOS, 5th century: famous recluse of Potamia, lawyer and ecclesiastical historian.

SPYRIDON, 4th century: Bishop of Tremithous and shepherd. Said to have attended the first Church Council in 325, where he proved the doctrine of the Trinity by reducing a tile to its elements – earth, fire and water. Always portrayed with tile and shepherd's cap.

TRIFYLLIOS, 4th century: Bishop of Ledra, friend and pupil of Spyridon.

TYKHON, 4th century: second bishop of Amathus, consecrated by Archbishop Epiphanios.

SOME OTHER POPULAR SAINTS

BARBARA, 3rd century: said to have been killed by her pagan father. Depicted richly dressed with crown and jewellery.

COSMAS & DAMIAN, early martyrs: called 'anaryiroi' or silverless, being doctors who healed without taking payment; they were twins.

DEMETRIOS, late 3rd c: soldier saint, usually mounted and often paired with St. George.

FORTY MARTYRS OF SEBASTEIA: Christian soldiers in the Roman army who chose to freeze to death in an icy lake rather than renounce their faith. Paintings show one of the guard taking the place of the sole defaulter who is tempted by a warm bath-house on the shore.

GEORGE, 3rd/4th c: soldier saint, usually mounted, usually slaying a dragon, often with small pillion figure of a youth saved from slavery complete with his master's water-jug.

KYRIAKI, unknown: female saint displaying the rest of the days of the week in medallions – an iconography peculiar to Cyprus; richly dressed.

MAMAS, 3rd century: a shepherd-boy who milked the wild deer; martyred at 15 or 17. His legend is beloved by the Cypriots: on his way to court to answer for non-payment of his taxes, Mamas saw a lion chasing a lamb. He rescued the lamb and rode into court on the lion, whereupon the governor remitted his taxes for life!

MARINA, late 3rd c: always shown in a bright red maphorion; popular martyr in post-Byzantine art.

MARY OF EGYPT, 5th c. (?): a prostitute from Alexandria, suddenly converted, who spent the rest of her life alone in the desert. Found by Bishop Zosimas who gave her communion.

NICHOLAS, 4th c: Bishop of Myra. Was present at the Council of Nicaea in 325. Miniature Christ and Virgin shown on portraits, bearing gospel and omophorion signifying his long-sought elevation to bishop's rank.

ONOUFRIOS, ca. 400: for sixty years a hermit in the Egyptian desert. Depicted naked behind a bush.

PARASKEVI, unknown: female saint whose name means Friday, she holds an icon of Christ on Good Friday, the "Utter Humiliation".

THEKLA, 1st century: one of the most famous female early martyrs, she was converted to Christianity by St. Paul.

THE SEVEN COUNCILS OF THE CHURCH

Held in Nicaea in 325 AD, Constantinople 381, Ephesus 431,

Chalcedon in 451, Constantinople in 553 and 680 and Nicaea in 787.

They were convened by the Byzantine emperors when needed. They are of the utmost importance because they defined once and for all the fundamental doctrines of the Christian faith. They also sorted out the Church's internal organisation and administration. The life of the Church in early Byzantine times was dominated by the edicts of the Councils, which were given imperial confirmation and the binding force of law.

It was in the first two convocations that the Nicene Creed was worked out as a precise statement of belief; and the second of 381 also brought together some brilliant theologians: Athanasios of Alexandria, Gregory of Nazianzos, Basil the Great, Gregory of Nyssa and John Chrysostom. These men are the leading Fathers of the Church. **In art** they are shown in the apse converging upon a painted altar in celebration of the Liturgy. The selection varies a little: in many Cypriot churches, their own Epiphanios, Spyridon or John the Almoner often figure.

SOME BASIC CHRISTIAN SYMBOLS

Chi Ro: ☧ Made from the first two letters in Christ – or ΧΡΙΣΤΟΣ
Fish: ΙΧΘΥΣ from ΙΗΣΟΥΣ ΧΡΙΣΤΟΣ ΘΕΟΥ ΥΙΟΣ ΣΩΤΗΡ Jesus Christ the Saviour, Son of God.
Ship: the Church, or the voyage of Faith.
Anchor: Hope; security in Faith; often a Cross and Anchor.
Lamb: singly represents Christ; a flock of sheep represents Christians.
Vine: Christ, 'I am the true vine'; birds feeding on grapes = the Eucharist.
Pomegranite: the unity of the Church – many seeds contained in a single fruit. (It also has a secondary symbolism of immortality and resurrection.)
Pelican: Christ's sacrifice – this bird was thought to feed her young with her blood.
The four Evangelists are represented by the four beasts of Ezekiel: Matthew by the man, Mark by the lion, Luke by the ox, John by the eagle.

DICTIONARY OF TERMS

Aer:	veil of silk for covering chalice and/or paten.
Amphora:	tall, narrow-necked jar for oil or wine.
Anastasis:	Christ breaking the gates of Hell; the Eastern Resurrection.
Aniconic:	devoid of imagery.
Architrave:	main beam across tops of columns; moulded frame round doors and windows.
Ashlar:	hewn or squared stone.
Ayiasma:	holy spring.
Ayios, Ayia, Ayii:	Saint (male, female, plural).
Baldacchino:	canopy over altar supported by four columns; the ciborium.
Blachernitissa:	depiction of the Virgin with hands uplifted in prayer and the Christchild in a medallion on her breast. (From an original in Blachernae Monastery.)
Catechumeni:	name given in the early Church to adults undergoing instruction preparatory to baptism; normally this took three years.
Cenobiarch:	head of a monastic community; (from Greek koinos, common + bios, life).
Champlevé:	lit. 'raised field', in which the ground is cut away to a design and the resultant hollows filled with coloured pastes or enamels, cp. cloisonné.
Cippus:	small, low pillar marking a Greek or Roman tomb.
Cloisonné:	in the Byzantine technique of enamelling, tiny cells, divided by thin strips of gold (cloisons), are filled with coloured glass and fired.
Corinthian capital:	the Byzantine developed from the Roman, but the acanthus leaf carving was more deeply undercut. Both kinds are encountered, the Roman being spolia.
Deesis:	lit. 'entreaty': Christ enthroned, with the Virgin and the Baptist each side interceding for mankind. The most powerful vehicle for prayer.
Diakonikon:	the room south of the apse where the sacred vessels are kept; used by the deacons. Could be a separate building in the early Church.
Dormition:	death of the Virgin. Apostles present in accordance with her wish; Christ holds her unblemished soul.
Eleousa:	Virgin of Tenderness.
Epistyle:	beam or architrave of an iconostasis or templon.
Finial:	carved decoration above an arch or pinnacle, generally foliage.

Guilloche:	Graeco-Roman and early Christian motif for borders, formed by two or more interwoven or plaited bands; generally used for mosaic floors.
Hodegetria:	'Conductress'. The most popular type of Virgin – holding the Child and pointing to Him as the way to salvation, the Child giving a blessing.
Hood-mould:	the drip-stone over a door or window.
Katholikon:	main church in a monastery.
Lunette:	semi-circular upper surface of a wall.
Machicolation:	openings formed for the purpose of defence at the tops of castles and fortifications.
Machicoulis:	such a defence projecting beyond the face of the wall above entrances, intervals being left open through which missiles could be dropped.
Nilotic:	scenes of Roman derivation featuring exotic fauna and flora from the river Nile.
Omophorion:	a long scarf looped over the shoulders and decorated with crosses; the principal characteristic of the liturgical dress of bishops.
Opus sectile:	inlay, mainly of marble and polished stone, cut into geometric shapes to form a pattern.
Orans:	Early Christian attitude of prayer with arms raised to shoulder-height and open hands.
Panayia:	lit. 'All Holy', referring to the Virgin.
Pantocrator:	Lord Almighty. Depiction of Christ holding a Bible in one hand and blessing with the other.
Parabema:	the sacristies, the compartments on either side of the apse.
Patriarch:	a bishop of one of the five principal Sees in the early Church, possessing jurisdiction over several provinces.
Pendentives:	the four curved triangles of wall which form the transition between the dome of a church and the piers beneath.
Phelonion:	vestment worn mainly by clergy; a chasuble.
Pithos, pithoi:	large storage jar(s) made of pottery.
Polystavrion:	a phelonion decorated with crosses; prerogative at first of the Patriarchs in the late 11th c., it became more general later.
Prothesis:	the room north of the apse where the Eucharist is prepared.
Quoin:	the external angle of a building, most commonly of ashlar blocks.
Repoussé:	ornamental metal-work hammered into relief from the reverse side.
Reveal:	internal side surface of an opening or recess.
Revetment:	facing of thin marble slabs on walls and pillars, usually carried up to meet the mosaics in the vaults.
Rhipidia:	long-handled fans for keeping flies off the Eucharist.
Rinceau:	a border-motif developed by the Romans in mosaic and metal-work and consisting of a continuous decorative foliate scroll of vine or acanthus, sometimes inhabited.
Soffit:	the undersurface of an arch or architrave.
Spandrel:	the almost triangular surface between one side of the outer curve of an arch.
Spolia:	materials and artifacts taken from earlier buildings for re-use.
Squinches:	small arches or niches across the corners of a square to facilitate the support of a circular dome.
Stavropegiac:	lit. 'fixed with a cross' – which is actually driven into the foundations. A term reserved for Patriarchical monasteries, independent of the local See e.g. Kykko, Makheras, St. Neophytos.
Synthronon:	Semi-circular seating for clergy in the apse of a Byzantine church.
Tessera:	a small piece of stone, glass etc. set in plaster to form part of a mosaic.
Theotokos:	Mother of God.

SOURCES:

Bank of Cyprus Cultural Foundation: The House of the Dragoman of Cyprus, Hadjiyeoryakis Kornessios, 1991.
C.D. Cobham: Excerpta Cypria, 1908 reprinted 1969.
Marc Dubin: Cyprus, the Rough Guide.
Camille Enlart: Gothic Art and the Renaissance in Cyprus, 1899. Translated from the French and edited by Sir David Hunt in 1987. Publ. by Trigraph Press.
Rupert Gunnis: Historic Cyprus, 1947 (second edition).
John Hackett: A History of the Orthodox Church of Cyprus, 1901 reprinted 1972.
W. Hepworth Dixon: British Cyprus, 1879.
Sir George Hill: A History of Cyprus, 1940-52, reprinted 1972.
Sir David Hunt: Footprints in Cyprus (editor), 1982. Publ. By Trigraph Press.
George Jeffery: A Description of the Historic Monuments of Cyprus, 1918 reprinted 1983.
Kevork Keshishian: Romantic Cyprus (11th ed. 1973); Nicosia, 1978.
F.G. Maier & V. Karageorghis: Paphos, History & Archaeology, 1984, Publ. by the A.G. Leventis Foundation.
G. Mariti: Travels in the Island of Cyprus, 1769. Translated by Cobham 1909 (2nd ed).
A.H.S. Megaw: The Basilica at Curium, Cyprus, 1974-5. (Report)
Philip Newman: A Short History of Cyprus, 1940 (2nd ed. 1953).
A. Papageorgiou: The Wooden-roofed Churches of Cyprus (in Greek), 1975.
H.D. Purcell: Cyprus, publ. in 1969.
Ian Robertson: Cyprus (in the Blue Guide series).
S. Sophocleous: The Despotic Icons of the Monastery of Megalos Agros, 1992.
David Soren: The Day the World ended at Kourion. (Article, Nat. Geographic, July 1988.)
J. & A. Stylianou: The Painted Churches of Cyprus, 1986.
Hazel Thurston: The Travellers' Guide to Cyprus, 1967.
Ioannou Tsiknopoullou: History of the Churches of Paphos, 1971 (in Greek).
D.C. Winfield: Asinou, a Guide; Panayia tou Arakos, Lagoudera, a Guide. Publ. by the Cyprus Dept. of Antiquities.
Marguerite Yon, Symposiarch at Lyons 1991: Kinyras, French Archaeology in Cyprus.
also
The Oxford Dictionary of Byzantium.
Timothy Ware (Bishop Kallistos of Diokleia): The Orthodox Church, publ. 1963.
D. Talbot Rice: The Byzantines 1962; Art of Byzantium, 1963.

INDEX

When a monument has more than one reference, the main description appears in heavier print.

287

The Author

GWYNNETH DER PARTHOG

Gwynneth der Parthog was born and educated in England, in Essex. She took a degree in English at King's College, London, obtained her Certificate of Education, and arrived in Cyprus in September 1954 to take up a position teaching English at the Victoria Girls' School in Nicosia.

Later, she married John der Parthog, an Armenian, and went to live in Kyrenia where she drove around in a battered car of 1930 vintage and kept donkeys (among other things). They had two children. Their home was seized by the invading Turkish army in 1974 and the family went to live in the U.K., where they still are.

Ties with the island remain strong and visits are frequent. Each year between 1982 and 1993, Gwynneth and John ran conducted tours from the U.K. – a general one entitled 'Treasures of Cyprus', and a more specialised Byzantine one to the painted churches. Gwynneth's interests include walking, poetry and the history of almost everything.

Judith Davis (illustrator)

Judith is no stranger to Cyprus; she lived here as a young child and has returned many times since. As an artist she deserves to be better known, and her sympathetic sketches reflect her love for the island and have added another dimension to this book.

OTHER INTERWORLD BOOKS ON CYPRUS

EXPLORE CYPRUS – Illustrated Guide/ Renos Lavithis
PAPHOS – Land of Aphrodite: Illustrated Guide / Renos Lavithis / ISBN 0 948853 15 3
THE TASTE OF CYPRUS – Cypriot Cooking / Gilli Davies / ISBN 0 948853 19 0
FLORAL CHARM OF CYPRUS – Illustrated Guide / Valerie Sinclair / ISBN 0 948853 16 3
MAKING OF MODERN CYPRUS – History – Customs/Dr. S. Panteli/ISBN 0 948853 09 3
APHRODITE CYPRIS – Mythology of Cyprus / Stass Paraskos / ISBN 0 948853 05 0
CYPRUS IN PICTURES – Pictorial Guide / Renos Lavithis / ISBN 948853 06 0

To obtain any of these books ask your local bookshop.